Responsible Public Speaking

Bobby R. Patton
Kim Giffin
Wil A. Linkugel

University of Kansas

Scott, Foresman and Company
Glenview, Illinois

Dallas, Tex. Oakland, N.J. Palo Alto, Cal.
Tucker, Ga. London, England

All illustrations in this book are by Jay Gold.

An Instructor's Manual to accompany *Responsible Public Speaking* is available. It may be obtained through a Scott, Foresman representative or by writing to Speech Communication Editor, College Division, Scott, Foresman and Co., 1900 East Lake Avenue, Glenview, Illinois 60025.

Library of Congress Cataloging in Publication Data

Patton, Bobby R., 1935-
  Responsible public speaking.

  Includes index.
  1. Public speaking. I. Linkugel, Wil A. II. Title.
PN4121.P315   1982   808.5′1   82-10675
ISBN 0-673-15363-0

Preface

All public speaking textbooks teach students an understanding of the speech communication process and how to research, organize, prepare, and deliver a public message. *Responsible Public Speaking* goes a step further and also teaches the importance of responsibility in communication behavior. It grew out of a deep concern for responsibility in public communication. In every age—and certainly in our own—it is essential that our colleges and universities intensify their effort to teach values emphasizing the worth and dignity of the individual. Responsibility in public communication means speakers exercising accountability to themselves and also to their listeners. Basic to this perspective is the Aristotelian factor of *ethos*—good will. This quality broadly encompasses the way speakers view their listeners: the attitudes they hold toward them and the respect they have for them. At the same time, responsible public communication requires that speakers be concerned for the benefit and welfare of their listeners.

Responsible Public Speaking is designed for the introductory Speech Communication course with a strong performance orientation. Three goals were central to its construction: (1) that the text be highly practical for the beginning speech student; (2) that the speech principles be grounded in current research data; and (3) that the book present a singular perspective: encouraging responsibility on the part of the speaker toward the listener.

Responsible Public Speaking is divided into three parts: Part 1, A Perspective on Speaker/Audience Communication (Chapters 1-4), explains the basic public speaking process and the responsibilities it involves, for both the speaker and the listener. Part 2, From Preparation to Presentation (Chapters 5-9), explains the process of preparing and presenting a speech. This includes Focusing on Ideas; Organization of Ideas; The Introduction and Conclusion of a Speech; Use of Voice and Bodily Action in Delivery; and Use of Visual Aids. Part 3, Preparing Specific Speeches (Chapter 10-13), explains the theory behind informative and persuasive speeches and illustrates the theory with sample speech material. A final section, Speeches for Study and Analysis, presents three speeches for students to study and analyze.

Part 3, Preparing Specific Speeches, employs a feature that will be especially useful to students. Each of the kinds of informative and persuasive speeches is illustrated with examples from an actual speech. Most of these are student speeches. Each speech example is analyzed in terms of the theory of that type of speech; the aim, in each instance, is to make the analysis instructional instead of critical (in the sense of rhetorical criticism). Each analysis is concluded with a Criteria Box that students and instructors can use for assessing that type of speech. Thus, students can better complete an oral assignment because they are presented both a valid example and a systematic method of evaluation.

Other key features enhance the book's usefulness. Each chapter is relatively self-contained to facilitate teaching flexibility. A section of Learning Experiences concludes each chapter; it includes behavioral objectives and exercises. In addition, the section on Speeches for Study and Analysis contains speech examples that can be used as the basis for written assignments and class discussions.

A detailed Instructor's Manual, available from Scott, Foresman and Company, will help you implement the use of this book in your course. It includes teaching suggestions; course syllabi; additional assignments and activities; and a variety of test items.

Responsible Public Speaking represents a collaborative effort involving a large number of people, including eight students: Steve Gibbs, Russell Hodge, Rebecca Martinez, Randy Schrock, Gregg Braun, Amy Vandoren, Jodie Wallace, and Shana Woodyard, who reacted to our ideas and our manuscript and helped provide us with examples. We also appreciate the constructive criticism of our reviewers: Bruce E. Gronbeck, University of Iowa; Gary D. Keele, California State Polytechnic University at Pomona; Kevin E. McClearey, Southern Illinois University at Edwardsville; Richard Nitcavic, Ball State University; Sharon A. Ratliffe, Golden West College; and Barbara Strain, San Antonio College.

We are indebted to many persons at Scott, Foresman and Company who contributed to the completion of this project: Barbara Muller was instrumental in the conceptual development and guided it through the various phases. Anita Portugal and Susan Strunk gave able technical assistance and Michael Anderson contributed guidance and encouragement. We are grateful for Scott, Foresman's expertise in Speech Communication.

If through this book your students learn methods, attitudes, and skills that will serve well both speakers and audiences in our society, our intentions will have been richly fulfilled.

Bobby R. Patton
Kim Giffin
Wil A. Linkugel

Contents

Part 1

A Perspective on Speaker/Audience Communication

Choices are the essence of speaker/audience communication. You choose whether to attend a speech and even while there choose whether or not to listen to the speaker. You choose whether or not to speak, and if you speak you have a number of choices to make as you formulate your message.

Our perspective is that everyone is best served by responsible public communication by a speaker who has concern and good will toward the audience. In this section we will present *responsibility* as the guiding principle of effective public communication and present a model to help you understand the extent and ramifications of choices.

1

Introduction to Responsible Public Speaking

 The term "public speaking" is likely to bring several images to your mind. Think about public speakers you have heard. Perhaps in your mind you picture a candidate for public office delivering a campaign speech; perhaps you see a minister or evangelist delivering an impassioned plea for salvation; perhaps you picture a statesman presenting a famous speech from history. Did you picture *yourself* in front of an audience? Probably not, because "public speaking" is outside the typical day-to-day experience of most of us. Yet from time to time virtually all of us are called upon to make planned presentations to a group of people. The purpose of this book is to help you to present yourself and your ideas to an audience on such occasions. Our goal will be to help you to develop a cooperative, trusting climate that will reduce tension and anxiety and produce mutual growth and enlightenment for both yourself and your listeners.

In this chapter we will emphasize the importance of public speaking and the value of responsibility in the public communication process. In addition, we will ask you to envision yourself accepting responsibility as a speaker.

THE IMPORTANCE OF PUBLIC SPEAKING

Can you imagine building a computer that could be given a specific topic or problem, fed a mass of relevant information, digest this mass, compare it with one's lifetime of personal experience, provide a simple brief of the essence of this knowledge, and then tell you what position or plan of action

should be adopted? Wouldn't that be a wonderful machine, the "ideal" computer? To date we know of no computer that can do this. But *you* can do this. A conscientious public speaker provides this service for listeners. To think of yourself as being able to do all of these things may seem a bit difficult. Probably it is much easier to imagine yourself simply giving a report based upon your unique experience or training. In some of your classes you will probably be asked to report on a subject or situation that you have investigated or researched. In this way you will likely be practicing the principles of public speaking in the near future.

If you are working while going to school, you may find it necessary to help other new employees become oriented to the work situation. They may need to become informed about the use of equipment, reporting hours worked, or providing information for social security forms or income tax. You should be able to imagine yourself as an experienced worker giving them the information that they need; if you do this for a group of new employees, you will be using public speaking principles.

These examples essentially consist of presenting short, informal speeches to inform others. However, sooner or later you are likely to find yourself wanting to ask other people to help improve a difficult situation by taking action of some kind. Such a situation might involve a committee of students working on a class project. Later in your life it may be a meeting of the local school board, or a community planning commission. You will wish you were the "ideal computer," able to collect information, analyze it, compare the result with life's experience, present the essence of this knowledge, and recommend a stand or plan of action that your colleagues or associates should adopt. You can do all of these things by preparing and presenting a persuasive speech. Perhaps you can't imagine yourself doing this well, but undoubtedly you can imagine yourself wanting to do so. Very likely you are reading this book because you are enrolled in a course designed to help you speak well in public. Your instructor's purpose, and the purpose of this book, is to help you to meet such situations effectively.

Meeting your personal need to speak well in a public meeting is a basic part of living in a democratic society. Skill in public speaking has long been recognized as a necessary part of the equipment of every educated man and woman in our culture. In our society the average citizen finds it difficult to avoid situations that occasionally demand public presentations. A variety of circumstances and situations call for one person to stand up before a group of people and talk.

Our democratic society with its emphasis on individual freedom and equality of opportunity requires that people act in concerted ways. Americans affirm the conviction that every person can acquire the knowledge necessary to form opinions and make decisions; democracy demands that knowledge be made available to all, rather than to the few (as in totalitarian systems). We cannot tolerate restriction and distortion and must cherish our freedoms of speech, press, and assembly.

THE VALUE OF RESPONSIBLE PUBLIC SPEAKING

With our freedoms go responsibilities. Public speaking involves making a number of choices. In fact, as you plan a speech, you *must* make choices. The responsible public speaker who respects the democratic system and has genuine regard for fellow citizens must select and present facts and opinions fairly. Such a speaker must not intentionally distort ideas or conceal materials that the audience would need in justly evaluating the arguments. We believe that the health and well-being of a free society depend upon the integrity of its public speakers.

The Meaning of Being Responsible

Hundreds of years ago a Roman teacher of public speaking, Quintilian, described an orator as a "good person speaking well." In essence we support this concept. "Good" can mean different things to different people. To some extent, it is defined by our society or culture; in the long run, however, each of us must define it for ourselves. For our purposes, "good" means having *a strong sense of responsibility to oneself and to others.* James Edward Doty has observed, "Authentic man has a deep sense of awareness of his own responsibility."[1]

This sense of responsibility is well expressed by the Golden Rule:

Do unto others as you would have them do unto you. Studies of the use of this principle (often called "prosocial behavior") show that many people do respond to the needs of others rather than simply in terms of measurable benefit to themselves.[2] Evidence exists that such behavior differs little across races or cultures. Further evidence suggests that many persons who do not practice the Golden Rule (and this includes a great many of us) do practice a principle of *reciprocity:* If you treat me well, I will treat you well—better than I would if you treated me unfairly.[3] The principle of responsibility means that a person accepts accountability to others in at least one of these ways. In addition, responsibility means that a person is *aware of his or her own conscience, and feelings of right and wrong.* Such persons are in touch with their inner selves and sense of morality. They do not compromise their values or change their beliefs merely to be in tune with others. They are both true to themselves, and assume responsibility toward others.

In essence, *responsible speakers are people we trust.* We take them at their word and count on their behavior. Long ago, Aristotle identified three characteristics of credible speakers: (1) Knowledgeable—such persons are well informed; (2) Good character—such persons are seen as reliable and honest; (3) Good Will—such persons are seen as genuinely caring about their listeners' welfare. Good will is what tends to put expertness and good character into action. Let's illustrate this principle: Larry Rhine, a highly knowledgeable speaker on agricultural trends, addresses an audience and does not bother to organize his thoughts in a meaningful pattern, or for that matter, to check his facts, because he fails to accept responsibility as a speaker. Additionally, he may not bother to search for interesting support materials, or to practice his speech in order to make the listening experience an acceptable one for his audience. What this speaker gives is a poorly prepared, relatively uninteresting, and not necessarily reliable speech. The speaker has not been dishonest, does not lack humility, or any of the other traits that generally are identified with good character. The speaker simply does not put forth his best effort because he lacks concern for the listening audience—that is, good will. Our concept of responsibility can thus be summed up in two dimensions: (1) the speaker being true to himself or herself; (2) the speaker possessing good will for his or her audience.

A responsible person is accountable to his or her conscience, and is seen by others as informed, honest, and *ready to act* in a positive way. A speaker who feels genuine good will toward the audience will not want to waste people's time with a poorly-prepared, poorly-researched, poorly-organized address; neither will such a person be content to bore the audience with monotonous and listless vocal delivery; nor will that person want the audience to feel discomfort and embarrassment because of the speaker's sloppy or uncontrolled bodily behavior. Whenever you address an audience you accept responsibility toward that group of people and owe them your best thinking and your best performance. Your knowledge, your integrity, and your dynamism must be translated into good will for those with whom you communicate. In short, when you are responsible, you become "a good person speaking well."

Benefits to You as a Speaker

Responsible interaction with an audience benefits the speaker in at least three ways:

    1. The first benefit is that you are more likely to enjoy good psychological health. You are more at peace with yourself, less inclined to be under stress, and more capable of using all your faculties, energies, and ability if you communicate responsibly with others. As Jourard has noted:

> We . . . have the capacity for entering into true dialogue with our fellows, disclosing what we think feel, and are planning . . . The interests of healthy personality are served if a person can disclose himself honestly and spontaneously to others.[4]

    2. A second speaker benefit is a greater likelihood of achieving a satisfactory long-range outcome. A sincere desire to provide sound and useful information or ideas can help coordinate one's effort with others, and establish warmer, happier relationships based on mutual respect. We make this claim not on the basis of faith or idealism, but on the near-universal experience of people: in all cultures lying and cheating are deplored and outlawed.

Figure 1-1   Characteristics of a Responsible Public Speaker

Trust of others is necessary for full and undistorted exchange of information. Irresponsible communication promotes a climate in which people withhold or distort some of their information as a means of gaining an advantage over others. This behavior may result in short-term advantages, but also promotes distrust and defensiveness.[5]

Studies indicate that as defensive behavior decreases and trust increases, two important changes can occur: (1) We tend to achieve heightened feelings of personal adequacy (improved self-image), and (2) We achieve easier acceptance of our temporary feelings of internal conflict (less anxiety).[6] The reduction of defensive behavior and increasing trust through the use of responsible communication are extremely valuable goals for the public speaker.

3. A third benefit is the opportunity to gain a wider, more functional perspective, especially with respect to understanding people's behavior. Such growth is enhanced by offering honestly one's ideas and listening to feedback and reactions from others. In this way, responsible communication provides opportunity for increased perspective along with self-evaluation and possibility for change.[7] Such an invitation will allow members of the audience to raise pertinent questions and state their opinions.

Benefits to Your Listeners and to Society

Benefits accrue to your listeners as you become a responsible speaker. Their needs and aspirations are more likely to be met. To the extent that you provide relevant, dependable information, they will be better able to make wise decisions.

As a society, we have many problems of economics, ecology, and human relations; these pose a serious challenge for us to develop responsible ways of communicating with one another.

As Franklyn Haiman of Northwestern University contends, our ethics should be based on the ability of people to make their own decisions. Admitting that people often make decisions irrationally, Haiman suggests that any speaker who "short-circuits" the thinking of his or her listeners and manipulates them into emotional decisions is unethical. In a democracy, the ethical speaker presents arguments and evidence so as to allow people to grow in their ability to govern themselves, which is the central tenet of democracy.[8]

YOUR VISION OF YOURSELF AS A RESPONSIBLE SPEAKER

Try now to picture for yourself the kind of behavior that you would like to have as a speaker. Deliberately imagine how you will look and sound; think through the things you would like to do. This is an important exercise because if you cannot in your own mind develop an image of yourself as a competent, responsible speaker with an audience, it is unlikely that you will be able to behave in that way. Vision sets boundaries on our ultimate potential.[9]

Help yourself to become a more competent, responsible speaker by deliberately envisioning yourself doing two things; for each of these you should try to create a picture of yourself "in your mind's eye" behaving in specific and particular ways.

Understand Your Listeners

Picture in your imagination how you would feel and behave if you clearly understood your listeners' needs and desires. Do this carefully regarding any topic or area on which you expect to speak to them. If you don't have enough information about their hopes or interests, seek to obtain this knowledge. Imagine yourself meeting these needs and interests; develop your picture of yourself and your behavior in as much detail as you can. In addition, envision your listeners responding to you in a favorable way because you are willing to consider their special needs and interest.

Figure 1-2   Your Vision of Yourself

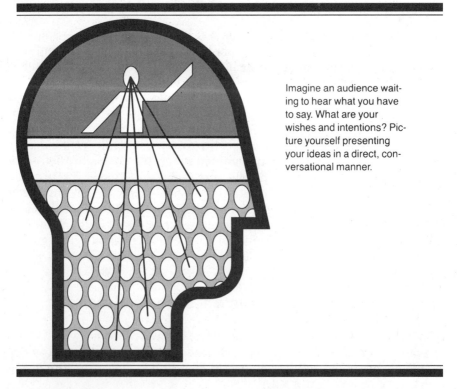

Imagine an audience waiting to hear what you have to say. What are your wishes and intentions? Picture yourself presenting your ideas in a direct, conversational manner.

Know Yourself as a Speaker

Can you imagine yourself being a dependable, knowledgeable person, talking to a group of listeners? Your most valuable characteristic as a speaker is your credibility; can you imagine yourself speaking to an audience in a way that *uses and protects* your credibility? In order to do this you will need to be clear in your mind regarding your *intentions* toward your listeners: do you really wish to help them understand, reach useful decisions, achieve their interests and needs? As you imagine yourself achieving these goals, do you present your ideals in a clear, well-organized fashion? Use words well? Have an attractive, expressive voice? Let your body talk freely? To the extent that you can create a vision of yourself doing these things well, to that extent you may be able to succeed in behaving in such a manner.

In both ways we have described, it will be valuable to be as specific as possible in forming an image of yourself behaving as a responsible speaker. Following through on this suggestion will take some time. Our experience with students indicates that, when well done, such imagining is well worth the time. We urge you to do it.

You can start right away to apply the principle of responsibility in communication. *First,* you can start by demanding such responsibility from other speakers anytime you listen to them. You can let them know that you expect them to be open and honest with you as you listen to their ideas. You can practice being aware of responsibility in speakers as you give them your time and attention. In effect, you can offer them a kind of contract: You will listen as carefully and attentively as possible, giving full effort to understanding their views regardless of your present beliefs on their topic; in return, you ask that they present the entire picture as they see it, omitting nothing, either pro or con, relevant to their ultimate position. Your expectation will be that, together, you can give the topic optimum exploration and consideration. The combination of your critical thinking and theirs should provide both of you the best possible result.

Second, you can start immediately requiring yourself to be as responsible as possible whenever you find others willing to listen to you express your ideas. Your ultimate responsibility as a speaker can be measured in terms of the degree to which your listeners are willing to hear and consider what you have to say. Ask yourself this question: what do you want from speakers when you agree to give them your attention? What do you require in terms of their responsibility for what they say? We suspect that you want them to be well-informed on the topic when you agree to listen to their ideas and that you want them to tell the truth as they see it. Competency and honesty on their part, insofar as humanly possible, are likely to be your criteria. Your responsibility as a speaker can be similarly determined: What you require of others is what you should require of yourself when others listen to you. Ultimately this requirement is the measure of your responsibility.

SUMMARY

The foregoing chapter has described our concern for responsibility in speaker/audience communication. Our society is based on democratic principles of equality under the law and a legal system predicated on the assumption that when people argue both sides of a case with all their abilities, justice can best be served.

We have identified positive values of achieving responsibility to both yourself and your listeners. Values to yourself include psychological health; realistic insights and decisions; and a broader, more useful perspective in your view of the world and its affairs. To your listeners will accrue more rational understanding of situations and conditions, more reliable decisions, and increased trust and cooperation.

Your *achievement* of responsibility as a speaker will be determined by your vision of yourself and your capability. To improve your vision of your potential you should try to picture yourself (1) understanding your listeners, and (2) knowing yourself as a speaker. Your ultimate responsibility can be determined by asking yourself: What do I require as a listener when I give my attention to a speaker? We have suggested that the answer will likely be: (1) Competence in terms of being well-informed, (2) Honesty in the presentation of thoughts and ideas, (3) Dynamism in terms of vocal and bodily behavior, and (4) Good will in terms of responsibility toward one's listeners.

LEARNING EXPERIENCES

Objectives

After studying this chapter, you should be able to *do* the following things:

1. Explain the importance of public speaking in a democracy.
2. Cite and explain five possible benefits of being responsible as a public speaker.
3. Identify your perceived strengths and weaknesses as a speaker. Discuss these perceptions with your classmates and instructor.
4. Create an image of yourself helping others to reach decisions.
5. Discuss your attitudes and capabilities of discerning responsibility in others.

Exercises

1. Working in pairs, interview and be interviewed by another member of your class. Learn as much as you can about each other that might influence speeches that you will give in class. Learn about hobbies, work experience, professional aspirations, and personal competence that make this person unique.
2. Based upon the information gained in the interview, introduce your classmate to the class. Stand in front of the room and speak directly to your classmates. Use as few notes as possible; strive for clarity. Respond to any questions that might be asked.
3. After you have been introduced by your classmate, expand on information about you by elaborating, clarifying, or correcting any information that you think might be confusing. Help the audience know "Who I Am."
4. Write a letter to your instructor assessing yourself as a speaker and identifying your aspirations for this course. Set goals for yourself. Be as candid as possible. Your instructor may respond to this letter and retain it as a basis for subsequent evaluation of your achievement of goals in the course.
5. Test yourself on this *People Quiz* prepared by John E. Gibson, "Lies, Lies, Lies—Can You Excell in Them?"[10]

True or False?

1. The adage that "It takes a thief to catch a thief" also applies to lying.
2. It is easy to deceive others, but it is costly to oneself.
3. People who excel in the practice of deception fall into a special personality category.
4. When a person tells a lie, the amount of guilt or stress that goes with it depends on the *kind* of lie and whether or not getting caught is likely, whether premeditated or not.
5. When a man lies, his eyes behave differently than a woman's do when she attempts a deception.

Answers

1. *False.* Studies at Harvard University on the psychodynamics of lying and the ability to detect deception in others found that "skill at lying was unrelated to skill at catching others in their lies."

2. *True.* The Harvard University study also indicated that, unfortunately for those of us who are trusting of others, "the ability to lie successfully appears to be a fairly general one," that a person with the intent to deceive others has a good chance of getting away with it without the other person actually realizing that he has been had. And it is interesting to note a further finding in this connection: People who effectively mask their deception attempts also effectively conceal *most* of their true feelings and emotions. And this makes it difficult, if not impossible, for them to enjoy a really close relationship with another human being. The individual who gets where he wants to go by manipulating others through deceit and dissembling ends up being a "loner" in its most unrewarding sense.

3. *True.* As studies sponsored by the National Science Foundation show, they are the *Machiavellian type*, people who excel in manipulating others and who are very effective in deceiving others when it serves their purpose to do so. The investigators found that "the Machiavellians seem to favor an especially theatrical style of deceiving, particularly when feigning positive regard: They tend to be 'hams' when they lie. Moreover, the hamming strategy appears to work quite well. People who tend to exaggerate sentiments of liking that they do not really feel, as well as people who exaggerate feigned feeling of disliking, are much less likely to get caught in their lies than are the less histrionic sorts."

4. *True.* It is observed in the same study that "among the many types of lies are ordinary white lies, proffered in the service of smoothing social interaction, lies of self-aggrandizement for purposes of making an impression or for personal gain and lies in which the deceived party is the intended beneficiary, as in physicians' cloaking of grim prognoses or parents' imaginative fabrications about sex and death." It is pointed out that: Lies vary in the degree of guilt or stress that they cause for the deceiver, the degree of involvement that they engender in the topic of the lie, the consequences of getting caught in the lie and whether the lies were planned and rehearsed or unpremeditated.

5. *True.* A study of the effects of lying, conducted by a team at Western Washington University, cites findings showing an interesting sex difference in the eye contact measurement of subjects when telling a lie or attempting to deceive. It was found that "Males increased their eye contact while lying, but the females' eye contact decreased."

NOTES

[1]James Edward Doty (ed.), *Authentic Man Encounters God's World*. Baldwin City, Kansas: Baker University Press, 1967, p. 1.

[2]For an excellent review of these studies see Robert A. Baron, Donn Byrne, and William Griffit, Chapter 7, "Prosocial Behavior: Altruism and Helping," in *Social Psychology*. Boston: Allyn and Bacon, 1974, pp. 225-264.

[3]Baron, Byrne, and Griffit, pp. 374-380.

[4]Sidney M. Jourard, *Healthy Personality*. New York: Macmillan Publishing Company, 1974, p. 168.

[5]Jack R. Gibb, "Defensive Communication," *Journal of Communication*, 11 (1961), pp. 141-148.

[6]Bobby R. Patton and Kim Giffin, *Interpersonal Communication in Action*. New York: Harper & Row, 1977, p. 77.

[7]See Carl R. Rogers, *On Becoming a Person*. Boston: Houghton-Mifflin, 1961.

[8]Franklin Haiman, "Democratic Ethics and the Hidden Persuaders," *Quarterly Journal of Speech*, vol. 44 (1958), pp. 385-392.

[9]An excellent presentation of this principle has been given by Kenneth Boulding, *The Image*. Ann Arbor: University of Michigan Press, 1956, pp. 3-18.

[10]"Lies, Lies, Lies—Can You Excel in Them?" by John E. Gibson from *Family Weekly*, February 8, 1981. Reprinted by permission of *Family Weekly*, copyright © 1981, 641 Lexington Avenue, New York, New York 10022.

2

The Public Speaking Process

We live in a world of processes. Everything around us and within us is constantly moving and changing. Nothing is static. Because of the difficulty in capturing an image of a fluid, ongoing continuous process, we tend to focus on limited aspects of a process in the form of events or experiences. An abstract process is far more difficult to conceptualize or discuss than a specific event or situation.

Consider an example of the distinction between events and processes. In the summer of 1979 a DC-10 crashed in Chicago with the tragic loss of 273 people. This event is memorable and was readily understood and discussed by people around the world. But less easily understood was the *process* that resulted in the crash. All components of the plane were examined and attempts were made from transcriptions and other data to reconstruct the ill-fated take-off attempt. The process could only be understood and analyzed by experts looking at significant components.

Such is also the case with communication. Public speaking occurs in terms of situations and speaking events. Take, for example, a president's inaugural address. The event is the president's inauguration. The situation involves a large group of people standing gathered around the steps of the nation's capitol. High governmental officials and dignitaries are in attendance, and the chief justice of the United States Supreme Court administers the oath of office. The president responds to this situation with a speech, thereby making the speech itself part of an event. However, the communication that occurs is a process. The speech manuscript is a thing—we can look at it, we can hold it, we can read it—but any communication that results from the speech is not a thing—it is a highly complex process.

In this chapter, we shall identify common misconceptions about public speaking, describe the components in the public communication process, present a visual model of the process, and discuss the interactive implications of that model. Although communication as a process has no discernible beginning or end, we can identify significant components. In Chapter 1 we stated that public speaking was a process; in this chapter we shall explain what we mean by that and the implications for you.

COMMON MISCONCEPTIONS ABOUT PUBLIC SPEAKING

There are some commonly held misconceptions about public speaking which might cause you difficulty. These misconceptions need to be examined so that we may more clearly understand the essential elements in the process.

Is There a "Right Way" to Speak in Public?   One common misconception is that there is one right way to speak in public. Years ago teachers of elocution attempted to standardize gestures and vocal inflections into a set of rules for students to follow. We do not believe that there is one "correct" way to make a speech. In a class several excellent speakers may have techniques as divergent as their personalities. While they may have certain traits in common—desire to communicate, sound organization of ideas, or interesting materials—their speaking styles may be quite different. Nevertheless, they all succeed in communicating with people in the class.

Can You Change Your Habits in Public?   Another common misconception is that you can speak well on the platform without changing your daily habits. Responsibility to yourself requires that you "be yourself." However, in so doing, you may follow your established habit patterns. For example, if your habitual posture is careless and slovenly, you will likely find yourself standing that way in front of an audience. You probably will not be able to change these habits unless you make a special effort. In order to achieve lasting benefit from the speaking opportunities available to you, you need to develop speaking *habits* that will serve you well.

Does Practice Make Perfect?   A third popular misconception is that practice in public speaking makes perfect. A speaker who makes speech after speech without reducing the number and size of his or her communication problems and without increasing the assets will merely strengthen existing habit patterns. A speaker needs practice, but the practice must afford an opportunity to habitualize changes in a beneficial direction. We agree with the person who said, "Practice does not make perfect; it merely makes permanent." Practice and feedback are necessary for us to decide what should be made permanent.

COMPONENTS IN THE PUBLIC SPEAKING PROCESS

For many years people viewed public speaking only from the aspect of the speaker. The speaker was thought to be the only significant variable, and student speakers were taught techniques that supposedly gave them the ability to influence any audience. Elocutionists in the nineteenth century even formulated gestures and bodily actions that they presumed would have certain predictable impacts upon audiences.

Modern communication scholars recognize that the speaker-centered approach fails to capture the essence of the process. *To speak* is not the same as *to communicate*. Communication cannot take place without willing listeners and a common code of meaning. Primarily through the use of speech/language, people communicate their needs, thoughts, feelings, and intentions to one another.

Language is often cited as the greatest achievement of the human race and the significant variable that distinguishes people from other animals. We learn how to think, feel, and judge through the aid of and within the constraints imposed upon us by the words, idioms, and syntax of our language. The experiences, dreams, and wisdom of past generations are subtly and ineradicably preserved in language. Language enhances the communication of meanings and the sharing of experience among a people, enabling us to form an enduring society and to create and transmit a distinctive culture.

The meaning of any statement is determined by the experiences of the speaker and listeners and by the total context in which the statement is heard. Accurate communication—mutually correct understanding of the meanings of the statements of each participant in a communication event—is possible to the degree that each person has experienced comparable wants, has faced comparable problems, and is able to identify comparable feelings. If people have had different experiences, or if they perceive the communication context differently, the meanings of the message will differ to some degree.

Human communication takes many forms: intrapersonal communication transpires within an individual; interpersonal communication involves spontaneous, face-to-face interaction between two or more people; in small group communication people meet together to examine and work with mutual concerns and problems; and in mass communication the sender is separated from the receivers by the media employed, such as radio, television, or the newspaper. While all forms of human communication have much in common, including the problems inherent in language, we are primarily concerned in this book with that unique type of communication known as public speaking.

Public speaking is unique in several ways. One person accepts the role of speaker while the others assume roles as listeners. This agreement allows the speaker to plan the message with the audience and context in mind. Unlike mass media communication, the audience is present and can give direct and immediate feedback to the speaker.

In the typical speaker-audience situation, we can identify ten components:

1. *Stimulus* — There is some reason *why* the speaker has been designated to address the group. The reason or reasons may be psychological drives within either the speaker or the audience; or the stimulus may be a holiday or an event such as a commencement ceremony. Every public statement has some reason for being. Unlike the spontaneous nature of much interpersonal communication, the public presentation is usually planned. There are times when a speaker is asked to stand up and address a group of people in impromptu fashion, without advance preparation, because he or she possesses some special knowledge or has some highly relevant ideas pertaining to audience concerns. But most "speeches" are prepared prior to the speaking occasion.

2. *Speaker* — The designated speaker constructs a message based upon past experiences, emotional-psychological state, and immediate goals. The speaker hopes to achieve some goal or serve some purposes, and by sound and sight presents the message to a group of listeners.

3. *Message* — Verbal messages in the form of a symbolic code and nonverbal cues in the form of gestures, stances, and intonation changes are transmitted by the speaker to the listeners. A discernible organizational pattern and logical development are needed for clarity and understanding.

4. *Channel* — Sound and sight are the main channels in speaker-audience communication. The presence or absence of a public address system affects the relationship. Speakers must be heard and seen.

5. *Audience* — For some reason a group of people is assembled to hear the speaker. Each member of the audience is unique in past experiences and reasons for attending. He or she makes a choice whether or not to listen to the speaker. The combination of individuals making up any audience is unique.

6. *Context* — Time, place, and occasion are significant variables. People respond differently to a speaker in the evening than in the morning, in crowded rooms than in open auditoriums. The reason for the meeting makes a difference.

7. *Effect* — Measurement of effect on audience behavior is sometimes difficult as the results may be immediate or long range. Even so, some possible effects are listeners' changes in beliefs, attitudes, self-concepts, and behaviors. In consideration of these various possible effects, an important consideration is the following: Did the speaker achieve his or her goal?

8. *Feedback* — By applause, attention, and overt show of interest, members of the audience give the speaker hints as to their responsiveness to the message. Negative feedback exhibited by inattention or hostility similarly provides the speaker a basis for gauging effect.

9. *Noise* — Any disturbances or problems coming between the speaker and his or her audience can be labeled "Noise." Such problems as static in the public address system, or less obvious distractions such as visual disturbances or emotional reactions in the minds of individuals may cause interference.

10. *Intra-audience Communication* — Audience members affect each other by their verbal and observable nonverbal responses to the speaker.

Within the public speaking process, each of these components affects all the others and the dynamics of the communication event. No two speaking events are ever the same, and even to "freeze" a speech through video recording omits the factors of timeliness and human presence that cannot be duplicated. In the chapters that follow we shall refer to these components as we examine the process in greater detail.

A MODEL OF THE PUBLIC SPEAKING PROCESS

As we have just indicated, communication is a set of complex behavioral patterns, not simply the articulation of a verbal message. Models are attempts to identify, simplify, and give focus to larger, more complicated objects, concepts, or processes. A model airplane, for example, attempts to replicate in smaller, simpler fashion the real object.

Probably no one model will ever be able to identify all of the potential variables in public speaking, for even if it were possible to apply labels to all conceivable elements, the size and complexity of the model would make it useless. We should once again emphasize that public speaking is a dynamic process, constantly changing, never static. All variables interact with one another, modifying and adapting to all situations.

Models based on information theory have sometimes been applied to human communication. Such models typically depict communication as a game of pitch and catch in which the talker pitches a message to the listener, who in turn throws a message back. Unfortunately, this model is misleading when applied to public speaking because it suggests that the communication process proceeds in only one direction at a time.

Figure 2-1 (see page 20) depicts in visual terms the ten components of the public speaking process. This diagram tells only a small portion of the whole story. Each component could be further examined as a complex process itself. However, this diagram provides an overview of major factors to be considered.

The first thing to note about this model is that public speaking always occurs in a context of place, time, and occasion. This larger context provides a significant backdrop. What has transpired before the speech, what the members of the audience expect, and the total circumstances create a special dynamic.

INTERACTIVE NATURE OF THE PROCESS

Public speaking is a process of complex behavioral patterns rather than simply the delivery of a verbal message. In our discussion of public speaking, we should remember that communication has many functions and facets, all of which influence one another.

Interdependence of Speaker and Audience

The speaker and members of an audience are interactive and exert mutual influences upon each other.[1] We realize that some speakers behave in ways totally oblivious to their audience. Some college professors, for example, lecture in the same way if one or a hundred people are present. They drone on from notes, speak in a monotone, and ignore questions from students. One might surmise that if such a person went to a class and *no* students arrived, he or she would still present the lecture in the same way. Without recognition and adaptation to the people present, such speakers are not engaging in responsible public speaking as we conceive it.

A study of interdependence of speaker and audience was conducted at the University of Kansas by Jon Blubaugh.[2] Students were hired to be members of an audience and were trained to give *either* positive *or* negative feedback to student speakers. When the audience reactions were *positive* the following behaviors were exhibited by the listeners:

1. constant eye contact
2. smiling
3. positive head nods
4. comfortable, but erect posture
5. notetaking
6. little or no movement of the body or limbs

Figure 2-1   A Model of the Public Speaking Process

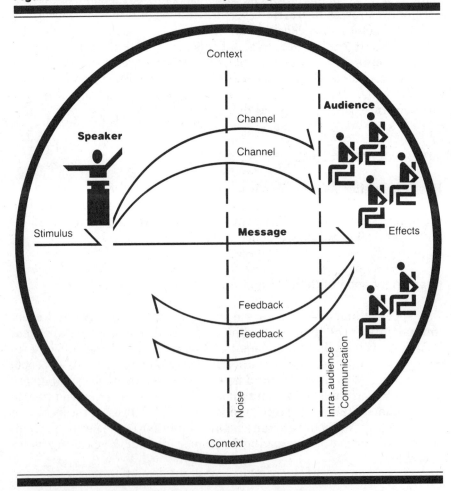

In the *negative* condition, the following behaviors were used:

1. no eye-contact
2. "slouch" posture
3. manipulating or "playing with" objects
4. manipulating, examining, or touching parts of the face or body
5. looking around the room or at others
6. frequent shifting of body position
7. "doodling"

Student-subjects were given twenty-five minutes to prepare a ten-minute speech on the topic, "What factors should be considered in the choice of a college or university?" The subjects were then randomly assigned either to positive or negative audience reactions and the speeches were observed and recorded through a one-way mirror.

What do you think were the differences in the speeches? Picture yourself giving speeches to audiences responding in these ways. As Blubaugh predicted, and as you might guess, the students receiving negative feedback spoke shorter periods of times, were less fluent, and spoke much slower, as if unsure of themselves.

In reality, most audiences are neither as totally positive or as totally negative as depicted in this study. Usually as a speaker, you will be able to make impact in such a way as to promote change in one direction or the other. The responsible speaker is prepared to communicate a message of value to the audience and will likely gain greater and greater positive feedback. Conversely, audiences will respond in negative ways to speakers who violate their expectations.

The interactive nature of the process is further apparent in the influence of audience members upon each other. Perhaps you have noted a difference in watching a humorous film on television and in seeing the same film in a crowded theater. The laughter of other audience members heightened your enjoyment and willingness to laugh. Such interaction among audience members is analogous to popping corn. Each kernel receives heat from a single force and pops independently. Yet each kernel also releases heat that affects the other kernels. When the various messages of speaker to audience, audience-member to audience-member, and audience to speaker are considered, we see a truly interactive process.

PREPARING TO SPEAK

The process of speaking, even rather informally, to a group of listeners involves specific steps in preparing and presenting your message. We will identify these steps, and attempt to make them more real and lifelike to you by telling you about the experience of one student. One young man, a college sophomore, was asked to prepare a speech to be given in his public speaking class, and to use it in a public speaking contest.

First, he considered the interests and attitudes of his classmates. He noted certain similarities between them and himself. He thought of a topic that had made a great impact on his own life—the handicapped brother with whom he had lived, had seen suffer daily, and from whom he learned personal lessons of courage and determination. His own life had been changed by this association. He believed that his classmates would benefit from learning more about this particular type of affliction—cerebral palsy. Thus emerges one major factor in the development of a public speech: (1) *Consider the interests and attitudes of your potential listeners in terms of what you have to offer.*

From the general topic of cerebral palsy, the speaker narrowed the focus to the lack of knowledge that then existed toward the problem. Instead of dealing with the multitude of specific problems such as schooling, access for the handicapped to public facilities, or public policy, he chose to deal with the feelings he had concerning the tremendous lack of data and the "sick jokes" that were then popular. Since he had only a few minutes to speak, he chose one idea. He thus accomplished a second factor in the process: (2) *Focus on one important idea for a particular presentation.*

After thinking about his own knowledge or information, the speaker did some additional investigation and research. He then prepared a simple outline that gave continuity to the various items of relevant information. He then did more research to fill in the gaps in his thinking. He thus met the third requirement: (3) *Organize your thinking.*

With special attention to the introduction and conclusion, the speaker went through the speech aloud to ensure that his ideas fit together and could be easily understood by his listeners. He selected key words that were especially useful in presenting his ideas clearly; in addition, he noted subpoints and examples that would help his listeners understand. Thus, he met another requirement: (4) *Develop your viewpoint with appropriate language and subsidiary ideas.*

The speaker felt strongly about his topic. He did not want to have to grope for words. He wanted to be free to establish contact between his listeners and to display the sincere feelings that he had. Only by practicing the speech could he achieve the confidence and directness that he sought. In this way he met the final requirement in preparing for his presentation to his listeners: (5) *Practice the verbal and nonverbal behaviors that will help you to achieve your purpose.*

An Example of a Student Speech

We believe that this young speaker was sincere and that he felt good will toward his listeners so that he wanted to share his thoughts and feelings with them. In his speech he demonstrated the essential requirements of being a responsible speaker.

Obviously, a manuscript cannot capture the full essence of the event. Even a video recording would omit the audience's reactions and many subtle message cues that we would detect if present. The written word is a medium quite different from the spoken word. However, we believe that reading a speaker's words will help clarify the principle that we are advocating. This student speech is a good example of responsible public speaking, and we want to share it with you in its entirety.

This speech was entitled, "What We Don't Know . . ." and was given in 1958 at Hutchinson Junior College (Kansas).*

In August, 1948, an unusual child was born in my community. His birth was a slightly abnormal one. He had received a head injury about which the doctor had hesitated to explain. As he grew older his parents began to wonder just what had happened. At one year he couldn't sit up and his baby-like incoordination was still very evident. At two years his arms and legs were stiff and uncontrollable and his head bobbed without purpose. His parents took him to several doctors who said he had some sort of spastic condition about which they, admittedly, knew very little. Then they took him to a chiropractor, who snapped and jerked his taut muscles until he screamed with terror. Finally, after nearly three years of hopeless endeavor, they discovered that the child was a victim of what is scientifically known as cerebral palsy. Now, after nine years of life, the child can still neither walk nor talk. His life, like the life of every cerebral palsy victim, is like living behind a huge looking-glass where everything is reversed. When he is told to relax, he becomes aware of his movements and becomes tense. When he thinks about his speech, he drools and grimaces and can't talk at all. Yet, he lives on. He lives on as though he is crossing a hypothetical plank ten stories high and never knowing if he will make it to the other side. Had his parent known sooner and proper treatment been available, it is difficult to say how much farther and faster the child would have gone.

To me, the victim which I have described is a brother. He could just as easily have been your brother, or even your child, because the condition with which he is afflicted does not discriminate. Cerebral palsy appears with regularity in all kinds of people in every geographic location. The rich and the poor, the educated and the illiterate must all suffer alike.

Certainly I am aware that this is not a new problem. I'm also aware of the fact that my discussing cerebral palsy will not wipe out its existence. What I do want to show you is how each year we are denying thousands of people the opportunity to lead useful and productive lives because few more than one out of every one-hundred cerebral palsy victims are getting the needed treatment. Years ago humble hearts moaned, "Nobody knows the trouble I've seen." The words of this Negro spiritual could very well apply to the

* "What We Don't Know . . ." by Robert C. Dick

cerebral palsy victim of today. For nobody knows the bitterness and humiliation which he has had to endure thoughout his life. If the grotesque figure of a cerebral palsy victim were to walk into this room today, his walk being the usual stumbling, halting gait, with one arm held stiffly at his side and the other wagging violently behind, what would we know about him? We would immediately realize that he looks and acts dreadfully different from us. But few of us would realize that only thirty years ago every cerebral palsy victim, just like him, was inevitably lost to society. Most of them were placed in institutions for the insane and feebleminded and the rest were kept at home, useless, hopeless drags upon their families. Yes, cerebral palsy was a shameful, frightening thing. But this fear was soon dispelled by a discovery—a discovery that over seventy-five percent of its victims can be reclaimed.

Now thirty years later, what further knowledge do we have of this disease? It is still comparatively unknown and until recently its research received barely one-fourteenth the amount of money that was going to polio. Yet in comparison, cerebral palsy constitutes over fourteen percent of the crippling population in every community—polio fifteen percent. Yet, nobody knows. Likewise, there are very few up-to-date clinics which provide the individual services of a physical therapist, occupational therapist and pediatrician, and in these the cost is from seven to fifteen dollars a day per child. Most rehabilitation centers are for children only. A few will accept from the increasing population of cerebral palsied adults but only in small numbers because, throughout the entire United States, facilities just haven't been made available. It takes seven very specially trained people to give twenty C.P. victims a chance for rehabilitation. Yet for every three thousand speech therapists graduating from our colleges and universities, there are jobs waiting for over twenty-five thousand. For every four thousand occupational therapists graduating, there are jobs waiting for over twenty-eight thousand.

Yet, even as science advances, attempting to solve the medical problems of this atrocious disease, the parents and families of these children must continue to face the daily dilemma of contact with discouragement and misunderstanding. The brilliant boy or girl who grows up to receive the rare fortune of treatment and education must face a possible lack of employment or vocational success due to the ignorance of the cerebral palsied in the outside world. Yes, he is still laughed at, feared, and turned away because he looks different and acts peculiar. The spastic victim has recently gained the center of attention as the subject of America's new "sick jokes." The Department of Health has reported that even many parents have mistaken C.P.'s alarming manifestations to be those of mental deficiencies and have actually been ashamed to bring their children to the attention of the medical profession.

It's time we learned of this dreadful affliction. Through public education we can build a better understanding of cerebral palsy. Since it may possibly never be cured, we must look upon it as a condition in which maximum improvement must be achieved. Yet, even all this—all the money and effort spent in attaining this—will be wasted unless final acceptance of the cerebral palsied is accomplished. These people are looking to us for help. They are looking from that hypothetical plank of emotional instability and despair. We can't close our ears to their cries, nor can we turn our faces from their deformed hands as they stretch out to us for help. They aren't asking for pity or condescension. They ask only for help, recognition, and understanding—just as polio is helped and recognized today. For only in this way can thousands of small sufferers hope for that opportunity without which, for them, the door leading from mere existence into real life will remain closed forever.

The speaker was Robert C. Dick. He is now Chairman of the Department of Communication and Theatre at Indiana University/ Purdue University in Indianapolis. The impact of the speech was memorable because of the authenticity in its developments and the skill demonstrated in its presentation. Probably you would like to know what has happened to the brother since that time. Fred still cannot walk, use his arms, or talk very intelligibly. He must be fed and given complete custodial care. But he has an exceptional mind and an amazing perserverence. He attended Hutchinson Junior College. Often he went all day without using the bathroom because he had a female attendant. He took exams orally and typed papers by putting on a headband with a stylus attached and pecked out one letter at a time on an electric typewriter. In that way he has written several articles and a chapter for a book. He completed his B.A. and M.A. degrees at Wichita State University and is presently working on his Ph.D. at the University of Kansas. Fred is also working part-time as a staff writer for the *University Daily Kansan*, the campus newspaper. His articles citing abuses of handicapped people have helped educate people to this problem with similar impact to his brother's speech of years ago.

Preparing by Visualizing

Golfer Jack Nicklaus has told how before every shot he takes, he "goes to the movies inside my head." He "sees" where he wants the ball to finish, in a specific small area of fairway or green. Then he "sees" the ball going there—its path, trajectory, and behavior on landing. Finally he "sees" himself making the kind of swing that will turn the first two images into reality. As Nicklaus says, "These 'home movies' are a key to my concentration—and to my positive approach to every shot."[3] In a similar vein, W. Timothy Fallway in *The Inner Game of Tennis* instructs people to picture hitting the ball where they want it to go and then to let it happen.[4]

In Chapter 1, we challenged you to picture yourself as a responsible speaker. With the model of speaker-audience communication in mind, we would now like you to be more specific and visualize yourself engaged in the process in a specific speaking situation. Please make yourself comfortable and try this experiment. Close your eyes and allow yourself to relax. Breathe in and out slowly and deeply. Allow an image to come to mind of a meeting room where you have been asked to give a talk. Picture yourself in the front of the room. Look across the room and notice details—the color of the walls, location of the windows, pictures on the walls, where the doors are. Now look at the chairs; notice how they are arranged. Look over the people in the room; notice the clothes that they are wearing. See if you recognize any friends or colleagues in the room.

Now imagine walking up to a table or lectern to begin your talk. Notice what the table is made of; put your hands on it and feel it. Take a few deep breaths until you feel calm, clear, and relaxed. Listen as the people in the audience become quiet. Allow the quietness to enter you and make you calm. Notice the people looking at you in a friendly, interested way. Now hear yourself begin the speech. Your voice is clear and loud enough for everyone to hear. Your speech is organized, interesting, and conveys exactly what you wish to say.

Figure 2-2   An Expanded Vision of Yourself

Rehearse the details of preparing to speak in your "mind's eye." Picture the details of the situation, including the people to be addressed, the layout of the room, and the positive reactions of the audience. Think of yourself as being poised and in control of your voice and body, using crisp, emphatic gestures. Your language is fluent and precise. You are a responsible speaker.

As you are speaking, you feel increasingly confident and comfortable. You can tell from the expression on your listeners' faces that they have understood what you've said and are stimulated by it. As you end your speech you hear excited talk among the members of the audience. Several people come up to you with questions and you answer them candidly and readily.

The goal of this exercise is to allow you to feel at ease while imagining the audience reaction. As you prepare an actual speech, other similar attempts at visualization can help you. They serve as "rehearsals" in your mind. Finally, however, ease in speaking to an audience comes only with experience. Your classroom should provide a supportive atmosphere in which you can consciously focus on skills development. That will increasingly allow you to reduce the amount of self-consciousness in subsequent speaking situations. Action is an important way to gain relief from excessive self-consciousness. Also, when you are expressing yourself and are not concerned with creating false impressions about yourself, there is less reason for anxiety and dissipated energy.

Communication is the process that promotes changes between and among people. They attempt to interpret the world and their role—to make sense out of the influx of perceptions—so that they can order and assign significance to the various components of their environment. It is now generally accepted that the vast majority of human behaviors are learned, that is, they develop as a consequence of persons interacting with their environment. It was primarily through our communication that we grew into what we are today, and through public communication we enhance this process.

SUMMARY

In this chapter we have examined three popular misconceptions about public speaking and identified the primary components of the public speaking process. We have also presented a model showing how these components interact. We have further emphasized the nature of the components, particularly the interrelationship between the speaker and the audience members.

In our model we depicted ten components that affect the complex process of public communication as indicative of choices that speakers and members of the audience make. These components will be cited in subsequent chapters. Positive and negative behaviors of listeners were shown to have genuine impact upon the behaviors of the speaker.

We identified five steps in the process of preparing a public speech and illustrated these steps by showing how a student went through these stages. Finally, we presented a visualization exercise in which you were invited to picture yourself "in your mind's eye" presenting a public speech. In the chapters that follow we will move from this mental image to the skills and orientation that you will need to accomplish your goals.

LEARNING EXPERIENCES

Objectives

After studying this chapter, you should be able to *do* the following:

1. Differentiate between a process and an event.
2. Cite and explain the misconceptions about public speaking.
3. Critique the model shown in Figure 2-1 and provide illustrations that either fit the model or require modifications.
4. Discuss your reactions to the visualization exercise. Were you comfortable and able to picture yourself in the situation? What caused you the greatest anxiety?
5. Give examples of positive and negative feedback behaviors. Cite other behaviors not mentioned in the text.

Exercises

1. Meet with a group of 4-6 classmates and discuss your conceptions concerning public speaking. Be able to supply personally observed examples that illustrate your points. Summarize your observations to the total class in the form of an oral report.
2. Use the model shown in Figure 2-1 as the basis for an analysis of an actual speech that you attend. For example, analyze a speech in your church or on your campus and show the way in which the ten components cited play a role. Your analysis should either be reported to the total class or to a group as your instructor directs.
3. Simulate the positive and negative feedback behaviors cited from the research of Jon Blubaugh. As time permits, have members of the class take two conditions for a couple of minutes. Compare your reactions and feelings.
4. Critique the sample speech on pages 23-25. What do you feel was missing by having to rely upon the manuscript? Discuss these judgments with your classmates.

NOTES

[1]We prefer the term interaction and use it in the way that some writers use transaction. See, David H. Smith, "Communication Research and the Idea of Process," *Speech Monographs*, XXXIX (August 1972); and Karen Rasmussen, "A Transactional Perspective," in Donald K. Darnell and Wayne Brockriede, *Persons Communicating*. Englewood Cliffs, NJ: Prentice-Hall, Inc., 1976, pp. 28-38.

[2]Jon A. Blubaugh, "Effects of Positive and Negative Audience Feedback on Selected Variables of Speech Behavior," *Speech Monographs*, XXXVI (June 1969), pp. 131-137.

[3]Jack Nicklaus and K. Bowden, "Play Better Golf," a King Features syndicated column dated 4-21-76.

[4]Timothy Galloway, *The Inner Game of Tennis*. New York: Random House, 1974, p. 59.

3

Your Responsibilities as an Audience Member

Receivers of messages determine to a great extent the success of the communication transaction. In Chapter 1 we described the responsibilities of the speaker in our society. We believe that the members of an audience have similar responsibilities.

As members of an audience we have considerable control over a speaker. We *choose* whether to attend the speaking event; our presence is a message that we are willing to hear what the speaker has to say. We can choose to attend psychologically, to listen. We can shut out the speaker by daydreaming or by engaging in mental argument. On the other hand, we may *choose* to be empathic or critical listeners. Our perception of the speaker will influence our willingness to listen. Additionally, our responses to the speaker will influence the speaker's subsequent behaviors. In this chapter we shall examine the potential choices of members of an audience and the responsibilities involved.

ATTENDING: YOUR PHYSICAL AND PSYCHOLOGICAL PRESENCE

As free agents, we decide how we want to spend our time, whether we wish to watch television, to attend a concert or a sports event, to take college courses leading to a degree, or to attend speeches.

Physical Attendance

At least six factors might influence you to attend a speech.

1. One factor is *habit*. You may go to hear a lecture because you always go to a particular series. Similarly, you may have a habit of

Owen Franken/Stock Boston

always going to church on Sunday morning, regardless of what the minister or speaker may have to say. Habit impels you to attend a particular event and expend your time and exert your energy to be there.

2. A second factor may be *external pressures*. For example, your roommate may convince you to hear a particular speaker on campus, or your parents may influence you to hear a particular topic discussed. If you belong to an organization, you may be expected to attend a meeting at which a speech will be given.

3. You may also go to a speech as a means of achieving a *desired goal*. If you have felt a need for new information, and you believe that a speaker can satisfy this need, you are willing to make an effort to hear the presentation. For example, when you are considering what to do after graduation, you would probably want to hear a speech discussing job opportunities for graduates in your field.

4. You also go to speeches for *psychological reinforcement*. You like to have your own beliefs and prejudices confirmed and validated. If you believe strongly in women's rights, an advocate of that position is likely to have your attendance at a public presentation.

5. Similarly, you may also like *to be identified as a member of a particular audience*. Just as people in business have corporate identities, you may wish to be seen and identified with particular groups. For example, Young Republicans or Young Democrats may meet to support a particular candidate. You may, in effect, be symbolically identified with the speaker and his or her cause. A speaker advocating gay liberation or a speaker in opposition may gain your attendance and response based upon your own beliefs or feelings. You also choose to

attend such events as funerals in order that you may symbolically identify with the bereaved family and other mourners.

6. Finally, a compelling reason to attend a speech is for *entertainment or the satisfaction of curiosity.* Humorists and people who have had unique or unusual experiences remain in popular demand. And topics such as extrasensory perception and flying saucers generally arouse curiosity and cause us to want to know more.

Psychological Presence

In all cases, as receivers of the message, you determine whether or not communication transpires. You determine this first by your physical attendance, and second by whether or not you "tune in" the speaker. Your psychological presence is determined by an impelling drive: the fact that the speaker has something to offer that you want. You choose whether to give the speaker your psychological presence.

Psychological presence has tremendous impact on the communication process. We all know what it feels like to talk to a person who is reading or daydreaming and obviously not listening to us. Remember how disruptive such nonattentive behavior is to our communication. The nonattentive audience has similar impact upon the speaker and the presentation of the message.

In an experiment on the impact of attending behavior, at a prearranged signal six students in a psychology seminar switched from the traditional student's slouched posture and passive listening and notetaking to attentive posture and active eye contact with the teacher. In the nonattending condition the teacher had been lecturing from his notes in a monotone, using no gesture, and paying little or no attention to the students. However, once the students began to demonstrate psychological attendance, the teacher began to gesture, to increase his verbal rate, and to create a lively classroom climate. At another prearranged signal later in the class, the students ceased their attentive gestures and returned to the passive state. The teacher "after some painful seeking for continued reinforcement" returned to the unengaging behavior with which he had begun the class. In the nonattending condition, the teacher paid no attention to the students and the students reciprocated in kind.[1] Both the teacher and students got what they deserved: reciprocated inattention. Attending made the difference; this experiment further illustrates the interactive nature of public communication discussed in Chapter 2.

Attending requires being psychologically "in tune" with the contexts in which the speaker presents the message. The responsible listener must be attuned to the various environments that he or she encounters—the physical setting, the internal states of the people present, and the larger societal mood of the times. Gerard Egan aptly observes:

> ... *Attending, therefore, involves the skill of listening to words, sentences, and ideas, to nonverbal behavior, to interpersonal situations, to the voices of particular cultures and to cultural differences, and to trends in society. Whoever constantly puts filters between himself and the "messages" coming from his multiple environments is not good at attending, fails to discriminate, and, ultimately, communicates poorly.*[2]

Attending, then, is the act of being physically and psychologically present.

In summary, we choose to go to a speaking event; we decide to give the speaker our attention; we are now ready to listen.

LISTENING

Just as we choose to attend, we also choose to listen. Contrary to a common assumption, the listener role is not a passive one; it requires active involvement if communication is to take place. We have all learned to "fake" listening, to appear to be interested in a classroom lecture while our minds are elsewhere, daydreaming or engaging in private planning.

In fact, we have become quite adept at *not* listening. In a society in which we are constantly bombarded with noise, we learn to close our minds to such distractions. Our brain selects those cues that have significance for us. This capacity to ignore insignificant noise is a genuine blessing, but it can lead to bad listening habits. The listener determines whether or not communication will take place.

Listening for Information

Much listening in a public forum has for its purpose the obtaining and retaining of some form of knowledge. Many experiments have tested audiences after listening to a speech to determine how much information they have retained. As Carl Weaver has stated:

> ... *In general, even in situations where the listeners were not facing the prospect of being called upon to speak next, they could remember only about 25 percent of the information called for in the test. They actually heard less than that, because at least some of them knew some of the information before the speaker said it.*[3]

Such experiments are merely rough approximations and cannot be considered totally accurate, yet they do suggest a problem we can observe both in ourselves and others: We do not hear enough of what is said.

Not only must you listen for the content of the message, but you must also seek to evaluate its credibility: Should you believe what is said? To what extent does it agree with your experience, the reported experience of other persons in whom you have confidence, and the general wisdom accepted by most people?

Listening for an accurate understanding of the message as well as seeking to assess its credibility are important functions for you to achieve whenever you're a member of an audience. However, although you critically seek to assess credibility of the message, you must do so in a way that does not limit (1) your ability to receive it, or (2) the speaker's ability to present it. If you are very judgmental, supercritical while trying to listen to a speaker, you may not be able to listen with an open mind. In addition, if your nonverbal behavior is negative, the speaker may become inhibited and falter in his or her presentation. It is not easy to be both open-minded and sensitive to credibility at the same time. However, this is exactly your responsibility as a listener to a public speech.

Listening for Decisions

Critical evaluation of ideas is essential to all of us in the decision-making process. However, to achieve this, we must hear fully what the speaker has to say—to hear him or her out, and to avoid giving the speaker negative feedback that will impede the full and free expression of thought and feeling. Usually this means suspending critical judgment until we understand the speaker's message. Too frequently we let our predispositions block new ideas or ideas contrary to our beliefs from entering our minds and fail to give them consideration. We have perfected the debater's technique of refuting point-by-point controversial ideas as they are presented to us.

Let's assume, however, that a speaker is authentically trying to communicate with us. What critical assessments do we make after we have given fair and empathic hearing to his or her address? Begin by asking yourself four questions: (1) What is the speaker really saying? (2) Does the speaker make sense? (3) Why should I believe this? (4) Why is this important?

1. *What is the speaker really saying?* In this first question our search is for the true meaning of the speaker's ideas. Are there hidden meanings? Are there double meanings? If the speaker's meaning appears to be obscure, we may search for probable reasons for his or her not being more explicit. Deliberate ambiguity is a common tactic of speakers who feign good intentions in order to deceive listeners. Irresponsible speakers are frequently vague; they fail to use names, numbers, dates, and places, but rely on generalities of all sorts. Terms such as *truth, freedom, progress,* and *the people's will* may be used; they mean vastly different

things to different people. If the speaker's meaning is not clear, ask clarifying questions at the end of the speech. If there is no formal forum period, you can quite often talk to the speaker privately for a brief moment after the speech.

2. *Does the speaker make sense?* There are four basic flaws in reasoning that you should watch for when you evaluate ideas: *non sequitur*, false causes, hasty generalizations, and the bandwagon appeal.

Non sequitur refers to instances in which one statement does not follow from another. If someone were to say, "Enrollment in American colleges is declining; I guess I don't need to worry about going to college," that person would be guilty of using a *non sequitur*. The mere fact that enrollments are declining says nothing about the value of a college education. This *non sequitur* is fairly obvious to most of us, but some of them are much more subtle and much more difficult to detect. Unless a listener carefully reflects upon the sequencing of a speaker's statements, such errors in reasoning often go unnoticed.

A speaker commits a *false cause* fallacy when he or she ascribes something as the cause of an effect when in reality it is not the cause at all. When someone tells an audience that we have to curb labor unions because the growth of labor unions has brought with it considerable unemployment, we can quite legitimately ask if a causal relationship actually exists between labor unions and unemployment. Doesn't a general business recession often cause rising unemployment? We should always test assumptions of causal relationships that a speaker may make. The following three questions are especially pertinent: Is the ascribed cause the real cause? Is it the only cause? Is it an important cause?

We are all given to *hasty generalizations*. "I once had a German shepherd dog that was very lazy. I just couldn't get it to do anything. I guess German shepherds just can't be counted on for much." Frequently we hear such statements in conversation. Similar statements find their way into public speeches. A hasty generalization occurs everytime we generalize about something from too few instances. In the above statement the "expert" on dogs generalized from a sample of one. It is important that a critical listener ask if the speaker's conclusions are drawn from sufficient examples. In other words, does it make sense to generalize from the data base the speaker is using?

The *bandwagon appeal* suggests that we should believe something because "everybody believes it"; or it suggests that we do something because "everybody is doing it." People may be convinced by this "follow the crowd" form of reasoning. In such cases people surrender individuality and bow to conformity. Whenever a speaker is trying to ground an argument in the thought that "it is commonly held" or "everybody seems to be doing it," the listener should be wary. Does it make sense to do something merely because there are others doing it? A number of college students each year commit suicide. Does it follow that therefore you should commit suicide?

3. *Why should I believe this?* Before making a decision on an issue we should become thoroughly acquainted with the available supporting data. If the primary reason for listening to a speech is to find important information about a topic and its corroborating evidence, you should raise the question, "Why should I believe this?" And if the speaker fails to answer the question during the speech, it is highly appropriate to ask questions about supporting evidence during the forum period. Since evidence is discussed in detail in Chapters 6 and 10, we will merely suggest at this time that you ask: (a) What is the source of the speaker's claims? Do they stem from the speaker's personal experience? Statistical data? The testimony of authorities? Specific examples? Direct observation? (b) Is the source of the speaker's evidence reliable? Is the source competent to observe? Is the source prejudiced or biased?

4. *Why is this so important?* Debaters have for years used a device known as the "so what" technique. It consists of questioning the importance of the opponent's arguments. The "so what" technique is equally useful in evaluating the ideas of a public speaker. A speaker may develop a point with meticulous care but fail to demonstrate that it has significance. If so, you should rightly ask, "So what?" "Why is this important?" Certainly most commercial testimonials should receive the "so what" treatment. A prominent Hollywood star smokes Marlboros. So what? A baseball superstar eats Wheaties. So what? If a speaker were to argue that you should oppose capital punishment because it was opposed by the greatest criminal lawyer of all time, Clarence Darrow, you should say, "So what?" What you should be interested in is Darrow's *arguments* against capital punishment.

This section on Listening for Decisions can be summed up with four words: *meaning, reasoning, support, significance.*

Listening with Empathy

As you listen both for information and to make effective decisions, you also need to be able to empathize with the speaker, that is, identify with the speaker's feelings and point of view. Gary Cronkhite has offered the following analysis:

> *Empathy—the ability to feel and understand what another person is feeling and thinking—is probably the most valuable asset a communicator can acquire. Empathy is both a cause and an effect of successful communication. In fact, cause and effect in this case blend so completely that in a broad sense we can say that empathy is communication.*[4]

Empathic listening can only occur in an atmosphere of responsibility and trust. Judgment and evaluation are typical and habitual human reactions. We have been accustomed to making quick judgments about whether or not something is desirable. We have learned to listen defensively with the intent of protecting our own positions. "I'll listen, but my mind is made up!" The problem comes when we don't listen to one another, when we make an evaluation of another person's point of view or frame of reference, before we understand it.

Research suggests the adverse affects of a judgmental audience. Jack Gibb made a detailed study of group behavior by analyzing tapes of discussions and reported three effects of judgment by the listener:

1. *The listener is prevented from concentrating on the message as sent.*
2. *The listener distorts the message.*
3. *The listener misses the cues that indicate the motives, values, and emotions of the sender.*[5]

Gibb's conclusion is that judgment arouses devastating doubts about ourselves that distort our ability to hear accurately. We believe that this principle applies to speaker-audience situations. A judgmental atmosphere creates problems for the speaker as well as the listener. No doubt you have been in situations where it was difficult to share your thoughts because the listener did not appear to understand or agree with what you were saying. The listeners in a judgmental condition may shake their heads in disagreement or interrupt the speaker. The speaker's attention may be diverted and delivery may suffer. It is frustrating to be put on the defensive when we are trying to communicate something important.

Listening with empathy requires that we temporarily suspend our own frame of reference and try to get into the speaker's inner world as he or she experiences it. This does not mean, however, that we necessarily agree with what the speaker has said, only that we genuinely understand the point of view and the feelings about it.

Empathic listening helps speakers understand themselves better. Carl Rogers has hypothesized that the more empathic our listening, the more willing and able the speaker will be to express feelings, give meanings to these feelings and try out new ideas.[6]

Empathic listening is a difficult skill, but we believe that it is such a powerful aid to communication that even when a person tries and only partially succeeds, the mere attempt may help the communication. Such an attempt is in itself an expression of respect for the speaker's views, a statement of caring in this situation, and most important, a desire to truly understand.

Improving Listening Habits

As with other communication skills, good listening habits can be developed. They can be learned and improved by persons who have desire and determination. William A. Conboy suggests five guidelines that can help people improve their capabilities as listeners:

1. *Understand the nature of listening behavior.* We often find that poor listeners are poorly informed *about* listening. Directors of

training programs in schools and in corporations frequently report improved listening performances following the "knowledge" phase alone in their courses.

2. *Know your own listening habits.* Listening improvement depends upon self-awareness. The first step is to conduct a self-inventory. Find out how many "spare-time" distractions you fall prey to in ten minutes of average speaking. Find out what kinds of nonlistening activities make up your listening profile. Self-awareness may make you self-conscious, but awareness of where you are is vital if you plan to build a bridge to where you want to be. The "Listening Profile" at the end of this chapter should assist in your self-inventory.

3. *Practice listening control.* Practice implies exercises, drill, and preparation *prior* to the moment of need. Too many of us never practice high-gear listening except at the moment of need. No football team would be successful if it never practiced before its crucial games. Workouts are needed in all sports to get the muscles and techniques toned up. Listening muscles and techniques need comparable scrimmages if the results are to be satisfactory when the chips are down. Once a week, choose a practice situation—a short talk on which you can test yourself. See how much you can remember after the talk. Try to reproduce it in its entirety. Sometimes it helps to record a speech as you listen, then attempt to reproduce it, then check your reproduction against the tape. Strive to improve your retention scores as you go along week by week. These scrimmages make a difference when the big game comes along.

4. *Create your own motivations.* Productive listening depends heavily on attention and concentration. These in turn depend heavily on motivation. In building better listening habits, it is sometimes useful to

Figure 3-1   The Three Types of Listening

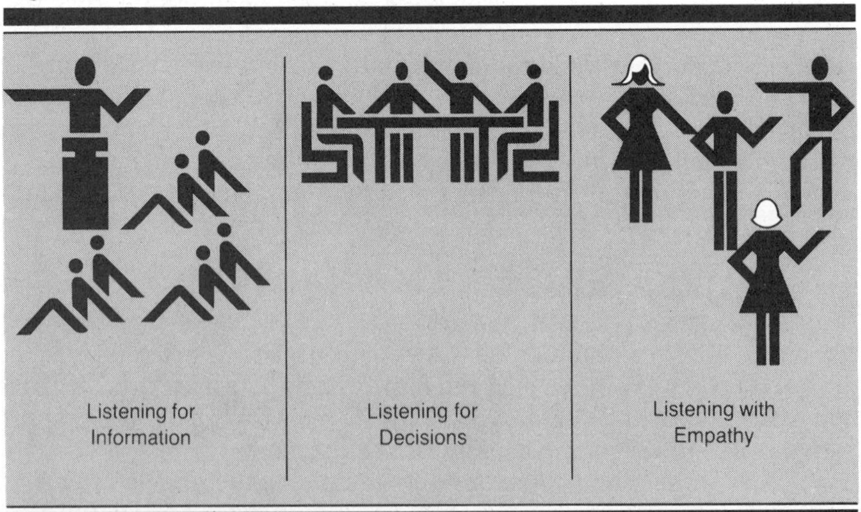

Listening for Information

Listening for Decisions

Listening with Empathy

supplement ordinary motivation with special techniques. For example, see how well you can anticipate the speaker's next point or the overall design of the speech. By actively searching for the speaker's master plan, you will be able to see each piece in better perspective. Tell yourself before a speech that you will be called upon to reconstruct it for someone else after the speech is over, that you will be responsible for a later accurate summary. Play the role of newspaper reporter. This is based on two sound principles of learning. First, we retain the details of an experience better when we *want to remember*. Second, we remember better those things which we *expect to use*.

Some expert listeners pretend to themselves that they will be quizzed about a talk afterwards, perhaps on a television quiz show. This capitalizes on the principle of *anticipated* gain as a source of motivation.

5. *Develop your own tools.* The preceeding four guidelines or suggestions establish the behavioral climate within which good listening habits can grow. Beyond these it would be misleading to identify too many specific rules or techniques. What succeeds for one person may not succeed for another. The tools used in listening must be appropriate to the individual using them. Notetaking is one good example. The amount of notetaking or the kind of notetaking a listener engages in will depend on that listener's needs and experience. Listeners-in-training should experiment with a variety of methods and devices, testing and choosing on the basis of personal results.

It is important that you make use of special tools for better listening, but it is equally important that your tools fit you as well as they fit listening. Don't borrow your neighbor's tool chest. Develop your own.[7]

PROVIDING HELPFUL CLASSROOM FEEDBACK

In most speech situations it is helpful to a speaker to receive feedback from the listeners. As a responsible and caring audience member you should seek to provide such feedback. In training programs and public speaking courses such feedback is essential. There is no question that it should be provided; the sensitive question is, how?

Having a positive attitude toward the classroom speech and giving your attention fully are prerequisites for intelligent feedback. We suggest that you concentrate first and foremost on the subject matter of the speech, next on the adaptation of the speech to this audience, and finally on the speaker's presentational abilities. You should be able to supply answers to three questions:

1. *What was the speaker's main idea and how was it developed?* The main idea may or may not have been stated explicitly by the speaker, but whether it is stated or not, you should be able to identify and remember it. Presumably the speaker composed the speech using materials and a pattern of organization as a means of making the

message understood and the purpose clear. Even if you cannot detect the exact pattern of arrangement, you should have a global impression of the cohesiveness of the speech: Did it all fit together? Being able to distinguish the main points in the body of the speech will help you answer the question about the speaker's main idea.

2. *Was the speech appropriate for this audience?* If you can assume that you are a typical member of the audience, you can decide how appropriate the level and content of the speech seemed to you. The significance of the topic to you, the amount of interest you sustained, and what you learned and felt as a result of the speech are important. Did the speaker bring the topic to life and communicate at a level you could comprehend?

3. *Was the speech presented effectively?* Be wary of concentrating too much on technique of presentation. Even if the speaker put on a good show, was that all that was accomplished? Since the delivery can either help or hinder the presentation, you should note the use of voice, body, and visual aids. Try to determine whether they added to your reception or distracted you.

Begin with these three points of concentration and then gradually develop more sophisticated goals for your listening.

If the speaker has planned a specific purpose in terms of potential audience response to the message, he or she should have some means of determining how successful the speech was. You, as a listener, can also have some means for helping determine the degree of success of the speech by deciding *after* the speech is completed what the speaker was trying to do. You can ask yourself such questions as, "What did the speaker expect me to learn, or how much was I influenced as a result of the speech?" If the speaker did or did not gain the desired response from the audience, to what do you attribute this result?

Having a constructive, positive, caring attitude toward the speaker is a prerequisite for feedback in the form of suggestions. If you have practiced active listening, then you may offer specific feedback in the following forms:

1. *Reflection of content understanding.* The goal of this feedback is to reflect to the speaker that you truly understand the content of the speech from the speaker's perspective. Paraphrasing and restating the ideas that you have received are appropriate.

2. *Degree of empathy.* Accurate empathy involves getting "inside the speaker." We should communicate to the speaker the degree to which we (1) understand and (2) share the same feelings about the topic.

3. *Areas for improvement and growth.* Underlying all constructive criticism should be the feeling: I respect and value you as a person. If the speaker wishes constructive feedback, you may identify concrete, specific barriers to your understanding. You may cite alternatives that occur to you regarding future presentations.

SUMMARY

Our role as a member of an audience provides several possible choices. First, we may choose to attend, involving the giving of both our physical presence and psychological attention. Listening requires an outpouring of energy and we must choose to give much or little of this energy.

Listening can involve the gaining of information as well as making decisions. As listeners, we can help determine whether or not the atmosphere is empathic and encouraging for a speaker, or defensive and hostile.

We have presented five guidelines to help people improve their capabilities as listeners: (1) Understand the motive of listening behavior, (2) Know your own listening habits, (3) Practice listening control, (4) Create your own motivation, and (5) Develop your own tools. As responsible listeners, you can, if given the opportunity, provide constructive feedback to the speaker. Such feedback should be based upon a positive, caring attitude toward the speaker. Finally, we have further suggested ways in which the classroom may be used in the development of these listening skills.

LEARNING EXPERIENCES

Objectives

After reading this chapter you should be able to *do* the following:

1. Analyze different audiences and suggest the possible factors that cause people to attend.
2. Discuss what factors you find important to your attending and listening behaviors.
3. Cite ways of improving listening capabilities.
4. Explain the concept of empathy.
5. Suggest ways of listening for understanding and for decision-making and for the speaker's content in an efficient way.
6. Give your classmates responsible feedback and criticism.

Exercises

1. With a group of your classmates (4-6 people), formulate a list of *all* the speaking events that you have attended in the last two months. Try to categorize these occasions and determine the *reasons why* you attended.

2. Rate the speeches reported in the group according to their interest to the listeners. What factors made the audience "tune in" to the speakers? Report to the total class.
3. To check on your capacities as a listener, you are encouraged to complete the following listening profile.
4. Share your listening profile with your instructor. Set personal goals in areas that you would like to improve.
5. Based upon the suggestions for giving feedback, write a critique of a public speech that you have heard recently.

Listening Profile

Answer the following questions and chart your listening profile by circling the question number in the appropriate chart division. Connect your circles for a continuous profile (see chart at end of the profile).

When Participating in a Communication Situation as a Listener, Do You:

1. Try to make sure that you are in good physical condition, rested and alert?
2. Prepare yourself by becoming as well-informed of the speaker's subject matter as time allows?
3. Allow for your own prejudices?
4. Sit facing the speaker and close enough to hear without strain?
5. Look at the speaker as he or she talks?
6. Give the speaker your undivided attention?
7. Avoid all controllable interruptions?
8. Compensate for unavoidable distractions such as noise, temperature, and poor lighting?
9. Allow ample time for listening, thus avoiding undue tension and stress?
10. Try to see things from the speaker's point of view?
11. Try to find the area of mutual interest in what is being said?
12. Keep an open mind?
13. Try to hear "what" is being said and not "how" it is being said?
14. Try to listen for nonverbal meanings—meanings given through tone, emphasis, volume, and gesture?
15. Try to encourage the speaker by your attention and willingness to listen?
16. Take advantage of your ability to discern and recall the speaker's main ideas?

17. Withhold evaluations of the ideas and beliefs until you understand them?
18. Upon completion of the communication write down the important points?

Usually:	1 2 3 4 5 6 7 8 9 10 11 12 13 14 15 16 17 18	Excellent
Sometimes:	1 2 3 4 5 6 7 8 9 10 11 12 13 14 15 16 17 18	Could use improvement
Seldom:	1 2 3 4 5 6 7 8 9 10 11 12 13 14 15 16 17 18	Work on these

NOTES

[1]A. Ivey and J. Hinkle, "The Transactional Classroom," unpublished paper cited by Gerard Egan, *The Skilled Helper*. Monterey, CA: Brooks/Cole Publishing Company, 1975, p. 62.

[2]Gerard Egan, *The Skilled Helper*, p. 63.

[3]Carl Weaver, *Speaking in Public*. New York: American Book Co., 1966, p. 59.

[4]Gary Cronkhite, *Public Speaking and Critical Listening*. Menlo Park, CA: Benjamin/Cummings, 1978, pp. 38-39.

[5]Jack Gibb, "Defensive Communication," *ETC*, 22 (June 1965), pp. 221-229.

[6]Carl R. Rogers, *On Becoming a Person*. Boston: Houghton Mifflin, 1961, pp. 330-331.

[7]William A. Conboy, *Working Together*. Columbus, OH: Charles E. Merrill, 1976, p. 74-77.

4

Your
Responsibilities
as a Speaker

 When you want to listen to music on the radio, you commonly dial directly to a favorite station because you assume that the channel will be clear and that the music will be to your liking. But if your favorite station is broadcasting a special talk show that does not appeal to you, you may turn the dial in search of something of interest. And if you hear a station that has a lot of static or fades in and out, you dial on until you find one with less noise. The next station you find may be free from noise but you don't like the music they are playing, and so you continue to dial until you find one that is both clear and is playing music you like. At other moments, you may turn on the radio in search of weather information, because you are planning an outing and the sky in the west is boiling with ominous, grey-black clouds. You may find a station that is giving weather news, but it is so noisy that it interferes almost totally with your listening. So you quickly flick the dial in the hope you will find a station that will meet your needs by giving you weather information on at least a relatively noise-free channel. If you find such a station, you listen intently, because you are receiving what you want and need.

RELATE IDEAS TO YOUR AUDIENCE

So it is with public speaking. Listeners want to hear a speech by a speaker who keeps the communication channel as clear as possible and who is presenting ideas that are adapted to their needs and interests. Although they cannot change the station if the speaker is not telling them anything of interest in a noise-free manner, they certainly don't have to pay

attention, and in some cases they can get up and walk out. Your target, therefore, in this chapter is to examine what you can do as a speaker to eliminate as much interference as possible from the communication channel and how you can relate your ideas to the needs and interests of the audience.

If you are the speaker, you should know that you have certain choices available to you that will help communication occur. If you have knowledge that you think will be of value to people or if you have ideas that you feel will help them to make wise decisions, your goal should be to help the listeners hear what you have to say. You will, therefore, want to clear the communication channel as best as you can and to present your ideas in a way that your listeners see value in them. In order to do this you must observe seven guidelines.

Avoid Irritating Your Listeners

Begin by recognizing that there are three common irritants you should try to avoid in public speaking: (1) needlessly arousing listeners' biases or prejudices, (2) using the listeners' time poorly, and (3) not making yourself heard.

Before your presentation you can ascertain some biases or prejudices held by a particular group of listeners. Many of these biases will be entirely unrelated to your topic or thesis. In the selection of your supporting materials be careful to avoid arousing known prejudices or biases of your listeners. You do not avoid telling them relevant facts that are unpleasant but demonstrably true; rather you avoid *needlessly* arousing negative responses. For example, in a speech on equal rights for women and men, there is no need to mention the controversial abortion question.

Both in preparation and in your actual presentation you should seek to avoid needless use of your listeners' time. For example, one successful speaker has found a workable formula for high-school commencement addresses—presenting two ideas in a ten-minute address. Audiences are satisfied that the traditional protocol has been met, and they are delighted at the consideration in the use of their time. They also have remembered and been challenged by the two main ideas:

1. In our culture we tend to see our world in two separate stereotyped categories: good or bad; moral or immoral; success or failure.
2. Because very few conditions or behaviors are entirely good, we often classify them in the remaining category— bad, immoral, stupid, failure.

Conclusion: We must use additional categories (fairly good, partly successful, sometimes immoral, as bright as most folks) to properly assess ourselves and our lives.

In any presentation, seek to be brief. Make your points, clarify them, support them, and move on. To many audiences a lengthy presentation—simply by reason of its length—is not very good, and they may cease to listen.

At the outset of the chapter we suggested that a common aggravation is listening to a radio station that fades in and out. This is a distracting factor: In public speaking you should speak loudly enough at all times so that all listeners can hear you easily. If people have to strain to hear you, your effectiveness will be reduced. A good rule to follow is to speak directly to the listeners in the back row during much of your speech; in that way, you will almost certainly project sufficiently so that all can hear. Additionally, if you are using a microphone, be careful not to turn away from it periodically, for if you do, you will produce a fade-in, fade-out effect. You can also produce aggravation by either standing too close or too far away from the microphone. In the one instance, you will be hard to hear, and in the other there will be an unpleasant distortion of your voice—much like static on the radio. The listening experience should be made as pleasant and as easy as possible.

Involve Your Listeners

You can involve your listeners and thereby encourage them to consider your ideas by asking them to respond to your ideas and by inviting them to ask questions during your presentation.

You can show respect for your listeners by making them partners in the speech process. If you feel that there is a "wall" between you and your listeners, you may get closer to them by moving from behind a desk or podium. You may also invite listeners' participation, and if they are reluctant, ask for specific help. One easy way is to poll the audience, asking for a show of hands in response to questions related to your presentation. For example, if you were to give a speech on the "double bind," you might raise the question, "How many of you have heard the term 'double bind'?" The members of the audience may offer possible definitions, and this interaction keeps you from either underestimating or overestimating their knowledge on your topic.

Audiences usually like to be included in the presentation and will volunteer to help the speaker. Simple matters, such as distributing handouts or helping you in a demonstration, may aid in removing barriers between you and your audience. We recall a student who spoke on maintaining the 55-mile-per-hour speed limit. In demonstrating the stopping distance required for speeds of 55 and 65 miles per hour, he requested two volunteers to stand as far apart as they thought the distance would be to stop at 65, then 55. The speaker then showed with a tape measure that there was not enough space in the classroom to show the distance demanded.

Consider the Special Interests of Your Listeners

As you begin your speech preparation, ask yourself why is this meeting taking place and why are these people willing to listen to you? Perhaps they need or desire information which you can provide. Or they may have problems for which you are suggesting solutions. Or perhaps you will need to raise their concern or degree of awareness toward a potential problem which affects them.

This assessment of special interests is usually based on how well you know the members of the audience and why you are designated as the speaker. If you have been invited to address a class as a representative of a service group, then you know that the people invited you because they want to learn more about your club. As we shall discuss in Chapter 5, you will be drawing from your personal resources as a speaker, what you know and have experienced, to meet the needs of this audience.

If you have ever left a speaking situation and said, "That was an interesting speech," try to recall why you said that. Chances are the speaker touched on something that was of special interest to you. Perhaps you like baseball, and the speaker told baseball stories. Perhaps you are strongly interested in improving interpersonal relationships, and the speaker provided some concrete insights regarding human relations. Let's take a concrete example of what might or might not interest you. When you were a freshman you might have listened most attentively to a speech on "College Requirements," but as a junior the same speech would have seemed tedious because you no longer had concern about the subject. What this example suggests is a theory of relevance: That which is highly relevant to us at any given time is interesting to us. People all have special interests and the better the speech relates to them, the more attentive the audience will be.

Consider the Needs of People

In his well-known theory of human motivation, psychologist Abraham Maslow presented a hierarchy of basic human needs.[1] He distinguished between primary needs, which are physiologically based, such as the need for oxygen, food, and water; and acquired needs, which are social in nature and may have cultural derivations. Maslow devised an elaborate hierarchy of needs. The hierarchy, starting with the most basic and, thereby, strongest drives, suggests that acquired needs are perceived as significant only after the more basic needs are met. This hierarchy is as follows:

1. *Physiological needs.* These include oxygen, water, food, maintenance of body temperature (may involve clothing and shelter), sleep, sex, and exercise.

2. *Safety needs.* These include avoidance of falling, loud noises, flashing lights, bodily injury, illness, pain, and other sources of anxiety or fear; in a general way a need for a safe, organized, orderly, predictable environment.

3. *Belongingness, or love, needs.* These include friends, sweetheart or spouse, children, affectionate relations with others, a place in a chosen group; a need for both giving and receiving love.

4. *Esteem needs.* These include high self-regard and respect from others; these may be met by self-estimations of strength, confidence, freedom, and by others' recognition of one's status, prestige, reputation, importance, or competence.

5. *Needs for self-actualization.* These include doing what we are fitted for, fulfillment of our potential, and becoming everything we are capable of becoming. When our basic needs such as hunger, safety, and belongingness are not met, we feel aroused to act in ways to meet those needs. Maslow's general hierarchy of needs varies somewhat from person to person, depending on inborn differences and past experience. A person's hierarchy will also vary from time to time because of the change that comes with satisfaction of needs, such as the lessened influence of hunger after eating.

Examples of speeches that use the hierarchy of needs. Let us now suggest how this hierarchy of needs may be used by a speaker.

1. *Physiological needs.* A group of people going to another country may need information about food and water. A person facing health problems may be concerned about how exercise can serve him or her. Individuals at different times in their lives are interested in how their sexual needs can be met.

2. *Safety needs.* As with physiological needs, people entering a situation that is calling for change in their environment, such as a trip to a new territory, want to know how to proceed in a safe, predictable fashion. If they are moving to a new part of the country, they will be interested in conditions that may pose problems. For example, a new resident in the state of Kansas may be interested in signs warning of tornadoes and what to do in the event of a storm.

3. *Love needs.* People may be concerned about the quality of their relationships with others. For example, college students may be concerned about new ways of relating to their parents that express love and care for them but affirm their own independence.

4. *Esteem needs* are typically met in public speeches by recognition and awards presentations. For example, an award may be given in recognition of outstanding service or a special accomplishment.

Figure 4-1   Maslow's Hierarchy of Basic Human Needs

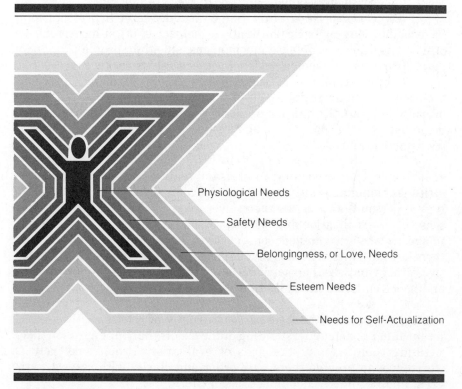

Physiological Needs

Safety Needs

Belongingness, or Love, Needs

Esteem Needs

Needs for Self-Actualization

5. Speeches of *self-actualization* are typically speeches that attempt to show a higher level of potential. For example, sermons and graduation speeches may exhort listeners to strive for their highest potential.

Adapt to the Attitudes of Your Listeners

An attitude is a relatively stable predisposition to respond in some consistent way toward a person, a group, a situation, or an idea. In order to accommodate your listeners' attitudes in a responsible way, you need to know why they are important to them. Based upon the needs of people, psychologist Daniel Katz has advanced a theory suggesting that people hold given attitudes that help them achieve basic goals.[2] He distinguishes four types of psychological functions that attitudes perform:

1. *Adjustment function.* Human beings typically seek to maximize rewards and minimize penalties. According to Katz, people develop attitudes that aid them in accomplishing this goal. They tend to favor a political party or candidate that will advance their economic lot—if they are in business, they likely favor a candidate who wants lower corporate taxes; however, persons who are unemployed will favor a candidate who seeks to increase employment and social welfare benefits.

2. *Ego-defense function.* Some attitudes serve to protect people from acknowledging basic truths about themselves or the harsh realities of life. They serve as defense mechanisms, shielding people from inner pain. "Projection" is such a device: People attribute to others traits that they find unacceptable in themselves, and in so doing, dissociate themselves from the traits. To the alcoholic it may be the other fellow who overindulges; to the failing student it may be the teacher who is incompetent; to the hostile and aggressive child it may be the other child who started the fight.

3. *Value-expressive function.* While ego-defensive attitudes prevent people from revealing unpleasant realities to themselves, other attitudes help give *positive* expression of central values and indicate the type of person they imagine themselves to be. Such attitudes reinforce a sense of self-realization and self-expression. A person may have a self-image as an "enlightened conservative" or a "militant radical" and therefore cultivate attitudes that support and represent such a perspective. Others may see themselves as being tuned in to the popular culture, and hence cultivate attitudes that reinforce this perspective.

4. *Knowledge function.* People seek some degree of order, clarity, and stability in their personal frames of reference; they search for meaning in and understanding of the events that impinge upon them. Attitudes help supply standards of evaluation. People may rely on stereotypes to provide them with order and clarity with respect to the great and bewildering complexities of life.

Examples of speeches adapting to audience attitudes. Speakers may adapt to attitudes of audience members in a number of ways.

1. *Adjustment function.* At an orientation program for incoming college freshmen a speaker may talk about activities at the university. The speaker may describe events or games that the payment of an activity fee entitles the students to attend without paying admission.

2. *Ego-defense function.* Any speech topic has the potential for touching on defenses that members of audiences use. For example, a classroom speech on overemphasis of athletics is likely to produce defensiveness from members of sports teams. Focusing on the ways in which overemphasis can be damaging to the athletes themselves may reduce the level of defensiveness of athletes who are listening.

3. *Value-expressive function.* Since this attitude function is concerned with those core values by which people define themselves—such as religious, well-educated, socially enlightened, liberal, and so forth—the speaker may show how his or her ideas assist the listener in implementing these values. A speech launching a clothing drive for the underprivileged might appeal to listeners who are generous and sympathetic. A speaker seeking greater support for higher education might draw the image of an enlightened person writing the governor of the state urging support for the state's educational system. The speaker will do well to point out that the listener's support of the measure will become widely recognized.

4. *Knowledge function.* People want to be knowledgeable about topics important to them. For example, a speech on "tax shelters" may help members of the audience, who think their income tax is too high, feel that they better understand the tax system, and have a clearer knowledge of how they can receive tax benefits.

Consider the Demographic Traits of Your Audience

An audience is a collection of individuals who are willing to give you a segment of time to hear from you. But, obviously, you cannot send a separate message to each one. You must deal with an audience in large part as if it were a unit—a single, collective entity with characteristics that you can average out into an approximate range. You, therefore, make some educated guesses about the characteristics of an audience that are important to your presentation, and plan and deliver your speech at a level that will engage the most alert listeners.

Suppose a student wishes to talk about one or another feature of President Reagan's programs. Factors such as *age, sex, race, group membership,* and *education* of audience members would need to be considered. For example, in 1981 President Reagan considered reducing social security benefits. A student discussing this topic would need to consider how age might influence the response of listeners. Older

Americans may be concerned about the possibilities of loss of income while younger people may be concerned about the cost of the system.

Reagan's attitudes toward women's rights may be viewed differently by women and men in a given audience. Similarly, Reagan's policies toward busing may cause greater emotional response to more members of one race than another. Both issues (women's rights and busing) will possibly be received differently by Republican and Democratic audiences, or audiences comprised of one or another religious affiliations.

The racial make-up of your audience may influence responses to topics or examples. Football coach Bart Starr once called a team meeting because he was concerned about leaks to the news media. To capture attention, and partially in jest, he brought a bullwhip to the meeting. Unfortunately, black players responded strongly to the prop. As one stated: "Can you imagine what the black guys thought when they saw a bullwhip? The first thing that goes through your mind is slavery days.... I know what I thought when I saw it: 'Does this go along with the job'?"

The level of education, experience, or sophistication of listeners should also be considered. An explanation of Reagan's tax program will have to be presented differently to a group of business school seniors than to a junior high school civics class. In any case be careful not to talk above the intellectual capacity of your listeners, but avoid with equal care any condescension to your audience.

Effective consideration of the demographic traits of your audience will help you adapt to your listeners in ways that will enhance your rapport with them and reduce potential barriers to communication.

Utilize Feedback From Your Listeners

Feedback—the way the audience responds to you and your message—enables you to assess the degree to which you are understood by your audience. The story is told of humanistic psychologist Carl Rogers and B. F. Skinner, the leading behavioral psychologist, disagreeing on the principle of behavior modification. Rogers was invited to speak to Skinner's students; without Rogers knowing it, Skinner told his students to respond favorably when Rogers moved to one side of the platform and to respond negatively when he stood in the center. According to the story, Rogers (without realizing what was happening) finished his talk way over to the rewarded (head nodding, eye contact, etc.) side of the platform. This story supports the research on the interactive nature of the speaker and audience behaviors cited in Chapter 2. The point for us to consider here is the value and effect upon us (as speakers) of audience feedback. It is a valuable tool for gaining and maintaining rapport with our listeners without sacrificing our personal integrity.

Observing your listeners can give you many useful clues concerning (1) the degree of attention they are giving your presentation, and (2) their attitude toward what you are saying. You should watch closely for attention clues such as, eye contact, distracting movements, coughing (a possible sign of boredom), members of the audience conversing among themselves, fidgeting, glancing at their watches, cupping their hands to their ears, and people leaving the room; these signs are straightforward and fairly dependable. Other signs of your listeners' attitudes toward you or your presentation are not nearly as dependable but are clearly worth noting. Shaking the head from side to side is a fairly dependable clue that the idea you are presenting needs more support. Sometimes a listener will suddenly turn to a neighbor and whisper emphatically; this could be a positive sign but more likely is an indication that your idea is in need of further explanation or support. Watching for feedback is a very useful way of adjusting to your listeners and modifying your presentation (not your basic ideas or stand on an issue). For a responsible speaker, the modification needed will be further or more careful explanation or support.

One of the best ways to become one with your listeners, to show that you trust them as you are asking them to trust you, is to offer to try to answer any questions they may wish to ask. You can clear up misconceptions, support points perceived by your listeners to be weak, and gain a rather strong advantage by showing that you believe enough in your own position to allow your listeners to ask questions. But the strongest impact is gained by demonstrating that you are a *part* of the interaction process; you and your listeners *together* are seeking to understand a topic or to solve a problem.

Do not be afraid that someone will confront you sharply about an alternative interpretation of events or an alternative solution to a problem. You may then use additional data or evidence (and listeners' time) to show that alleged arguments against your position are invalid. An early research study demonstrated that presenting arguments pro and con, with the weight of evidence supporting the advocated position, is significantly more effective than simply presenting one side of an issue.[3] A question giving you such an opportunity can work to your advantage.[4]

Of course, you run the risk that some less informed or prejudiced person may try to attack your stand. You must be prepared to meet such a situation without loss of your credibility—your respect by your listeners. Respond with facts and evidence; clarify your position as needed. Treat your adversary as a well-intentioned person seeking the common good but temporarily in error. Research evidence shows that if you can meet such questions and still maintain an image of being well-informed and highly reliable, your listeners will respond with stronger commitment and greater acceptance of your ideas.[5] Whatever you do, maintain your composure. Do not try to "beat" or ridicule your opponent; try, instead, to maintain the trust of those who are listening.

There is fairly good research evidence that, like Carl Rogers with

Skinner's students, whether we are aware of it or not, as speakers we are significantly influenced by the behavior of our listeners. Positive reactions will aid our motivation to present our ideas forcefully and in a positive way. Negative reactions such as visible loss of eye contact and distracting movements will tend to heighten our tension and diminish our motivation to be positive and forceful. These negative reactions by our listeners can affect our presentation without our realizing what is happening. The point to remember is this: Be aware of your reactions to negative responses of your listeners and compensate appropriately. Try to be more clear, more explicit in your explanations of your ideas; provide more supporting arguments and evidence for your proposals. Try to turn the reaction tide from unfavorable to favorable so that your own speaking behavior will become more natural, positive, and forceful. In this way, you can properly utilize your audience feedback.

SUMMARY

In this chapter we have identified some of the choices that you as a speaker must make as you approach a speaking situation. As guidelines, we have suggested that you consider the interests, needs, and attitudes of your audience, and that you present your ideas clearly and consider listener feedback. We have suggested three possible irritants that should be reduced: biases or prejudices, poor use of audience time, and not making yourself heard. We have suggested that you try to involve your listeners by inviting them to ask questions during your presentation.

We have emphasized from the beginning of this book the importance of the interaction with the audience. In this chapter, we emphasize the importance of utilizing feedback from your listeners. Although much of the adaptation must be made at the time of the presentation, you can think ahead and decide how you plan to maximize such feedback.

LEARNING EXPERIENCES

Objectives

After studying this chapter, you should be able to do the following:

1. Analyze the demographic characteristics of your prospective audience.
2. Determine the hierarchy of basic human needs in a given speaking situation.
3. Distinguish between the four types of psychological functions that attitudes meet.
4. Adapt to a given audience by noting their feedback.
5. Envision how you would respond to both negative and positive cues from an audience.

Exercises

1. Working in a group (4-6 people), formulate a questionnaire that you think would help you learn about a given audience. Try the questionnaire on other groups in the class and respond to the questionnaires that they have prepared. What did the questionnaires have in common? Would this information help you in adapting to a given audience?
2. In your group, discuss the seven guidelines suggested in this chapter and apply them to actual audiences, such as your church congregation or local clubs. What are the collective traits and predispositions of these groups?
3. Use the *Feedback Sheet* on pages 55-56 on a speaker that you hear. Compare your reactions with your classmates. What do the differences tell you about evaluating the communication process?
4. Ask members of your classroom audience to utilize such information as is on the *Feedback Sheet* in your subsequent speeches in class.
5. Give a short speech to the class describing a group of which you are a member. Indicate biases, prejudices, special interests, and attitudes of the group.

Responsible Public Speaking Feedback Sheet

Speaker _____

Circle your responses, please

Listener _____

		Yes		Undecided		No
I. Introduction:						
1.	Did the speaker attract your interest in the topic?	1	2	3	4	5
2.	Is the speaker qualified to speak on this topic?	1	2	3	4	5
3.	Is the purpose and direction of the speech clear?	1	2	3	4	5

Comments:

II. Body:

    1. Are the ideas clearly structured?   1   2   3   4   5

    2. Is the supporting material interesting?   1   2   3   4   5

    3. Is the supporting material adequate?   1   2   3   4   5

    4. Are the relationships between ideas clear?   1   2   3   4   5

Comments:

III. Delivery:

    1. Does the speaker seem poised and knowledgeable?   1   2   3   4   5

    2. Were there disturbing mannerisms that distracted you?   1   2   3   4   5

    3. Did the speaker have contact with you?   1   2   3   4   5

Comments:

IV. Conclusion, etc.:

    1. Did the speech pull together at the end?   1   2   3   4   5

    2. Did the speaker achieve his or her purpose?   1   2   3   4   5

    3. Was the audience attentive and supportive?   1   2   3   4   5

Comments:

NOTES

[1]Abraham H. Maslow, *Motivation and Personality*. New York: Harper & Row, 1954, pp. 80-106.

[2]Daniel Katz, "The Functional Approach to the Study of Attitudes," *Public Opinion Quarterly*, Vol. 24, 1960, pp. 163-204.

[3]Carl I. Hovland, Arthur A. Lumsdaine, and Fred D. Sheffield, "The Effects of Presenting One Side Versus Both Sides in Changing Opinion on a Controversial Subject," in *Readings in Social Psychology* (Theodore M. Newcomb, et al., eds.). New York: Holt, Rinehart & Winston, 1947, pp. 566-577.

[4]For a general review of research on this principle, see William J. McGuire, "Inducing Resistance to Persuasion: Some Contemporary Approaches," in *Advances in Experimental Social Psychology* (Leonard Berkowitz, ed.). New York: Academic Press, 1964, pp. 191-229.

[5]Wallace R. May, "Effects of Situational Stress on Fluency, Rate, and Proximity Behavior of College Student Speakers: Explicated by a New Model of Situational Effect," unpublished doctoral dissertation, University of Kansas, 1977; also see James C. McCroskey and Virginia P. Richmond, *The Quiet Ones: Communication Apprehension and Shyness*. Dubuque, IA: Gorsuch Scarisbrick, 1980.

Owen Franken/Stock Boston

Part 2

From Preparation to Presentation

In the previous four chapters we have presented a perspective of the public speaking process based upon the belief that responsibility in communication is essential. In the next five chapters we present an overview of the process of preparing and delivering the public speech. In Chapters 10-13 we go into much more detail concerning the preparation and development of informative and persuasive speeches.

We believe that an overview of speech preparation and delivery is essential at this point in the book because you will be asked by your instructor to start practice presentations before you have had the opportunity to study the book in its entirety. Your later practice speeches can be given a fine-tuned treatment by utilizing information presented in the later chapters.

5

Focusing Your Ideas

We hear a great deal about the world's energy shortages and the problems with energy supplies for the future. One source of energy not in short supply is human energy. We expend energy writing; we expend energy reading; all of life's activities provide energy outlets, and we choose when and how to expend energy. In a broad sense, life itself is energy. The human body radiates several forms of energy that can be easily measured by scientific instruments. Each of us is surrounded by an aura of radiant heat that can be perceived by a sensitive hand from several inches away. Scientists can measure this heat by thermistors and infrared sensors.[1]

Our communication, both verbal and nonverbal, can be examined as a utilization and expenditure of energy. The speaker is a center of vibrancy, emanating waves that radiate out through space and time and respond to and interact with the energy waves of other living creatures. Your first task in preparing for a speech will be to focus your energy and ideas in a way that will give direction and intention to your presentation.

ENERGY AND INTENTIONALITY

Many people have tried to identify the characteristics that distinguish humans from other animals. One distinctive characteristic is the capability of human beings to direct and sustain energy expression. This capability is what we called *intentionality*. The structure of the human brain enables us to delay responses in order to choose the most advantageous ones, but this directing capacity is of little or no value unless we also have the energy to implement that choice. Since there are

various sources and levels of human energy, some of which work for us while others work against us, it is important to know how to mobilize the energy we need, how to prevent creation of excess amounts, and how to channel all that we have. Energy undirected by intelligence can be wasteful and sometimes destructive; but intelligence unsupplemented by a constructive force of energy is lifeless and ineffective. No matter how finely we tune a car's engine, it will not run without gas; no matter how logical and correct our intellectual solution of a problem, there will be no change or improvement until we put our ideas into action.

Psychologist James F. T. Bugenthal has described or defined the crucial importance of intentionality as follows:

> *Intentionality is the process through which we bring to focus our being. Through our intentionality we may direct the diffuse array of our wants and needs, our information and interests, our talents and strengths, our hopes and fears — in short, our whole being.*[2]

Public speaking is an opportunity to focus energy through *intention*. A key difference between what we define as "interpersonal communication" and communication between speakers and audiences is that the latter is more frequently and more systematically planned.[3] Intention, as related to public speaking, then, means that you have clarified your own thinking and are prepared for the opportunity to talk. Directing your communicative energy through intentionality involves a clear consideration, determination, and specification of what you want to communicate and systematic attention to all of the factors that bear upon your achieving it.

The essence of public communication is the intention behind it.

Intention involves your *choice* of purpose, target, or goal. If you choose to share your experiences and ideas with an audience, you must assume responsibility for ordering and recreating them so that your listeners may understand and share them.

Planning does not preclude spontaneity, however. With experience in talking to an audience, you will likely become more at ease, more adaptive—in short, more spontaneous. Remember when you first learned to drive. Each operation required your total attention and concentration. With experience and practice, however, you were able to relax, listen to the radio, carry on a conversation, and still handle the car responsibly and effectively. Likewise, with your communication before audiences, spontaneity need not be permanently sacrificed in public speaking.

SELECTING YOUR SUBJECT

Occasionally you may have little or no control over the subject or topic of your speech. The instructor in your speech class will assign a topic or a group will ask you to talk on a particular subject that is familiar to you. Frequently, however, you have considerable latitude in selecting your topic. Initially, this element of choice may be a mixed blessing, because as a beginning student, you may view the selection of an appropriate subject as an obstacle. You can be sure that you have the right topic if you have lived with it, made it your own through experience and reflection, and talked about it in informal situations. For example, you may have raised and trained dogs or horses, taken them to shows, loved some specific animals, and invested time and energy learning things your classmates have often thought about but had no opportunity to experience. Perhaps you have been a member of a swimming team, competed in races, felt the heartbreak of losing and the thrill of finishing first. Or maybe you have the best jazz record collection of any owned by your acquaintances. To choose a subject for a speech, focus on what you know best and enjoy most. Ideally, your chosen subject should combine your personal resources and the interests and needs of your audience.

Your Personal Resources

In selecting a speech subject, begin by examining your *personal resources* to discover a potential subject that will meet the needs of this audience and this occasion. Before turning to external sources, concentrate on your present and past environment, your interests, beliefs, feelings, desires, attitudes, and experiences. Dip into your memory and search your background for those significant aspects of your life that made a vivid impression on you. Dismiss such rationalizations as "I'm not well informed" or "Nothing I know anything about would interest anyone else." Be confident that your insights and experiences are potentially of interest and benefit to others.

We emphasize the personal nature of your communication; you are the only person able to give this particular speech. Public speaking is a direct personal relationship of one human being with others. In contrast to writing and reading, there is no intervening agency of paper and ink. While it is difficult, if not impossible, for us as writers to reveal much of ourselves as persons to you, it would be possible, necessary, and desirable that we do so if we were giving a speech to you. Much of your communication training has probably been in writing rather than in speaking. Consequently, you must make adjustments in your style. You may have a somewhat impersonal tone in written communication. In spoken communication, however, you not only are allowed to talk about yourself, your activities, your thoughts and feelings, your knowledge and ignorance, your loves and hates, your attitudes and beliefs; you are *impelled* to do so by the nature of the form of communication that you are using.

Few of us can talk about ourselves—our hopes, desires, ambitions, efforts, mistakes, failures, achievements, and triumphs—without having some strong feelings. In an informal speech situation, where you are free to choose your subject matter, your personal feelings should be expressed. They will be of interest to your listeners, help them to see you as a real person with lively emotions and genuine depth, even if they don't always agree with you. Your thoughts on such topics as the way to be a true friend, your favorite music, an athlete you admire, your hopes for a career in art or electronics, your problems in finding a worthwhile job—all of the subject areas that have been important to you, about which you have strong feelings—can be of real interest to your listeners.

Your personal resources are tied to experiences that are entirely your own. Your experience is everything inside you. It includes mental ingredients—thoughts, attitudes, memories, beliefs, opinions, and judgments. In addition to these mental components of your experience are your internal physical components: body sensations, feelings, emotions, bodily movements, and postures. While external happenings stimulate your experiences, they do not cause or create these experiences. For example, an orchestra playing a particular selection of music serves as a stimulus for anyone hearing the music, but each person's actual experience of the music is unique. Just as each person's response to the music is highly individualized, so do we all respond somewhat differently to every stimulus. The words and actions of others, the events that take place in the world, the physical objects that we encounter—each of us creates our own experience of all these things.

An experience, then, is the unique series of internal events that you create for yourself as you process what happens in the world outside yourself. These inner experiences become inner realities that are just as real as physical realities perceived through your senses, such as wood, metal, light, and sound. The fact that your experience and internal reality are unique provides the major impetus and challenge for communication, which, as we have said, means sharing the experiences, worlds, and realities of one another. The communicative challenge for you is to recreate your inner reality for others so that they may understand and share the experience.

Thus, you cannot select an appropriate subject for your public speech by lifting ideas secondhand from some hastily read book or magazine article. Instead, you must dig deep into your experience and bring forth some of the ideas that are stored there. You may examine such areas of your experience as:

1. *Early years and upbringing.* Explore topics that pertain to your family, childhood, and schooling—incidents, hopes, setbacks, triumphs—that stand out vividly in your memory after years have gone by. Perhaps you were in gymnastics, tried out for cheerleading, or were chosen for a special exhibition. Or maybe you took piano lessons and suffered through a very trying experience in a recital. Most of us have had hopes, setbacks, and at least some minor successes in our early years.

2. *Special areas of knowledge.* Probe your life and experiences to find areas in which you have special or unusual knowledge. Without realizing it, you may be an expert in certain areas of endeavor. You may have expert knowledge in swimming, canoeing, camping. Or you may have unusual information about first aid, life-saving, or caring for small children. Your work experiences may have given you special information about coding data or choosing hi-fidelity components or selecting tasteful clothing. Think carefully about your personal background for areas of specialized information.

Figure 5-1 Your Areas of Experience

1. Early Years and Upbringing
2. Special Areas of Knowledge
3. Hobbies and Recreation
4. Peak Experiences
5. Beliefs and Convictions

3. *Hobbies and recreation.* Your natural enthusiasm about something you do for sheer enjoyment will reveal aspects of your personality inaccessible by any other means. Many of you enjoy certain kinds of music—jazz, rock, classical, country-western. Some of you have built and flown model airplanes or have customized a car. Travel—a special trip or camping adventure—any of these may make a topic for a speech. An unusual book you have enjoyed can be described for your listeners.

4. *Peak experiences.* Identify and describe highlights of your life that have made a great impact on you. Moments of crisis as well as moments of glory are rich sources of contact with an audience. Perhaps your basketball team won a regional tournament. Perhaps you worked very hard at ballet but had to drop out of a major performance. Some of us, in a moment of crisis—a street fight, an auto accident, even a disagreement with a teacher—found courage and capability inside ourselves that we didn't know we had, but helped to change our lives. Many of us have had parents who have separated, creating a crisis in our lives and consequent personal growth. Some of us have had religious experiences that altered our lives in some way. All such moments of crisis can make good speech topics.

5. *Beliefs and convictions.* Define and explain issues on which you have a firm and clearly thought-out position. If you have devoted considerable time and energy to the study of important issues, you probably have a core of material from which you can build a speech. Such issues as changing liquor laws, college major requirements, enrollment procedures, minimum wages, treatment of "delinquent" children—all of these and many more subject areas can make excellent speech topics for you.

Do not reject possible topics too quickly. Consider each idea long enough to think through its potential interest value to the audience, how it might be focused into a main idea and subordinate ideas, and whether it is a subject you can speak about with confidence, ease, and conviction. Do not reject a potential topic because you feel it is too personal or too trivial for your audience. Perhaps a slight modification—relating to a larger topic or focusing it more sharply—will make it more suitable. And remember, the more you are personally involved with a topic, the more interesting it will be for your listeners.

Discuss such possibilities with your classmates to test their interest and seek their suggestions for narrowing and modifying. We suggest that as a classroom activity, you meet in small groups (of four to six people) to discuss potential topics for everyone in the group. Standard categories—personal experiences, occupational experiences, beliefs, hobbies, special skills, travels, courses of study, life goals, views on controversial issues—may help your group to arrive at several topics that each member of the group could use as a potential subject for development. Ideas can be exchanged on what would be interesting and valuable for others to learn from your topic.

NARROWING YOUR SUBJECT

Based upon your background and experiences, the needs, interests, and expectations of the audience, and any special demands of the situation, you have now selected a general topic that you think would be appropriate. Your next task is to narrow that topic so that it fits the requirements of the speaking situation. One way to focus your thinking and give your speech direction and impact is to examine and identify your purpose in speaking.

Your General Purpose

Public speaking has traditionally been divided into three general purposes: to entertain, to inform, and to persuade. The speech to entertain is a specialized speech usually reserved for professionals in the entertainment field, or for experienced speakers in after-dinner situations. We have therefore elected to concentrate our attention on two general purposes: helping your listeners understand (the informative presentation); and helping your audience reach decisions (the persuasive presentation). Chapters 10-13 will be devoted to the explicit development of these two types of speeches. Although it is useful to categorize speeches according to these general purposes, recognize that rarely are the categories totally separate from one another. You may, for example, choose to use entertaining materials freely in speeches to help your listeners understand. Or you may need to inform your listeners in order to help them reach decisions.

Your Specific Purpose

Identification of the general purpose of your speech determines the specific type of preparation required. From the general purpose, you must move to your specific purpose which identifies explicitly what you want your audience to know, feel, believe, or do. This identification of specific purpose is similar to the central idea or thesis of a written theme. The specific purpose should guide you as you prepare your message, and it should guide your listeners as they receive and comprehend it. You cannot expect an audience to take the trouble to unravel your specific purpose. You must have it clearly in mind, and you must state it explicitly and reiterate it when necessary.

For example, suppose you have chosen as a topic, "Jogging." There are many possible specific purposes stemming from this subject. Some informative purposes are: to explain what jogging does for the body; to explain the proper equipment for jogging and its importance; to show the effects of jogging on certain types of people; to show what our cities are doing to promote jogging; to demonstrate the proper techniques for jogging; to explain possible problems and dangers of jogging. Some persuasive purposes might be: everyone in the audience should become a jogger; our schools should do more to establish habits of jogging; federal programs should be established to promote jogging. Unless you select a specific goal, it is unlikely that you will be able to develop a well-organized speech.

In narrowing your topic and identifying your specific purpose, do not try to cover too much. An attempt to show in fifteen minutes that our federal tax program should be restructured will prove most difficult to handle. Limiting yourself to one aspect of our tax laws, such as tax incentives to business to experiment and innovate, would likely be more effective. It is usually better to take a limited area and explain it fully than to give cursory or superficial treatment to a larger area. To borrow from the terminology of photography—do a close-up, not a panoramic shot.

Write out your specific purpose just as you would a telegram; try to reduce the number of words to a minimum and be as direct and precise as possible. Be careful, however, that you don't oversimplify or overstate. You will likely be showing that something is *probably* or *possibly* true, or that your research has convinced you that a given course of action should probably or possibly be taken. If, for example, after studying the relative merits of electric and gasoline-driven automobiles, you find the evidence to be inconclusive or contradictory, you should adapt your specific purpose to reflect this indecision. Instead of saying that one is clearly superior at this time, you may merely discuss the pros and cons.

While formulating your specific purpose, ask yourself questions such as these: Is this topic as specific and concrete as I can make it? Does it state more than I know or want to show? Does it reflect the audience's interests and needs? Does it summarize all that I want to present? (We suggest that you formulate several specific purposes that you feel qualified to speak on and then discuss these statements with your classmates.)

RESEARCHING YOUR TOPIC

With your specific purpose clearly in mind, you are now ready to start exploring your topic through *research*. Your first source of material is yourself. Therefore begin listing what you know about the topic. Remember where you obtained your information; that source may give you more. If you have selected a subject on which you are well-informed, your task may be to exclude material rather than to search for more. For most topics, however, you will want or need to supplement your present knowledge with research. For such reasons you should first analyze what would likely be the best sources—an interview with someone (such as one of your professors) who knows a lot about the topic; the library for books or periodicals; resource centers on your campus or in the community that are concerned with your topic (such as Common Cause, the Chamber of Commerce, or a Women's Resource Center); firsthand observations of an event related to your topic (a visit to a courtroom if you are speaking on the jury system, for example).

Notetaking

Common to all types of research is the need to take careful *notes*. Never depend upon your memory if you wish to retain particulars; an "unforgettable" quotation may elude you ten minutes later. Use note cards of uniform size (3 x 5″ or 4 x 6″) so that you can arrange them into a variety of sequences or remove the ones you do not plan to use. Later when you are organizing your speech, you may wish to spread the notecards on a table and group them under appropriate outline headings. Make all notes as complete as your purpose warrants. *Be accurate:* all direct quotations should be exactly what the author wrote; all paraphrases should correctly represent the author. Each card should contain a complete identification of the source, so that you can properly credit your sources and so that you can go back and locate additional material, if necessary. Include the full name of the author(s), title, publisher, date of publication, and page number. (See the illustration of a sample note card below.)

Figure 5-2 Sample Notecard

NUMBER OF AMERICANS   SURVEY
ABLE TO SPEAK ANOTHER LANGUAGE

"Fewer than 25 per cent of all Americans can speak, read, or write any language other than English, according to a survey at the University of Michigan for the President's Committee on Foreign Languages and International Studies." (national telephone survey of 962 persons)

Malcom G. Scully, "Most Americans are Monolingual, Survey Finds," The Chronicle of Higher Education, July 2, 1979, Vol. XVIII, No. 17, p. 8.

The information you gather may fall into such categories as:

1. *Significant facts and ideas.* Facts and ideas will form the central core of your speech. If a fact or idea makes a strong impact on you, make note of it. The fact may be of historical significance, or provide details of incidents or subjects.

2. *Examples, illustrations, and specific instances.* Such materials will serve to make your speech clear and concrete rather than vague and abstract.

3. *Statistical information.* Statistics are often important to demonstrate the extent of a problem or to quantify a factual situation.

4. *Quotations and testimony.* You may find that the concept that you are trying to explain has been expressed so vividly and aptly that you want to use a direct quotation. Experts and famous people may be quoted in support of your points and add credibility to your position.

5. *Jokes and anecdotes.* Jokes and humorous stories that apply directly to points you are making add interest and enjoyment to your message. Be sure they are in good taste and appropriate to the audience and the occasion.

6. *Human interest stories.* Unusual examples that involve people have a high interest level and can make abstract ideas concrete.

These categories of material will be developed in detail in Chapter 6, pp. 76-93.

This phase of gathering materials is more than merely finding support for your ideas. It should be part of your process of learning and expanding your concepts to make you a more effective communicator. After you have researched and become saturated with your subject, you will produce an *original* speech that is different from your sources. The speech must reflect *you* in a responsible way, revealing your individuality. Regardless of how much you already know, research will help you validate your thinking and also provide additional support for your ideas. You can never be *certain* of your ideas in any absolute or dogmatic sense. However, your research should lend the proper qualifications and objectivity that will give your presentation the greatest impact and value to your listeners.

Suppose, for example, that you are considering the general topic: Sex discrimination against women in the job market. Perhaps you are interested in the subject because you feel that you were discriminated against as a woman when you recently applied for a job. Does your personal experience prove the general existence of discrimination in our society? Clearly not. You may have misinterpreted the situation and been rejected, not because you are a woman, but because of your age, or your lack of experience in the field, or the presence of a better qualified applicant.

Another way you might assess whether or not sex discrimination exists is to resort to common sense, what everybody "knows" to be true.

But people differ in their assessment of "what everybody knows to be true." And even if everybody agreed, we may all be totally wrong, as when "everybody" believed the world was flat.

Still a third way would be to read what a number of contemporary writers have to say about job discrimination against women. If you have been interested in this topic for some time, you may have been clipping and saving relevant magazine and newspaper articles which you can now review for facts and ideas for your speech.

Use of the Library

For further material of this kind, you need to go to the library. You could check the following sources:

1. *The card catalog.* If you cannot find a book under "sex discrimination," look under "women" and "employment" for books on the topic. You might find Kate Millett's book, *Sexual Politics*, for example.

2. *Magazine indexes.* The most useful of the general periodical guides is the *Readers' Guide to Periodical Literature.* This guide is published twice a month, so you will need to decide the time period you wish to explore. For your purposes, you might locate the article by Harold Lawrenson, "The Feminine Mistake," published in *Esquire* magazine, January 1971 (pp. 82-83, 146-147, 153-154). There are other periodical guides which might be consulted for more technical or specialized topics.

3. *Newspapers.* Most large libraries subscribe to *The New York Times* and also to the *Index* for that publication. Information from other daily newspapers is not well catalogued, so if you begin to clip articles of interest from your daily newspaper, soon you will have a file of ready reference material.

4. *Statistical references.* For many topics, *The Statistical Abstract of the U.S. Government*, or a major almanac may prove useful.

5. *Pamphlets and bulletins. The Bulletin of the Public Information Service* provides an index to the pamphlets of many government bureaus, foundations, and societies.

6. *The librarian.* Most librarians welcome the opportunity not only to help you on a specific topic, but also to teach you generally on the most efficient use of the library. Don't be afraid to ask for help.

Until you know a great deal about a topic, you may be tempted to believe something just because it is in print. If you read widely enough, you will find contradictions and differences of opinion even among foremost experts. The two particular references cited above (Millett and Lawrenson) are directly opposed to each other. Unfortunately, many of us, when we read about controversial topics, merely select materials that reflect our own opinions. Our biases may obstruct our capabilities for objectivity and true honesty. Remember that authorities are merely people like ourselves who have opinions and value judgments. Constantly ask, "How do they know what they say they know? What is their evidence?"

If personal experience, common sense, and reading do not provide sufficient information to focus your thinking, what can you do? We suggest additional explorations are possible through observation, interviews, and surveys.

Observation

Since the general question of whether or not job discrimination against women exists in all jobs is extremely difficult to answer, you might decide to limit your question to the extent to which job discrimination exists at your own university. An examination of the university directory might be useful to determine the number of women and men in various employment categories (secretaries, professors, security officers, etc.). An examination of the hiring record of the university for the past three years might also be worthwhile. These numbers, however, do not tell the complete story. How many people applied? What were the qualifications of the applicants? Be careful that your observations are not aimed at merely confirming a preconceived conclusion.

Psychologists Zimbardo and Ruch give us the following "Moral" for observations:

> When we report on "the way things are," we really mean the "way they seem," given what we have been conditioned to notice, how we define and measure what we are looking for, and what others want us to see.[4]

Interviews

If your own capacity to observe and validate job discrimination against women is insufficient, you may decide to interview people who are in a better position to observe and judge the situation. If your university has an Office of Affirmative Action, you might wish to interview one of the staff. Or you may find it useful to speak to one of the deans or someone from the hiring office to gain their perspectives on hiring.

As a rule, people when approached tactfully are willing to spare a few minutes to answer questions in their areas of expertise. Don't expect someone else to do your work for you. Be sure to plan your questions in advance, explain clearly the purpose of the interview, and do not overstay your welcome. Take careful and complete notes so that you don't misquote or misuse the information received. Be sensitive to the possible biases of the people you interview, and ask the basis for their information and opinions. If you seem to be getting a one-sided view, try to interview someone else to get a different perspective.

Figure 5-3 Researching Your Topic

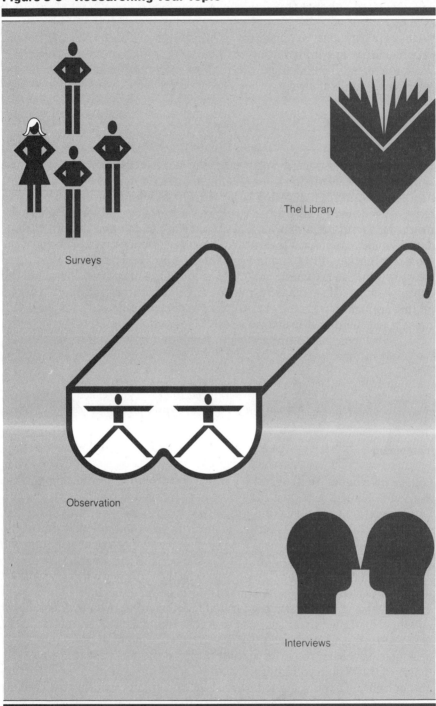

Surveys

Surveying large groups of people is so expensive and time-consuming that sample surveying is usually preferable. The general idea of sample surveying is to interview a small group of people, selected so that they *represent accurately* the larger population. The Gallup Poll, for example, selects approximately 1500 persons as a cross-section of the American voting population and has made extremely accurate predictions of voting behaviors.

You may use surveys to determine attitudes, opinions, or experiences. For example, you could ask a representative sampling of college students, "Do you think job discrimination against women is a problem?" or "Has your sex/gender influenced your opportunities for employment?" Rather than simple "yes" or "no" responses, a scale of 1-5 (with the points identified as 1-never, 2-rarely, 3-sometimes, 4-often, 5-always) can provide greater specificity.

Be particularly careful in drawing conclusions or generalizations from surveys. Are you certain that your sample truly represents the total population? Do you know that the respondents told the truth? Did the respondents interpret the questions in the same way? Even in the best of circumstances, with large, representative samples and sophisticated interpretations, only probabilities can be concluded. (Discuss with your classmates polls in which you have participated, such as television viewing and response to mailed questionnaires. How honest were you and did the general conclusions reflect your input?)

All of these approaches to researching your speech will serve to give you greater focus and provide a fund of data that you may choose to include in your actual presentation. In the next chapter, we shall discuss how you can organize and outline your ideas into patterns that will help you communicate with an audience.

SUMMARY

Our ideas and our energy tend to be diffused until we focus them. In this chapter we have discussed ways of gaining focus through identifying our intention and selecting a subject that reflects our personal resources and the needs and interests of the audience.

You are a vast storehouse of potential speech topics that with the right audience in the right circumstance will be mutually beneficial. *You* are the generator and creator of messages that reflect your experiences. Such experience can be of benefit to others if you are willing to share. In this world of processes and change, we recommend a stance of humility and candor. We cannot afford to be dogmatic and arrogant concerning our knowledge; the "facts" of today may become the "myths" and jokes of tomorrow.

To validate and supplement your personal data we have cited various sources: taking notes, the library, observations, interviews, and surveys. Such research will help you to gain greater focus on relevant ideas. As you analyze the speaking situation, you should identify your general and specific purposes in order to give your speech the maximum direction. This focus is the first step to successful interaction between you and an audience.

LEARNING EXPERIENCES

Objectives

After studying this chapter, you should be able to *do* the following:

1. Explain the importance of intentionality to a speaker.
2. Inventory your personal resources and list ten or more topics that you could speak on.
3. Through feedback from your classmates, identify topics that interest them and information that they would find useful.
4. State several specific purposes for possible speeches that can be discussed with classmates.
5. Identify the types of research sources that would be appropriate for the topics selected.
6. Recognize that information from research and personal experience is subject to change.

Exercises

1. Meet with a group of your classmates and determine four topics that each member of the group could speak upon that would reflect unique expertise and would interest members of the class. Help each other generate additional ideas that will aid the development of the speeches.
2. Utilizing the topics generated in the group, formulate specific purposes for the four speeches determined above. Have your instructor provide feedback and suggestions.
3. If you have not done so, take a tour of your local library. Report on where the various types of materials can be located. Take one of your topics and inventory the extent of library holdings relating to this topic. Prepare a research bibliography on this topic.

4. Prepare and administer a questionnaire and interview on your topic. Report on any problems that you encountered and the results of your survey.

NOTES

[1]George Leonard, *The Ultimate Athlete.* New York: Viking Press, 1974, p. 62.

[2]James F. T. Bugenthal, "Intentionality and Ambivalence," in *Interpersonal Behavior*, edited by Anthony G. Athos and John J. Gabarro. Englewood Cliffs, NJ: Prentice-Hall, 1978, p. 517.

[3]For the detailed distinctions see Kim Giffin and Bobby R. Patton, *Fundamentals of Interpersonal Communication.* New York: Harper and Row, 1971, p. 196, Chapter One.

[4]Philip G. Zimbardo and Floyd L. Ruch, *Psychology and Life*, 9th ed. Glenview, IL: Scott, Foresman and Company, 1975, p. 41.

6

Organizing and Supporting Your Ideas

Once you have determined your specific purpose, completed the bulk of your research, and tested your data, you are ready to begin organizing your ideas. Perhaps the instant you see the word *organization*, your inclination is to protest, "I'll bet now you want me to outline; I hate outlines." Unfortunately, many people regard outlines as "busy work." Such people would, however, be unlikely to start a long trip without looking at a map, or start building a house without a blueprint. The outline of your speech serves the same functions: to guide you, to retain your intended course; and to eliminate unnecessary detours or delays. Curiously, Quintilian, the Roman rhetorician, used this same metaphor in explaining the importance of proper arrangement.

> ... speech, if deficient in that quality, must necessarily be confused, and float like a ship without a helm; it can have no coherence; it must exhibit many repetitions, and many omissions; and, like a traveller wandering by night in unknown regions, must, as having no stated course or object, be guided by chance rather than design ... just as it is not sufficient for those who are erecting a building merely to collect stone and timber and other building materials, but skilled masons are required to arrange and place them, so in speaking, however abundant the matter may be, it will merely form a confused heap unless arrangement be employed to reduce it to order and give it connexion and firmness of structure. ...[1]

We all gather speech ideas haphazardly in life and we must give order to them before presenting them to others. Outlines provide useful ways of organizing our experiences and ideas so that others may understand them clearly. For some, distaste for outlining stems from

their early education when a teacher overemphasized the mechanics of outlining to the neglect of the purpose of the outline—idea development. Perhaps they were chastised for using a small letter when a number should have been used, and so on. The mechanics of outlining are important, but in and of themselves they are useless: what matters is effective structuring of ideas. We will therefore treat outlining as a building process—the building of a coherent, clear, and cogent message, stripped of unessential distractions. To a significant degree your listeners will judge the quality of your ideas by the clarity and logic of the design of your presentation. Numerous research studies support the suggestion that your presentation should be well organized.[2]

A speech typically consists of three parts: the introduction, the body, and the conclusion. Since the body of the speech contains the essence of the message, we will treat it first. This sequence is not all that unrealistic since many speakers prepare the body of their message before they develop their introduction and their conclusion.

ESSENTIALS OF ORGANIZATION

The body of the speech consists of a series of main points and subpoints that are designed to achieve the speaker's specific purpose. Main points should generally be few in number; from two to five is commonly recommended. An audience finds it hard to remember, and to follow, a long series of points. A useful first step in arriving at the best possible organization is to make a comprehensive list of the ideas that you have accumulated on your topic, and then work through this list looking for the main thoughts. Suppose you are a tennis player and want to address your class on the game of tennis. Your purpose is to inform this nonplaying audience of the essentials of the game. You begin by jotting down what you consider the main topic areas to be examined. Your list may look something like this:

1. The history of tennis
2. The rules of tennis
3. The strategy of the game
4. The serve
5. The forehand
6. The backhand
7. Rushing the net

You have listed what you consider seven topics to be discussed—too many for your speech. A moment's inspection will tell you that the seventh point, rushing the net, should be used as a subpoint under the broader heading of strategy, and that the fourth, fifth, and sixth points can be regrouped under the heading "fundamentals," and may serve as subpoints to that heading. Not only does this reduce your main points to four in number but it also makes them *parallel in significance*—namely, on the same level of generalization or classification. It is also useful to make them parallel in form. If one is a question, make them all questions; if one is a statement, make them all statements. Because of the symmetry that results from similarity of form, the audience will find them easier to remember. For a speech on tennis, the key words "history, rules, fundamentals, and strategy" can easily be retained by the average listener.

The next step in developing your outline is to look for a natural and logical pattern for arranging your points. By *natural* we mean that certain topics intrinsically divide themselves into main points often called "stock" patterns. A talk on the broad subject of the United States Government can readily be dealt with under the headings of the "legislative, executive, and judicial branches." A talk on college life can easily be divided into such categories as "social, academic, and economic." Any college student would be concerned about each of those three topics. "Stock" approaches can be used to divide numerous subjects. For example, you may want to determine if your subject can be partitioned according to one of the following patterns: local, state, and national; political, economic, and social; past, present, and future; problem, causes, and solution; background, characteristics, and accomplishments; resemblances and differences; specific to general; general to specific; theory and practice. Other types of listings may be spatial, such as East to West, or a classification of types, such as hunting dogs, watch dogs, and show dogs. These stock patterns will usually make organization a simple task and are a great help to the listener.

But what do we mean by a "logical" pattern? Let's go back to your speech on tennis to illustrate this attribute. Recall that you have four main points: rules, strategy, fundamentals, and history. If you order those four points in their most logical sequence, surely history would precede a discussion of strategy, fundamentals, or rules. Thus logically the first point will be:

I.   History of tennis

Which should be next? Assuredly we need to know the "rules" of the game before knowledge of strategy or fundamentals of play will do us much good. Thus the second point will be:

II.   Rules of tennis

Which should come next—strategy or fundamentals? In all probability we should know the fundamentals of playing before strategy will do us much good. So you will complete the arrangement of your speech thus:

III.   Fundamentals of tennis
IV.   Strategy of tennis

The idea of *logical thought progression* is integral to the organization of any speech. Listeners should be led logically from one point to the next and they should be made to see the progression of your thinking. The same is true for the development of any of the main points in the body of your speech. Let's illustrate logical progression by using the fourth point: strategy. Probably you would introduce the point by defining it—explaining what you mean by "strategy." Strategy can then be broken down into two logical components: offensive and defensive. Thus your outline would shape up something like this:

IV.   Strategy of Tennis
    A.   Definition and explanation of strategy
    B.   Offensive strategy
    C.   Defensive strategy

Then in turn offensive and defensive strategy would be divided according to the topics that need to come under it. Perhaps as offensive strategy you want to examine "the serve," "rushing the net," "moving the ball from side to side," and "the element of surprise." Now your outline will look like this:

IV.   Strategy of Tennis
    A.   Definition and explanation of strategy
    B.   Offensive strategy
        1.   The serve
        2.   Rushing the net
        3.   Moving the ball from side to side
        4.   The element of surprise

Each point and subpoint will be developed in this manner until your outline is complete. Actually, the general subject of "tennis" is too broad for the average student speech; for a five- to seven-minute talk your entire speech may be limited to "the strategy of the game of tennis." Then your main points would be: I. Definition, II. Offensive strategy, III. Defensive strategy.

In public speaking, a pattern or type of outline is a way of ordering and arranging your major ideas so that they make sense to your listeners. It is a means of avoiding the appearance of rambling, of having been poorly prepared, or presenting scattered thoughts or ideas. It can help your listeners believe that you have given careful thought to your topic—which as a responsible speaker we will assume that you have done—and that you have found a way of comprehending the major issues. An outline should help you avoid this vexing distraction: "Oh, yes, I meant to mention one other very important consideration . . ." Quite properly, Arthur Koestler in his book, *The Act of Creation*, has observed: "Preparing to say something, whether it is a single sentence or a public lecture, is to set a hierarchy in motion."[3] That hierarchy involves ordering and arranging ideas.

Figure 6-1   An Outline Going from the General to the Specific

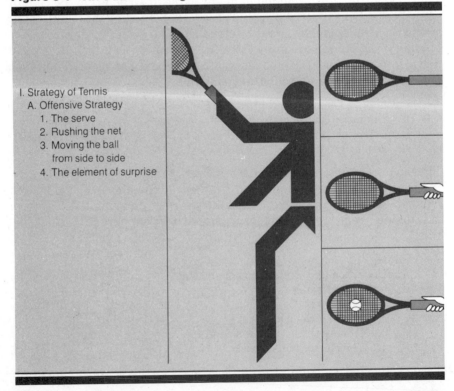

I. Strategy of Tennis
  A. Offensive Strategy
    1. The serve
    2. Rushing the net
    3. Moving the ball
       from side to side
    4. The element of surprise

CHOOSING YOUR SUPPORTING MATERIALS

As you focus on the subject, you will find yourself making statements or assertions that are in need of support. This need occurs both when you are trying to persuade someone to adopt a proposal and when you want that person to understand the nature of an event or process. The term "supporting" materials is apt; just as your outline will be a frame, the supporting material will give your speech clarity, believability, interest, and impact. As a rule, the supporting materials make the difference between an ordinary speech and a really good one.

In writing and speaking, abstractions should not be stacked on top of each other in succession but should always be followed by concrete data—supporting materials. In the late 1940s, Rudolph Flesch published two books, *The Art of Plain Talk* (1946) and *The Art of Readable Writing* (1949). In these books Dr. Flesch advocated "up-and-down writing" so that a speech or a composition consists of a series of "peaks and valleys," the peaks being the abstract thought and the valleys the concrete examples, illustrations, and comparisons. Flesch said: "As a rule, you should never stay at the abstract level for long; as soon as you get there, turn around and plunge again into the down-to-earth world of people and things."[4] Such "up-and-down" levels of abstraction protect against both misunderstandings and dullness.

Types of Supporting Materials

Before we suggest how you might integrate supporting materials into your outline, let's take a look at five types of supporting materials that are available.

1. Background Facts. Background facts provide much needed specificity to your speeches. Poorly prepared, poorly presented speeches tend to be overly general and fail to utilize specific factual information. A native American student makes effective use of background facts as he develops the backdrop to the problems of contemporary native Americans.[5]

In 1804 a policy of concentrating the Indian tribes on reservations was initiated; in 1825 the so-called Indian Territory had been acquired; and by 1840 five large tribes had been settled on its lands. Then for the next 50 years, the Indians of the Middle and Far West waged an unequal struggle to keep open their hunting grounds. But the westward progress of the white man could not be stayed, and by the end of the century the Indians were all safely confined on reservations. In making the western plains safe for white habitation, the officials employed all the devices of a cruel penology to break the spirit of the tribesmen.

As the War Department, during the 70's and 80's, pursued the relentless wars of pacification by extermination, wiser policies began to take place in Washington. In 1871 the farce of treaty-making with the Indians was ended and Congress took over supervision of the tribes. Until 1924, however, an Indian could become a citizen only by naturalization. Finally, in 1924, Congress gave full citizenship to all native-born Indians. Yet the 350,000 Indians living on reservations remain under the guardianship of the Office of Indian Affairs and are, therefore, in the curious position of being both citizen and wards of this nation.

Let's rewrite part of the above passage in a more general way, without specific support, and see how much impact it loses.

The federal government began a policy of concentrating Indian tribes early in the nineteenth century and soon a number of large tribes were settled upon what came to be known as Indian Territory. But as America expanded westward and pushed farther and farther into Indian territory, the plains tribes felt compelled to fight to preserve their land. The War Department responded with a policy of pacification and extermination. Later in the century Congress took over supervision of the tribes. Yet it wasn't until the 1920s that Congress gave full citizenship to all native-born Americans.

Didn't you find the first passage far more interesting and informative? The first passage is specific; it makes good use of factual background data, the second is general and unsupported.

2. Specific Examples, Illustrations, and Human Interest Stories. A second way to support your outline is to use specific *examples*, illustrations, and human interest stories. These materials add more interest value to your speech than perhaps anything else. We discuss them together because they are very similar. When we refer to a *specific example*, we mean a brief reference to an event, object, person, or relationship. For an example of this form of support, we turn again to the native American speaker who described the problems of contemporary Indians.

Land set aside for reservations is notoriously unsuited for agriculture. Yet, if, in a perverse mood, Manitou does smile and oil is found, the whites somehow manage to rob the Indian. For example, the Indian Commission was to pay the Navajos $100,000 for oil royalties. To this date they have not received one cent—all the money supposedly went to build a bridge. Three thousand starving Navajos, and the Bureau built a bridge from which curious tourists can come and gape down upon the remnants of a once proud Navajo nation!

Illustrations may be either factual or hypothetical and they do what the term says: they illustrate. For an example, we turn back to 1886, when Thomas Henry Huxley tried to explain "The Method of Scientific Investigation" to English workingmen. He did it with hypothetical illustration.

> *Suppose you go into a fruiterer's shop wanting an apple—you take one up, and, on biting, you find that it is sour: you look at it, and see that it is hard and green. You take another one and that too is hard, green, and sour. The shopman offers you a third; but, before biting it, you examine it, and find that it is hard and green, and you immediately say that you will not have it, as it must be sour, like those that you have already tried.*
>
> *Nothing can be more simple than that, you think, but if you take the trouble to analyze and trace out into its logical elements what has been done by the mind, you will be greatly surprised. In the first place, you have performed the operation of induction.*[6]

Human interest stories are extended examples used for purposes of illustration. If listeners can identify with the people in the story, they will most likely internalize and remember the point being made. News programs such as *60 Minutes* make large problems understandable by focusing on one small segment of the problem; for example, by looking at how one person or family is affected. You can do the same in your speech.

As with other types of supporting materials, the number and kind of details used in telling a human interest story are quite important. As an artist may attempt to create a picture that a viewer can recognize and appreciate, the speaker must "paint" enough mental images to allow the audience to picture and follow the action.

The native American student, in discussing contemporary Indian problems, concluded a narrative about what happens to an Indian child with a brief human interest story. We think that you will agree that it is the human interest story that gives impact to the point the speaker is making.

Historians often point with pride to the remarkable accomplishments of the Indian schools. These writers perhaps never have attended an Indian school. But here is exactly what happens.

At the age of six the Indian child is taken from his parents and placed in a reservation boarding school. In some instances, that child is never allowed to return home until he has reached the free age of 18. Once at the understaffed and poorly equipped school, the child attends classes half-days. The remainder of the day he is made to work at hard industrial labor: in the fields, bakery, or in the laundry— child labor forced upon six-year-old children who are heartsick and bewildered at being torn from their parents' arms.

At night the child goes to a dormitory where he shares a bed with two other children. Every boarding school from which I could obtain statistics admitted that it was overcrowded from 40 to 60 percent beyond capacity. Then, when the Indian child rebels or runs away from these conditions, he is caught, brought back to school, flogged, and kept on a restricted diet for weeks. If he is fortunate, he won't be placed in chains at night.

Let me state you the documented case of a young Indian boy named Taloole Esculante. Homesick, this child ran away from the school but was caught and returned. There he was beaten until unconscious and left for dead. But Taloole was still alive—alive enough to crawl, stumble, and somehow reach his home about 200 miles away, and there he told his story and died in his aunt's arms. The death certificate for Taloole read: "death due to spinal meningitis."

The most useful sources of such stories are your own experiences. While you may utilize stories that you've read or heard, be careful to identify which experiences are your own. The personal element involved in an event you have experienced reflects your individuality and helps your listeners identify with you. Observe how one speaker used a human interest story to illustrate his point:

> I have a friend—an old shipmate in New Haven, Connecticut—whom I visited a few years after the war. He was such a good father that he should have lost his amateur standing. He had four children, aged from junior high school into high school. After I had sponged off him for dinner he said, "Now Jenk, tonight is the family board meeting." And he said, "It'll only take a few minutes, but we must get it out of the way." And I said, "The what?" And he said, "The family board meeting!" He said, "Would like to come?" I said, "Try to keep me away."
>
> The dinner dishes were all cleared away; the family sat around the table. . . .
>
> Then Dad said, "Now, I've got a surprise for you. You remember I went down to Cincinnati last month to the association of my professional group, and I delivered a paper down there. I didn't tell you they paid me $500.00, and so," he said, "I'm setting $200.00 of it aside for the income tax. I'm keeping a hundred; I did the work. And I'm giving Mother a hundred because she keeps the family together. Then we're cutting it down, and each one of you youngsters gets twenty-five bucks." The kids all cheered. But never after that did Dad have to explain what the income tax was. It was two hundred out of Dad's five.[7]

This illustration not only tells a story in which the speaker was personally involved, but it gets additional interest from the use of dialogue. Moreover, the point of the illustration is perfectly clear.

Be willing to fill your examples with relevant details and relive your experience as you relate it. While unrelated details are likely to be boring, the details of a crucial story should be sufficient to allow the audience to project themselves into the picture that you are creating. The more that you can relive the experience through action and excitement, the greater will the audience be able to empathize. This capacity to tell a story is a learned one and one that you can develop. Examples will make your speeches memorable, interesting, and easier to understand.

3. Statistical Information. Statistics are numerical examples. As indicated in Chapter 5, reservations and appropriate qualifications should always be cited. The source, the data, the sample, and any possible investigator bias should be considered before you use statistics to support your ideas. As the old saying goes, "Figures don't lie; but liars figure."

On the other hand, statistics may be the best way to describe a problem or a situation such as unemployment or the balance of trade. For example, if you are planning to major in a foreign language, how many jobs are there likely to be? Numbers provide the answers.

The young Indian student used statistics to show the health problems of native Americans as follows:

And how faithful to its charges has been the Great White Father's representative, the all-powerful Indian Bureau? After almost 80 years of direct congressional control, former President Truman in 1950 saw the need for improving conditions of the Navajo and Hopi Indians. He signed a 10-year improvement program. After four years of that program had elapsed, hearings were held on the progress of the program and here are some of the findings: The average length of life of a Navajo was 20 years; the Navajo death rate from tuberculosis was 913 times that among the whites, from dysentery 13 times, from measles 29.5 times.

A good speaker will attempt to make statistics meaningful to the specific listeners being addressed. Sometimes numbers are so large that the average person has no point of reference to give meaning to them. It is the speaker's task to do this for the listener. Observe, for example, how President Ronald Reagan sought to do this in his address to a Joint Session of Congress on a "Program for Economic Recovery," February 18, 1981:

> Our national debt is approaching $1 trillion. A few weeks ago I called such a figure—a trillion dollars—incomprehensible. I've been trying to think of a way to illustrate how big it really is. The best I could come up with is to say that a stack of $1,000 bills in your hand only four inches high would make you a millionaire. A trillion dollars would be a stack of $1,000 bills 67 miles high.

Since statistics tend to be hard to visualize, you may decide to present them through the use of such visual aids as graphs, charts, or tables of data. Sometimes visual aids may be reproduced and distributed to all listeners; on other occasions they may be presented on an opaque projector. In general, such devices are a useful complement to your speech if the contents truly clarify the idea. Although visual aids require considerable work on your part, this should not prevent their use. Remember a clear presentation of your ideas is your goal. (The subject of visual aids will be explored in more detail in Chapter 9.)

4. Quotations and Testimony. Use the words of other people to support your message when these words are spoken by persons whose opinions your listeners respect. Showing that experts agree with your thinking will help listeners to appreciate the quality of your ideas. The process can be viewed as a rather reasonable or logical one: Your thinking is supported by experts; positions supported by experts should be accepted; therefore your listeners should concur with your thinking.

Studies have shown that the *expertness* of the "expert" is not always the primary or sole consideration; his or her *reliability* and *favorable intentions* (as seen by listeners) are of overriding significance. Thus, use of testimony by some expert who is not respected may produce a boomerang effect of negative instead of positive influence.[8]

The value of using supporting testimony from "authorities" relies heavily upon your listeners' perception of these experts, especially their reliability and their attitudes toward goals and values important to your listeners. Support for your ideas by experts is usually helpful; support by experts who are *trusted* by your listeners is of greater value. For example, a speaker arguing that the United States government should change its national policies to help hungry people may cite:

> *In 1980, the Presidential Commission on World Hunger called on the United States to make elimination of hunger the primary focus of its relationships with developing countries.*

Quotations may also be used to clarify and intensify your thinking. For example, the speaker on World Hunger believes that empathy with the world's poor is necessary to demonstrate our humanity. He states:

> *Saul Bellow has a marvelous little exchange in his book,* Mr. Semmler's Planet. *"I thought everyone was born human," says a woman to an old man. "It's not a natural gift at all," replies the man. "The capacity is natural, the rest is work."*

As a responsible speaker, before using testimony, you should be able to answer affirmatively the following questions:

1. Is the quotation from a person who is known and respected by this audience?
2. Is the quotation totally accurate?

3. Is it taken from the person's area of expert knowledge? (not quoting an athlete on nutrition)
4. Is the statement based on firsthand knowledge, rather than bias or personal interest?
5. If the person were in the audience, would he or she approve of your use of their testimony?

5. Jokes and Anecdotes. A sense of humor is a prized asset for any speaker. If you have the ability to make light of a local situation or the occasion, don't refrain from sharing this side of yourself. Humor that is original and relevant, growing out of the situation or directly applicable to a point that you are making, is more likely to succeed than an old joke or story from *Reader's Digest*. For example, one speaker used the following humorous anecdote in his speech:

> *Professor A. C. Knudson of Boston University used to tell his students a story about Ralph Waldo Emerson's habit of jotting down notes in the night. He kept a pad, a pencil, a candle, and matches beside his bed to make it just as handy as possible for him to record his magniloquent thoughts. In those days matches came in the form of a wafer-thin board with teeth. One night Emerson awoke, groped for the matches, broke off one, and tried to light it. No fire. He broke off another and tried it. Nothing. He kept at it until he had broken off all the matches and then, with unphilosophical chagrin, he went back to sleep without recording his sleepy-time thoughts. The next morning he was unable to recall those thoughts, and this upset him, but he was even more distressed when Mrs. Emerson said to him, "What has happened to my tortoise-shell comb? All the teeth are broken off."*

Professor Knudson then proceeded to connect this story to one of his points: we must be careful of jumping to conclusions with insufficient data.

You may even be able to share stories that have caused you to laugh at yourself. Whenever possible, build humor out of your own experience, and when you use anecdotes for humorous effect, adapt them to suit the audience and the points they are intended to support. For example, a physician in his introduction to a speech on a medical subject to a lay audience told the following joke on himself:

> *As a doctor I was interested in the use of ether as an anesthetic and had a dose administered to myself. As I was going under, a great thought framed itself in my mind—I believed that I had grasped the key to all mysteries of philosophy, a final solution to the central problem of existence. When I regained consciousness I was unable to think of it. But I had to recapture it, for it was of vital importance to mankind. I arranged to have myself given ether again and determined that I would speak the great thought so that a stenographer could write it down. This time, just before the ether took full effect, I had the vision again, and I spoke the words and they were written down as follows:*
> *The entire universe is permeated with a strong odor of turpentine.*

This story served to reduce the pyschological distance between the speaker and his listeners. Audiences today tend to expect more humor than audiences in the past; this expectation is tied to the clever speeches on television and the recognition that laughter is a release from tension and a bridge between people. Don't believe, however, that you have to imitate Johnny Carson if you are to succeed. Instead, rely upon the type of humor that you do best.

INTEGRATING SUPPORTING MATERIALS INTO YOUR OUTLINE

Having examined the types of supporting materials you can choose from, let's return to your outline of "the strategy of playing tennis." Your outline, when completed, might look something like this:

IV. Strategy of tennis
    A. Definition and explanation
    B. Offensive strategy
        1. The serve
            a. Explain strategy involved
            b. Example of Tracy Austin

Figure 6-2 Types of Supporting Materials

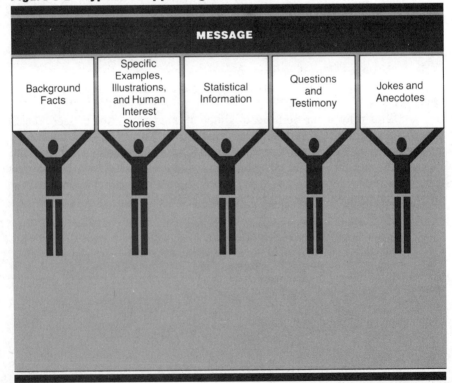

MESSAGE

Background Facts | Specific Examples, Illustrations, and Human Interest Stories | Statistical Information | Questions and Testimony | Jokes and Anecdotes

2. Rushing the net
   a. Explain strategy involved
   b. Examples of great players who are skillful at rushing the net
3. Moving the ball from side to side
   a. Explain strategy involved
   b. Use drawing on board to illustrate
4. The element of surprise
   a. Explain strategy involved
   b. Personal example of how I surprised my opponent in a championship match

Sometimes in order to see more clearly the relationship between ideas, speakers prepare full sentence outlines of their addresses. For example, Bill Link, in preparing an address on the "Joking Cowboy," developed the following outline of the body of his speech:

General Purpose: To inform the audience about Will Rogers.
Specific Purpose: To identify and explain the sources of Will Rogers' humor.
Title: "The Joking Cowboy"

I. Much of Will Rogers' humor stems from his pretense of being an ignorant and illiterate cowboy.

First Main Point or source of Will's humor.

A. Will's trademarks when he spoke were a big wad of chewing gum, a tousled forelock, and a rumpled blue serge suit.

Three subpoints are used to develop how Will pretended to be an ignorant and illiterate cowboy.

B. His Oklahoma drawl was a natural one.

C. He usually began by claiming that all he knew was what he read in the papers.

D. Will discovered early that by playing the "fool character" he could say and write things that otherwise the public would have resented.

The fourth subpoint tells the audience what the significance of Will's pretense at ignorance and illiteracy was.

   1. Will was accepted as a kind of "court jester."
   2. His audiences were delighted with the incongruity between his pretended ignorance and his common sense remarks.
   3. People were seldom offended by Will's humor.

II. Will liked to ground his remarks in some element of the truth which he extended just beyond the realm of probability.

Second main point or source of Will's humor.

A. Usually the truth was not extended to the point of burlesque.
    1. Burlesque would not have allowed a serious edge to Will's humor.
    2. Pure burlesque would not have provided Will with the almost universal audience that he did have.

B. At the same time, Will extended the truth far enough so that the audience caught its absurdity.
    1. His remarks on the London Naval Conference of 1930 illustrate this technique.
        a. Will suggested that other nations were going to sink ships that were old relics; the British ships, for example, fought the Spanish Armada.
        b. The U.S. by contrast, Will said, was building two ships to sink.
    2. The terms of the treaty Will described were basically true. But Will wanted the listener to think that the U.S. had been bested in diplomacy again.

III. Much of Will's humor is based upon the element of surprise.
    A. He liked to insert a real "shocker" in the midst of a series.
        1. Once Will suggested that unemployment problems could be cured right "at home."
        2. Will said: "Why right where you are, look around and you see lots of things to do, weeds to be cut, fences to be fixed, lawns to be mowed, filling stations to be robbed . . ."
    B. As a listener you followed his listings complacently, and were caught by surprise when he inserted his "shocker" about "filling stations to be robbed."
    C. This technique resembles a practical joke—which Will loved.

IV. Sometimes Will's humor was satirical.

The first subpoint explains the outside limits Will used and tells why this was important.

The second subpoint pinpoints how far the truth was extended and explains why this was humorous.

Use of a specific example to support and clarify the subpoint.

Explanation of why the London Naval Conference example is humorous.

Third main point or source of Will's humor.

Illustration of how the element of surprise worked.

Use of a specific example.

Explanation of why the specific example is humorous.

Further explanation of why the specific example is humorous.

Fourth main point or source of Will's humor.

A. He especially employed satire when he wanted to use humor as a weapon.
   1. Pompous political figures
   2. Foolish legislation
B. He usually feigned ignorance when he wanted to attack the hypocrisy of others.
   1. Will once sought to expose the hypocrisy of the Stell Trust.
   2. Will said: "Mr. Gary says that it will take time [to change the work schedule]. You see a man who has been working for years for 13 or 14 hours a day, and you cut him down to 8 and you have a physical wreck on your hands."
      a. Will of course meant exactly the opposite of what he said.
      b. The satire was obvious.
C. Will often functioned as a "rhetorical humorist."
   1. By a rhetorical humorist I mean that Will's quips embodied a serious message.
   2. This message was usually clear to the average listener.
D. Due to Will's sunny disposition he seldom offended anyone.
   1. His quips were delivered in fun and with a smile.
   2. People he attacked usually laughed with him.
   3. Thus Will's humor had impact; yet he was invited to dinner by those he lampooned.

Annotations (right margin):

First subpoint explains occasions when Will employed satire.

Points 1 and 2 give specific examples for subpoint A.

Explanation of how he used humor as a weapon.

Use of a specific example.

Explanation of the specific example's humor.

Explanation of the effect of Will's satire.

Defines a term introduced: "rhetorical humorist."

Explains persuasive value of much of Will's humor.

Explains why Will's satire made few enemies.

Transitions to be used:

Between points 1 and 2: "As the cowboy philosopher, Will liked to ground his remarks in some element of the truth which he would extend just beyond the realm of probability. The element of 'truth' was a second vital source of Will's humor."

Between points 2 and 3: "Coupled with the element of the truth quite often was Will's third important source of humor: surprise."

Between points 3 and 4: "The illiterate Oklahoma cowboy, who dealt with the truth, and was fond of surprising his listeners, sometimes turned to satire as a source of humor."

SUMMARY

The body of your speech becomes more fully developed as you plan the supporting materials that you may use. From available facts, examples, statistical data, testimony, anecdotes, and human interest stories you choose the support that will make your points clear and acceptable to the audience.

As you develop each main point, state what it accomplished and how it is related to your specific purpose. Similarly, subordinate points should be orally presented in such a way that the audience is aware of the relationships and connections between ideas. As you complete the development of a point, briefly review, summarize the materials presented, and state their application to the point in question. Redundancy may be required because an audience may not always let you know if an idea is unclear.

LEARNING EXPERIENCES

Objectives

After studying this chapter, you should be able to *do* the following:

1. Classify the data that you have assembled in your research according to the types of supporting materials described in this chapter.
2. Practice telling stories that paint word pictures. Ask for feedback on the images received.
3. Outline the body of a speech, using main points, appropriate subpoints, and supporting materials.
4. Be able to discuss different methods of ordering or arranging ideas.

Exercises

1. Prepare a topic outline for one of the speech topics that you have selected. Go over the outline with members of your classroom group and work to improve the outline in terms of the suggestions made in this chapter.
2. After discussing your topic outline with your classmates, prepare a full sentence outline of your talk. Note carefully the relationships between the main points and subpoints of your outline.

3. Plan and present one of the types of supporting materials suggested in the chapter. For example, tell a story or a joke to the class. Consider how this material could be used in a full-length speech.

NOTES

[1]Harold E. Butler (trans.), *The Institutio Oratoria of Quintilian.* Cambridge: Harvard University Press, MCMI, III, Book VII, Pt. 2-3.

[2]See Raymond G. Smith, "Effects of Speech Organization Upon Attitudes of College Students," *Speech Monographs,* 18 (1951), 292-301; and Ernest Thompson, "An Experimental Investigation of the Relation of Effectiveness of Organizational Structure in Oral Communication," *Southern Speech Journal,* 26 (1960), 59-69.

[3]Arthur Koestler, *The Act of Creation.* New York: Macmillan, 1964, p. 592.

[4]Rudolf Flesch, *The Art of Readable Writing.* New York: Harper & Row, 1949, pp. 164-165.

[5]"A Second Century of Dishonor" by Ted Jackson. Copyright ©1957 by Ted R. Jackson. Reprinted by permission of the author.

[6]Wil A. Linkugel, Ronald R. Allen, and Richard L. Johannesen, *Contemporary American Speeches,* 2nd ed. Belmont, CA: Wadsworth, 1969, pp. 27-28.

[7]Jenkin Lloyd Jones, "'Let's Bring Back Dad': A Solid Value System," *Vital Speeches of the Day,* May 15, 1973, p. 474.

[8]See Herbert C. Kelman and Carl I. Hovland, "Reinstatement of the Communication in Delayed Measurement of Opinion Change," *Journal of Abnormal and Social Psychology,* 48 (1953), pp. 327-335.

7

Introducing and Concluding Your Speech

The science of physics has proved that it is harder to start and stop the movement of an object than to keep it stationary. The same principle appears to function with speeches. Special attention, therefore, must be paid to the introduction and conclusion of your speech. If you have outlined the main ideas of your speech and determined your supporting material, you are now ready to turn your attention to the "start" and "stop" of your speech.

PLANNING YOUR INTRODUCTION

Do you believe that first impressions play an important role in interpersonal relationships? If so, then it should be easy to appreciate the critical function of the speech introduction. A good beginning will capture the attention of your listeners and involve them with your thinking. At the same time, a good beginning can greatly boost your self-assurance.

The first question prospective speakers commonly raise about speech introductions is: How long should it be? The answer is that it should be as long as necessary. Length should be governed by the subject, purpose, audience, and occasion. Usually a brief introduction is sufficient. Sometimes, however, it may be expedient to use as much as one third or one half of your speech preparing your audience for your subject; you may, for example, need to alleviate hostility in order to make your listeners receptive. For most speeches, the introduction should not take more than one fifth of your allotted time. A two-minute introduction for a

ten-minute speech is probably ample. Introductions that are especially prolonged often bore the audience before the speaker even gets to the body of the speech.

A second common question is: When should the introduction be prepared, first or last? Cicero, the ancient Roman orator and statesman, answered this question emphatically by declaring that the introduction should be prepared last, after the body and conclusion have been carefully worked out. Despite such authoritative advice, the best time to prepare your introduction is when one occurs to you. Successful speakers have prepared introductions first, last, and halfway in between. The important consideration is that the introduction fulfill its vital functions.

As a general rule, the introduction to your speech should do three things: (1) Gain the attention and interest of your audience, (2) Establish your credentials and your reasons for speaking on your subject, and (3) Give direction to your speech by revealing your topic and perhaps giving an overview of your presentation.

Gain the Attention of Your Audience

The first few moments of your presentation are particularly important because your listeners begin to make immediate judgments about you and your message. You must gain their attention and their interest by both the delivery and the content of your message. Eye contact, a relaxed yet active body, a voice that is adjusted properly to the environment, and a genuine effort to achieve rapport with your audience will be effective *physical* means to gain attention. Your speech itself should also be attention getting. You will thus want to consider the following methods by which your content can attract listener interest.

1. A Remark That Shows Relationship Between Your Topic and Your Audience. In a speech to college students on the topic, "Requirements for a Major in your Program," you might say:

> *Over half of the graduates from this school changed their major at least once; on an average, each change of major costs the student seven hours of credit. At the rate of $30 per credit hour, that is a cost of $210; to say nothing of the cost of time.*

2. A Human Interest Story. Sally Webb, a student at Southeast Missouri State College, began a speech on the problem of stereotyping with the following human interest story:

> *In the local newspaper of my community recently, there was a story about a man named Virgil Spears. He lived in a small town about 40 miles from my home. He had served five years in the Missouri State Penitentiary for passing bogus checks. When he returned to his family, Mr. Spears couldn't find a job. Everyone knew he was an ex-con and everyone knew that ex-cons aren't to be trusted. Finally, in what was described as calm desperation, he walked into a local barbershop where he was well known, pulled a gun, and took all the money the barber had. Up to this point it had been a fairly routine robbery, but then something unusual happened. Mr. Spears didn't try to get away. He got into his car, drove slowly out of town, and waited for the highway patrol. When they caught him, he made only one request. He turned to the arresting patrolman and said: "Would you please ask that the court put my family on welfare just as soon as possible?"[1]*

3. A Vivid Illustration. Daniel R. Crary, when a student at the University of Kansas, provided a good example of beginning a speech with an illustration. He began a speech on population density in the following manner:

> *In Los Angeles, California, during rush hour on a heavily traveled, fog-shrouded freeway twelve-lanes-wide, a woman's car blew a tire, careened to the side of the lane and stopped. But out of the fog came another car which could not stop in time, and it struck the first . . . and another and another until one of the worst automobile accidents in history had involved a string of 200 cars, over a mile long, and had resulted in one death and several injuries.[2]*

4. A Humorous Remark. A visiting Russian speaker comparing East vs. West, said to an American college audience:

> *I have just visited Rome, Paris, London, and New York. Do you know what I saw? I saw the decline of capitalism. Do you know what I thought? A beautiful way to go.*

President John F. Kennedy, desiring to establish a congenial relationship with his audience, gave us a good example of beginning a speech with humor in an address in Miami at the opening of an AFL-CIO Convention:

> *I'm delighted to be here with you and with Secretary of Labor, Arthur Goldberg. I was up in New York stressing physical fitness, and in line with that Arthur went over with a group to Switzerland to climb some of the mountains there. They all got up about 5 and he was in bed—got up to join them later—and when they all came back at 4 o'clock in the afternoon, he didn't come back with them. They sent out search parties and there was no sign of him that afternoon or night. Next day the Red Cross went out and they went around calling "Goldberg—Goldberg— it's the Red Cross." And this voice came down the mountain, "I gave at the office."*[3]

5. An Appropriate Quotation. President Kennedy was noted not only for his wit but for his ability to make good use of pithy quotations in his speeches. He began a speech on "The Intellectual and the Politician" at a Harvard commencement ceremony, by drawing from Prince Bismarck:

> *It is a pleasure to join with my fellow alumni in this pilgrimage to the second home of our youth.*
>
> *Prince Bismarck once remarked that one third of the students of German universities broke down from overwork; another third broke down from dissipation; and the other third ruled Germany. As I look about this campus today, I would hesitate to predict which third attends reunions (although I have some suspicion), but I am confident I am looking at "rulers" of America in the sense that all active informed citizens rule.*[4]

6. A Personal Experience. Our own experiences often are a good source for a speech introduction. Jane Van Tatenhove, a student, reached into her storehouse of experience to begin her speech titled, "An Echo or a Voice?"

> *"Jane, do you consider yourself to be a Christian?" A friend asked me this question as we were drinking tea and munching shortbread in a brightly lit cafe in Edinburgh, Scotland. I thought that perhaps the minister whom we had heard preaching on Princess Street, the Hyde Park of Edinburgh, had prompted this question. But when I answered yes, he quickly said, "Then tell me something, Why are you feverishly hurrying in and out of the shops of Edinburgh in an attempt to find a skirt to match the green sweater you bought in England? I thought Christians were not supposed to be so concerned with the material aspects of life." It wasn't until later that I began to realize the penetrating nature of this question. It haunted me, "Jane, do you consider yourself to be a Christian?" Evidently my friend could not tell by actions that I was a Christian.*[5]

7. Show Common Ground With Your Listeners. You and your listeners will likely believe in or stand for many similar principles. In addition, you may have had similar experiences or conditions in your background. Such similarities are often referred to as "common ground." In your introductory remarks you may help to achieve a favorable psychological climate for your main ideas by referring to such common ground, thus reinforcing existing favorable attitudes of your listeners regarding you or your topic. Of course, you must be careful that you make accurate assumptions regarding the background or experiences of your audience. No one looks sillier than a speaker who errs in the "just homefolks" approach, such as a speaker "raised in Indiana down on the farm" opening up to a class mainly composed of students from the inner city. On the contrary, a proper approach to seeking identification with your listeners might look like this:

> It is a pleasure to visit my old high school and talk to you students who are enrolled in shop. Five years ago I took some of the same classes you are taking. Later I obtained further training and experience in electronics in the U.S. Navy. Last year I was able to borrow enough money to set up my own repair business here in town.

Establish Your Credentials

Audiences typically want to know why you selected this particular topic and why you are qualified to speak on it. In other words, what makes you credible? As a consequence, we suggest that in your introduction you consider carefully the following factors:

1. Your listeners should perceive you as informed, reliable and dynamic—a person of integrity. Your entire life should be seen by your listeners as honest, sincere, and genuine.
2. Your listeners should know that you are genuinely interested in them even though you may see things differently than they do.
3. Your listeners should believe that you are acquainted with and understand their thinking about your topic even if they disagree with you. You must help them see that you understand their beliefs but that, for valid reasons, you have come to believe differently.

In other words, your reputation should have preceeded you, and it should show that you are knowledgeable about your topic, interested in your listeners, and reliable as a person. It can be helpful to have someone who has high credibility among your listeners introduce you. If possible, that person should review and reinforce your credibility to your audience. Numerous research studies have shown that this procedure can influence the effect of your presentation.[6]

In your own introduction to your main ideas you can modestly review your qualifications for speaking on that topic. Research has shown that a review of your capability for gaining valid information (for example, special training or experiences) can be helpful.[7] A number of studies show that this usually is true but not always, and that it must be done with tact and careful consideration of your relationship with your listeners.[8] Be careful that you do not claim more than they are likely to believe. Consider for example how unobtrusively one student speaker established his credentials when he spoke on "Building Your Own Hi-Fidelity Tape-recording System."

> Building your own hi-fidelity tape-recording system is a very complex operation. Since I have been in college I have built fifteen systems for my friends and acquaintances at a small profit to myself. I'll not try to tell you all the problems you may encounter, but I will explain some of the most severe problems involved. As we go along, please bear with me—I'll try to make things as clear as I can and you can ask questions whenever you wish.

Most people believe in treating others fairly, at least as they have come to know fairness. Asking for a fair hearing, an unbiased evaluation of your ideas, can be a useful request in your introductory remarks. This request must be made with courtesy and sincerity; it should not be an artificial ploy. In return, you must be prepared to be as trustworthy as you know how to be as you go on to present your ideas.

An appeal for a fair hearing cannot be effective if you provide any basis for suspicion or the appearance of subterfuge. You must give something of value to your listeners in return. We suggest that your request might be of this order if you expect your audience to disagree with your position:

> I would like to ask you to give my ideas a fair hearing. Please evaluate them carefully with as much objectivity as possible. And I'd like to offer something in return; to be as honest and sincere as I know how to be. I'm suggesting a little contract, a trade: your fairness in hearing me in return for my candid honesty in talking with you.

Focus on Your Topic

Throughout your introduction never let your audience lose sight of the main target or thrust of your talk. Each of the things that we have suggested that you may do in your introduction is important, but as you do them you will need to help your listeners come back to a focus on the main theme of your talk.

Teachers of public speaking have traditionally suggested to their students that at the end of their introductory remarks just before they discuss the first of the major points of their speech, they should state their thesis or theme of their presentation. This can be done in a very few words, as clearly, directly, and briefly as possible. It could sound like this:

I wish to review our present method of assigning football tickets to students, assess its effects, and suggest a way of improving this procedure.

As you focus your listeners' attention on your topic you will need to clarify your intention for this specific audience. Do you intend to help them understand a complex principle or procedure, such as the calculation of the amount that is withheld from their paycheck to be sent in for social security? Do you intend to share your thinking with them on a common problem such as a dangerous condition (inadequate safety) on the jobs in your plant? Such a clarification of your specific intentions regarding your presentation to this particular audience should be done in the introduction right after you state the thesis or specific purpose of your presentation.

The native American student referred to in the previous chapter established his credentials and clarified his specific intentions to his speech class with the following introduction:

As I have listened to my fellow students this morning discuss so capably grave international problems, serious social evils, and crucial domestic policies—problems affecting millions of people—it has occurred to me that it may seem ill-considered to devote my few minutes to discuss matters that directly concern less than 350,000 men, women, and children. But unlike my fellow students, I am not considering judicious policies that should be adopted to meet the needs of the *other* fellow, I am talking about *my* people. They are important to me. I think they should be important to all Americans. Perhaps it is because of the proud Cherokee blood that runs in my veins or perhaps it is because of my study of the Indian problem in the Far West that I have a great sympathy for the Indians in their fight for survival. "The Indian problem," you may say, "why I thought that was settled years ago. I thought that now all Indians own oil wells, drive fine cars, and make fortunes in Hollywood!" I am sorry to be obliged to destroy your complacency, but let me tell you the story of the contemporary Indian as I know it.

Following the clarification of your intentions is a good time to provide the preview of your major ideas. For example, you may tell your listeners:

In talking to you about tennis this morning, I want to touch on four main topic areas: history, rules, fundamentals, and strategy. First, a few words about the history of tennis.

Observe how James K. Wellington, speaking on the "Fundamental School Concept," opened his address by forecasting what was to follow:

> *This morning I would like to do several things:*
> 1. *I would like to point out to you why I feel that fundamental schools are a realistic alternative to achieving the goal of quality education.*
> 2. *I would like to tell you why I believe they are a viable alternative.*
> 3. *I would like to comment on my opinion of the current state of education.*
> 4. *I would like to tell you why I feel that we must achieve better results from our educational efforts.*[9]

Immediately after forecasting the main ideas of your speech, start dealing with them one by one. The statement of specific purpose and overview lets your audience know what to listen for and provides a basis for cohesion. We recall a speech teacher once saying that the key to a clear speech was threefold: "Tell them what you're going to tell them; Tell them; and Tell them what you told them." Seldom will you have reason to keep your audience guessing about your content. This overview should merely be a brief statement of key words, phrases, or questions that constitute the main ideas to be developed in the body of your speech.

In summary, we offer for your inspection an introduction a student prepared on the topic of "Double Binding."

Introduction to a Speech on Double-Binding

A. Gaining Attention: "Have you ever felt that you had to leave but knew you had to stay?"

B. Reinforcing Favorable Attitudes: "An understanding of the double-binding process can help us solve common dilemmas."

C. Establishing your Credentials: "I am taking a very unusual psychology course in solving personal psychological problems; many of us in the class have found ways of understanding and solving some of our personal problems."

D. Eliciting a Fair Hearing: "I know you may think I'm not an expert; you are right, I'm not a psychiatrist, only a student like yourself. But I have learned some things that work for me and they might work for you. I'll try to be as clear and informative as I can, and after you hear me tell about the double-bind, you can judge whether or not this information can be of value to you."

E. Focusing on Your Topic: "I want to tell you how double-binding is done, sometimes by well-meaning people who mistakenly think they are trying to help us."

PLANNING YOUR CONCLUSION

As with the introduction, special attention must be paid to your conclusion. This is your last opportunity to pull your points together and to make them remembered. A final summary is often advisable, particularly in an informational presentation. In addition, the conclusion ideally should have impact or heighten interest, add to the meaning of your speech, and leave the audience in an appropriate mood. The same techniques that were employed in your introduction to attract attention are also useful in the conclusion.

Two important purposes can be served by your conclusion: (1) It should help your listeners remember the essence of your thinking—the main ideas and their relationship to one another; (2) It should help you to achieve responsible outcomes, related to the purpose of your presentation.

Review Your Main Ideas

A concise restatement of your thesis and a brief summary of your main ideas can provide additional impact for the essence of your thinking and will help your listeners give final consideration to accepting your view. You may have generally led them to believe as you do, but they may not be able to explain if someone were to ask them *why* they believed this. Such a review can help them to leave equipped with answers for others who were not present. In addition, research evidence indicates that at a later time they are more likely to maintain this belief if they can remember your reasons, that is, your main points.[10]

Figure 7-1   Beginning and Ending Your Speech

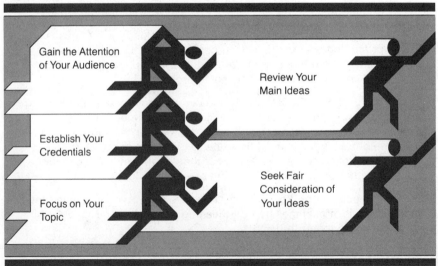

Gain the Attention of Your Audience

Establish Your Credentials

Focus on Your Topic

Review Your Main Ideas

Seek Fair Consideration of Your Ideas

Note how skillfully Adlai Stevenson, a two-time Democratic presidential candidate, summarized this eulogy of Winston Churchill:

> The great aristocrat, the beloved leader, the profound historian, the gifted painter, the superb politician, the lover of language, the orator, the wit—yes, and the dedicated bricklayer—behind all of them was the man of simple faith, steadfast in defeat, generous in victory, resigned in age, trusting in a loving providence and committing his achievements and his triumphs to a higher power. [11]

A commencement speaker, talking on the subject of "The New Furies: Skepticism, Criticism, and Coercion," closed his address with a summary:

> Let me conclude by suggesting that if you will invert these three hostile forces and if you will guide your own life by their opposites—an unwavering faith in principles you believe to be sound, instead of a corrosive skepticism; a persistent encouragement for that which is right, instead of criticism for that which is wrong; and a friendly persuasion, rather than angry coercion to advance the causes you believe in—if you can order your life by an affirmative rather than a negative posture, you will be surprised by how much you can accomplish and perhaps equally surprised by how much fun you have in accomplishing it and how many friends you made along the way. [12]

Sometimes a story can be used to emphasize the main ideas of your speech and leave the audience with a feeling that reflects your stated intention. The native American closed his speech as follows:

Indians are great story tellers. One night an old Indian man told me this pointed legend which epitomizes everything I have tried to say to you today: And the Great Spirit looked down upon the earth and said to one of his huntsmen, "Go and bring me the two most desolate things you can find in the world." The huntsman brought him the bones of an Indian baby and an Indian tent in which the fire had gone out. The Great Spirit held them in his hands, and then he looked down upon the earth where the white men were running back and forth in their frenzy for gold. And he said, "Oh White Men, White Men, what have you done with my people?"

The students in the class and the instructor were left with a lasting appreciation of the problems of the contemporary Indian.

Seek Fair Consideration of Your Ideas

This book emphasizes the importance of your responsibility as a public speaker—your honesty and sincerity in presenting your ideas. This basic philosophy will serve you well as you seek fair consideration of your ideas by your listeners.

Our approach is grounded on a psychological principle called *equity theory.* A fair amount of careful thinking and empirical investigation has gone into the development of this theory.[13] Its basic tenets have been expressed most clearly by J. S. Adams.[14] In essence, *equity theory* holds that one person's response to another's behavior is generally governed by a norm of reciprocity; if one person provides another with a useful resource, the other person will tend to respond with provision of a similar resource.[15] Specifically, if one person presents to another accurate information and interpretation of it, the other person will tend to respond in kind; if one person gives fair consideration to another's ideas, the other person will tend to respond with similar behavior.

Cross-cultural research tends to show that in most parts of the world this equity principle holds true, at least for the majority of people.[16] It is not true to the same degree for all cultures, nor is it likely to be true for every person you meet. The personalities and response patterns of some people have been damaged by harsh or severe experiences. You may meet some persons who live in terror, view the world with severe anxiety, or respond to you with undeserved deep hostility, anger, or hatred. Even so, most of your listeners will respond to you with fair consideration of your ideas if you demonstrate to them that you are sincerely interested in their needs and views. This, then, becomes your primary objective as a responsible person seeking to help others understand their world and solve their problems: *Seek their fair consideration of your ideas.*

Your ultimate goal as a responsible speaker should be to have your listeners *convinced by their own knowledge and reasoning* after giving fair consideration to your ideas. Presumably, their prior information plus yours will lead them to the same conclusions you have reached; if not, then you should compare their data and reasoning with yours. Maybe you have made a mistake; maybe their information is more accurate or extensive than yours; maybe their interpretation of it or their reasoning is more objective and valid.

Keep an open mind as you compare your thinking with that of your listeners. Ask yourself these questions: What data are necessary for a complete collection of relevant information? Are we sure we know all that is necessary? Have we missed something important? Then ask these additional questions: Is there more than one way to interpret these data? Can different conclusions reasonably be derived?

If you have done your thinking well in ways we have suggested, then you should be willing to compare your ideas with those of your listeners. Your goal should not be that they *must* agree with you; rather, *you should want them to be convinced that your thinking* (when they clearly understand it and have given fair consideration to it) *is a proper basis for them to adopt your position.*

In the long run, you should seek to allow your listeners to consider data from their own experiences and make their interpretation of it.

Then you should seek to *add* to their data and to show them how your conclusion makes sense. As you ask them to consider this new fund of data and its meaning, *your ultimate goal is that they will be convinced that your position is correct on the same basis that you, earlier, became convinced of it yourself.*

SUMMARY

In the introductory section of your presentation, you will need to gain your listeners' attention, establish your credentials to speak on the topic selected, and focus the audience's interest on your specific purpose.

You should plan an ending for your speech that shows you have concluded your remarks. Typically, you will summarize and attempt to make some final impact on your listeners' thinking. In all of your presentations, you should keep in mind responsible goals for your presentation. These outcomes should be (1) fair consideration of your ideas by your listeners and (2) beliefs or actions based upon adequate evidence and reasoning.

LEARNING EXPERIENCES

Objectives

After studying this chapter you should be able to *do* the following:

1. Formulate several ways that you can likely attract the attention of audiences.
2. State your credentials to speak on the topics that you have selected and outlined.
3. Plan how to state your specific purpose. Check these statements for clarity with your classmates.
4. Prepare a conclusion that includes both a review of your main ideas and an appeal for consideration of your ideas.

Exercises

1. Prepare and present a speech introduction to your classmates. Did the introduction capture attention, state your qualifications, and prepare your audience for what is to come? The test will be whether or not the audience wants to know more.
2. Analyze the introduction and conclusion of a speech that you have heard or read.

3. Prepare and present a conclusion to the speech that you earlier introduced. Work on an approach to gain a fair consideration of your ideas.
4. Unscramble the following outline concerning the preparation of a speech.* Organize the sentences so that a logical speech outline results. In each blank in the outline form, write the number of the appropriate sentence.

Central Idea: A speaker prepares a speech systematically.

1. At least a week before the date of his or her talk, the speaker selects a subject.
2. What is their knowledge of my subject?
3. Then the speaker analyzes his or her prospective audience and occasion.
4. The speaker determines his or her personal, general, and specific purposes.
5. In what kind of environment will I be speaking?
6. The speaker outlines the introduction and conclusion of the speech.
7. What is their background?
8. Am I competent to speak on it?
9. The speaker divides his or her central idea into its component ideas.
10. During the days remaining before the talk is given, the speaker practices it aloud, extemporaneously.
11. Having studied audience and occasion, the speaker prepares the talk itself.
12. Will it be suitable for this occasion?
13. What is their intelligence?
14. What are their attitudes toward me and toward my subject?
15. The speaker checks this subject by asking and answering four questions.
16. If his or her choice fails to satisfy these criteria, the speaker selects another subject which does.
17. What are their interests?
18. The speaker outlines the body of his or her talk.
19. Can I interest this particular audience in it?
20. The speaker asks and answers at least two questions about the occasion.
21. Is it too large or too small for the time limit prescribed?

From pp. 225-26 of "Testing Ability to Organize Ideas" by J. Calvin Callaghan from THE SPEECH TEACHER, Vol. XIII-No. 3, 1964. Reprinted by permission of the Speech Communication Association.

22. The speaker asks and answers at least five questions about his or her listeners.
23. The speaker writes out a one-sentence summary of the body of his or her speech.
24. At least two weeks before they are scheduled to deliver a speech, effective speakers make certain that they thoroughly understand what their audience expected them to do when it invited them to talk.
25. What will be my role in the total program?
26. The speaker phrases a provocative title for it.

Fill in the appropriate numbers from the list of statements.

I.

II.

    A.

        1.

        2.

        3.

        4.

    B.

III.

    A.

        1.

        2.

        3.

        4.

        5.

    B.

        1.

        2.

IV.

    A.

    B.

    C.

    D.

    E.

    F.

V.

NOTES

[1]Sally Webb, "On Mousetraps," *Winning Orations, 1963,* Evanston, IL: The Interstate Oratorical Association, 1963, p. 31.

[2]Daniel R. Crary, "A Plague of People," *Contemporary American Speeches,* Wil A. Linkugel, R. R. Allen, and Richard L. Johannesen, Eds. Belmont, CA: Wadsworth Publishing Co., 1965, p. 212.

[3]*Public Papers of the Presidents of the United States, John F. Kennedy.* Washington, DC: U.S. Government Printing Office, 1962, p. 786.

[4]John F. Kennedy, "The Intellectual and the Politician," *Representative American Speeches: 1956-1957,* A. Craig Baird, Ed. New York: H. W. Wilson Co., 1957, p. 165.

[5]Jane E. Van Tatenhove, "An Echo or a Voice?" *Winning Hope College Orations,* Holland, MI: Hope College, 1966, p. 115.

[6]Paul D. Holtzman, "Confirmation of Ethos as a Confounding Element in Communication Research," *Speech Monographs,* 30 (1966), 464-466.

[7]James C. McCroskey, "A Summary of Experimental Research on the Effects of Evidence in Persuasive Communication," *Quarterly Journal of Speech,* 55 (1969), 169-176.

[8]Theodore H. Ostermeir, "The Effects of Type and Frequency of Reference upon Perceived Source Credibility and Attitude Change," *Speech Monographs,* 34 (1967), 137-155.

[9]James K. Wellington, "A Look at the Fundamental School Concept," *Vital Speeches of the Day,* January 15, 1977, p. 215.

[10]H. C. Kelman and C. I. Hovland, "Reinstatement of the Communication in Delayed Measurement of Opinion Change," *Journal of Abnormal and Social Psychology,* 48 (1953), pp. 327-335.

[11]Adlai E. Stevenson, "Sir Winston Churchill," *Washington Post*, January 1965, p. A5.

[12]John A. Howard, "The New Furies: Skepticism, Criticism, and Coercion," *Vital Speeches of the Day*, July 15, 1974, p. 60.

[13]Uriel G. Foa and Edna B. Foa, *Societal Structures of Mind*. Springfield, IL: Charles C. Thomas, 1974.

[14]J. Stacy Adams, "Inequity in Social Exchange," in *Advances in Experimental Social Psychology*. New York: Academic Press, 1965, pp. 267-299.

[15]Alvin W. Gouldner, "The Norm of Reciprocity: A Preliminary Statement," *American Sociological Review*, 25 (1969), 161-178.

[16]Foa and Foa, *Societal Structures of Mind*.

8

Presenting Your Message: Voice and Action

Now that you have organized and developed your speech, you are ready to think about issues related to delivery. I. A. Richards has aptly observed, "... What is said depends on how it is said, and how it is said on what is said. What we say and how we say it are inseparable. ..."[1] Thus, an indeterminate portion of your message is carried to your audience by vocal and bodily cues. For example, the tone of your voice as well as your bodily movements provide data about your attitude toward the verbal message, about the intended purpose, about the degree of urgency in the message, and about your attitude toward the audience.

Such information does more than merely direct the listener's attention to the central theme and structure of your speech. Your nonverbal behavior helps the listener understand your intention, notes the values you hold, and determines the direction of your thoughts. The greater the congruence between your verbal and nonverbal messages, the greater your capacity to communicate effectively. Congruence is the term we use to indicate matching of your words and your behavior. Edward Hall has written, "when a person says one thing but really believes something else, the discrepancy between the two can usually be sensed."[2] When we find ourselves thinking, "I don't know what it is about him, but he doesn't seem sincere," it is likely due to a lack of congruence between the person's words and his behavior. Because nonverbal behaviors tend to be less conscious, we tend to believe them more than linguistic messages, if the two are incongruent. If a speaker says she "is happy to be here," but her voice and posture do not reflect this enthusiasm, we believe her actions more than her words.

We tend to recognize degrees of congruence or incongruence in all public speakers. With some speakers we recognize that in most areas they not only consciously mean exactly what they say, but the expressed feelings match that which is said—whether it is anger, affection, competitiveness, or cooperation. We feel we know precisely where these speakers stand. With other speakers we recognize that what is said is almost certainly a front, a facade. We wonder what these speakers really mean; we wonder if they know what they feel. We tend to be wary and cautious with such individuals.

YOUR VOCAL COMMUNICATION

It is difficult for current generations to appreciate the rapport and effect Franklin Roosevelt was able to achieve through his vocal communication in his radio addresses to the nation. His timing, his inflection, quality, and his vocal dynamism were such that radio listeners who had never seen the man felt certain of his integrity and good will. For sheer magnetism, Roosevelt's radio speaking voice may have been unequaled. Clearly, a speaker's voice attracts the attention of listeners, helps them to focus on central concepts, and allows them to know the speaker's feelings about the topic. Regardless of the message being sent, a voice can be interesting if it is varied in loudness, time, pitch, and quality. If the voice is monotonous in any of these four variables, it will tend to be dull and uninteresting.

Loudness, Time, Pitch, and Quality

We have all probably had the experience of trying to hear a speaker whose voice is not quite loud enough to be heard. Listening, which is hard enough work under good conditions, becomes intolerable. After some strain and failure, we quit trying. A beginning speaker should always be conscious of the people in the back row, especially early in the speech. People who can't hear tend to give fairly obvious feedback in most instances; they turn their heads slightly, they whisper to their neighbor, asking, "What did the speaker say?"; and they may even cup their hands to their ears. Speakers who are sensitive to these cues can tell quite readily if their listeners can hear. Loudness is one of the primary delivery issues which beginning speakers commonly have to confront.

Have you ever noticed that a successful comedian like Johnny Carson gets much of his effect through timing of his lines? The appropriate rate and the appropriate change of rate give fine meaning to what is being said. Generally, our rate of speaking should be lively and energetic, not slow and listless. To be sure, we don't want to rattle off words, but we certainly don't want to lull the audience to sleep. A rate that moves along briskly, but slows down for emphasis, is the desired goal. A well-placed pause can also produce a definite impact.

Pitch is important to vocal communication in two respects: (1) the overall pitch level should be pleasing—not high and squeaky, and not so low that the voice sounds like it is scraping on the bottom of a barrel; and (2) pitch inflection gives color and meaning to what is being said. You can read the manuscript of a speech which you found very funny when you heard it, and discover that without the speaker's peculiar vocal inflections, the written form of the speech is relatively humorless. Effective vocal inflection can give brightness, color, and life to one's message.

Quality is best explained on the basis of the timbre or tone color of the voice. Many adjectives are commonly used to describe the attributes of quality in voices. We speak of a voice as clear, husky, harsh, nasal, guttural, rotund, and so forth. Although the voice of the average adult is determined by physical structure, quality can be modified and improved somewhat by voice training. If you happen to have problems with your vocal quality, you may want to ask your teacher about the aids that are available in your school for voice improvement. Unfortunately, not all of us are blessed with the vocal quality of Ronald Reagan or Barbara Jordan. Nevertheless, we should try to make the most of what we have.

The most common problem with vocal communication is monotony. The speaker whose voice is colorless (without variety of pitch) may lack confidence and may not want anyone to know his or her true attitudes, emotions, likes and dislikes, or judgments. This person says everything in a monotonous, noncommittal way that does not signal any true feelings. Listen to your voice on a tape recording and consult with your teacher as to how you may achieve greater vocal dynamism. To a great extent, whether or not an audience likes to listen to you speak depends upon your vocal attributes.

Pronunciation and Diction

The mass media and our social mobility have made us aware of the differences in speech patterns among people from different parts of the United States. Linguists now tend to agree that all of the major dialects are equally correct. You need not drastically change your speech to communicate effectively. Indeed, very little is so distracting as someone feigning an acquired accent or speech pattern. The educated people of your own area provide the basis for a reasonable standard of diction and pronunciation. Careful articulation, of course, is needed, for intelligibility when a number of people are listening. But the average student need not correct many mistakes in pronunciation. However, if you say "fud" for *food*, "fur" for *for*, or consistently mispronounce a sound, attention should be called to this departure from the norm. Speech is a tool and should not call attention to itself.

Fluency and Clarity

American audiences prefer their speakers to be fluent. Fluency is not merely the process of saying words rapidly; fluency of presentation includes apt choice of words, fitting emphasis, and clarity. This trait can only come with practice and experience. As a beginning student, you should not expect to demonstrate exceptional fluency, especially on topics that you have not studied thoroughly.

Clarity is the degree of similarity between the speaker's meaning and the meaning received by the listeners. Thus, clarity is relative. At best, our words can only approximate our meaning, and we can only partly say what we intend to say. Clarity is obviously the result of interaction; both the speaker and the audience must participate in its achievement.

An audience cannot read a speaker's mind and sometimes speakers are unaware of what they are saying:

> *"Man, you know; it was something else. You know, it was a gasser! Why, you know, what they said and what they did you wouldn't believe!"*

No, the audience doesn't know. What is known is that the speaker says "you know" too much. Why do people need to assume "you know"? This unnecessary phrase has entered our usage because the words are used automatically, unthinkingly to cover thinking time between sentences. "You know" is more refined than "uhhh," which was once a prevalent crutch for speakers. A valid use of "you know" may be to provide a bridge between the speaker and listeners. If "you know" it, we have something in common, and you're more likely to agree with us and give us some positive strokes in return. "In other words" is another kind of hedge that allows us to repeat something to be sure that we have made our point with our listeners.

We recall a speaker who repeatedly said, "I'll be honest with you," or "to be honest . . ." When you sit back and think about it, what do such statements imply? First, we might assume that the speaker hadn't been fully honest with us except when he prefaced his comment with that phrase. Or, perhaps, he'd really prefer not to be honest with us. We get the definite impression that there may be times when he isn't honest or he thinks that his story is so unbelievable that we could consider him dishonest. In any case, doubt is implanted in our minds, for why else would he have to call our attention so frequently to his intent to be "honest"?

As listeners, we have a responsibility to "tune in" to these things, and also to give the speaker some feedback of our impressions. Only then can we confirm whether the message we are getting is what the speaker really wants us to hear. Or, in the case of an incongruent message, only then can we determine what is the dominant intention.

Figure 8-1   Factors of Good Vocal Communication

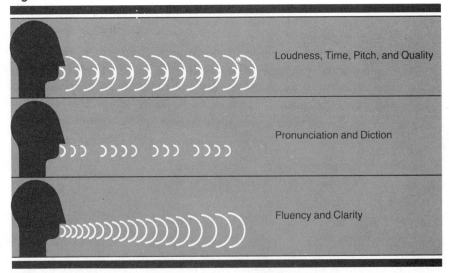

YOUR BODILY COMMUNICATION

The appearance and bodily mannerisms of a speaker play an important part in the audience's response to that person. Bodily behavior greatly enhances the speaker's effectiveness, and is related to the quality of "poise." The importance of physical behavior to communication is well indicated by the tremendous popular interest in "body language." The responsible speaker will be especially concerned with the congruence between his or her verbal message and bodily cues. Three topic areas warrant attention under the heading of bodily communication: (1) personal appearance, (2) eye and facial movements, and (3) bodily postures and gestures. In all three areas you have choices, and thus can influence the way that you are perceived.

Personal Appearance

There is considerable evidence that the general impression we form of another person significantly influences the way we respond to that person.[3] One of the most important factors in such an early impression is a person's general appearance. Studies have shown that appraisals of others are made easily and with little conscious awareness. In a few minutes perceivers form an image of another person that will guide their responses. In a study by Barker, for example, strangers who had no opportunity to interact verbally showed significant agreement with each other in their impressions of personality traits. Preferences for working together were correlated with these impressions. After several months of working with one another, 55 percent of these subjects reported the same impressions and working-partner choices.[4]

Clothing, cosmetics, and jewelry often represent a personal choice and are frequently taken as clues to the way people will respond to us in certain circumstances. Clothes and personal effects serve many purposes—protection, concealment, sexual attraction, group or organizational affiliation, status, role, and self-expression. One study found significant correlations between clothing choices and personal behavior. Subjects scoring high in *decorative* dress were found to be "conventional, conforming, and submissive," while those high on *economy* were "responsible, efficient, and precise."[5]

Clothing retailers and advertisers believe that dress is a way of expressing one's self-concept. A study by Compton of clothing choices and desired self-image tends to support this belief.[6] Further studies have shown an association between dress and perceived status with consequent differences in response behavior.[7] There is some evidence that persons are influenced by perceived differences in status clothing; in a well-known study, pedestrians were more influenced to cross "against the traffic lights" by well-dressed (high status) persons so doing than by persons poorly dressed.[8] Even small items of personal appearance may influence observer's responses. One study (in 1952) showed that the use of lipstick affected potential responses of males to females.[9] Another study has suggested that wearing glasses may produce more favorable judgments of intelligence and industriousness.[10]

Although the studies completed to date can only be taken to be suggestive of a relationship between personal appearances (including apparel) and predictable response behavior, it is clear that we ordinarily are influenced by it in a fairly dependable way. In one study, subjects, including students, police cadets, and schoolteachers, judged persons whose apparel *did not match* to be *less credible* than persons whose clothing matched. "Matching" elements included sport jackets, fringed leather shirts, blue jeans, "dress slacks," and "dress shirts." When apparel did not appear to present a clear, composite picture, observers reflected doubt and suspicion.

Your appearance thus reflects both how you think about yourself and how you want others to think of you. *If you respect yourself and respect your listeners, you will make choices that reflect this respect.* These choices should be reflective of sincere feelings about self and others.

Eye and Facial Movements

There is the old saying that the eyes are the windows of the soul. It is in the listeners' eyes that we look to check their level of understanding and agreement. When we look at our listeners it is apparent to them that we are concerned about them and their understanding of what we say. Of all of the visual cues that the speaker may send to listeners to tell them that he or she is concerned about their understanding and acceptance, eye contact is the clearest sign.

When a speaker merely talks *at* the audience, rather than *to* the audience, the listeners tend to perceive the speaker as unconcerned or insincere. We expect the personal contact of the meeting of the eyes. Similarly, the smile has been identified as the most primitive of human responses and the earliest evidence of recognition and acceptance of another person.[11]

The meeting of the speaker's eyes with members of the audience establishes a bond. Experienced speakers learn to look from one member of the audience to another, and, in effect, interact with each member for a while. Sociologist George Simmel has called the mutual glance the "purest form of reciprocity." He states: "By the same act in which the observer seeks to know the observed, he surrenders himself to be understood."[12] This mutual glance indicates a willingness to be involved with each other, as well as the absence of fear, hostility, or suspicion. Such contact is vital to communication.

Bodily Postures and Gestures

Elocutionists at the turn of the century were attempting to codify postures and gestures by rules and conventions that are similar to our oral language. Teachers taught their pupils what each gesture "meant" and how to use it to communicate the proper mood or idea to an audience. This approach was later rejected because of its mechanical and artificial nature.

In recent years, social scientists have again studied postures and gestures and attempted to "read a person like a book." We can tell a great deal about another person by his or her bodily communication, but problems result when we attempt to use generalized rules in order to create a certain impression. We stated earlier that when there is incongruity between verbal and nonverbal messages we tend to believe the nonverbal one. This reaction is based on the belief that nonverbal communication is less conscious and more revealing of a person's true internal state than are the words. To make our nonverbal communication appear conscious and strategic then defeats the basis of its impact.

The rejection of artificiality in our postures and gestures, however, does not ensure that we will "be natural." The very activity of standing in front of an audience is not a natural state but a learned one. It may be "natural" for us to appear nervous if we are the focus of attention; the public speaker must learn to control anxiety in such a way that it does not distract from the presentation.

One important step for the beginning speaker is to eliminate distracting movements. You may be able to observe yourself on a videotape recording or ask members of the audience to note postures and gestures that distract from your message rather than reinforce it. Conscious effort is needed to correct such distractions. Sometimes merely the knowledge that your shuffling or nervous gestures are distracting to your audience will serve as a motivation to eliminate them.

Our bodies generally betray deception. Participants in one study were asked to give a short speech and either try to be very persuasive toward one position or neutral and objective. The speeches were videotaped and shown to judges who scored the bodily movements of the speakers on a number of dimensions. When the speakers were trying to be persuasive, they engaged in higher rates of head nodding and gesturing, more facial expression, and higher degrees of speech rate, speech volume, intonation, and smoothness of speech than when they were trying to be objective.[13]

Experiments were also conducted in which participants were asked to give persuasive arguments in favor of issues in which they *did not* believe as well as issues in which they did believe. When the speakers were being deceitful and trying to convince an audience of something which they did not believe, they had less frequent body movements, they leaned or turned away from the audience more, smiled more, and talked less (more slowly), with more speech errors.[14] It appears that people are more animated in their movements when they believe in what they are arguing for, and more controlled and contained when they are being deceitful.

Gestures, particularly hand and arm movement (but including other elements of bodily movement: head-nodding, slumping, foot-shifting, etc.), perform several functions: illustrating an idea, expressing an emotional state, and signaling by using a conventional or agreed-upon sign.

Illustration of an idea or object is usually connected to verbal speech. Nonverbal illustrations are *iconic*, that is, they show movements or relationships (shape, distance) with hands, arms, etc., that show *similarity* to an object or condition. They are especially useful in describing an idea that is difficult or inconvenient to explain in words, by use of pointing, showing tempo or rhythm, showing bodily movements, spatial relationships, and direction.[15] One study has shown that people who have *greater* verbal facility also use *more* gestures.[16]

Although facial expressions generally are more dependable for inference of an emotional state, gestures and hand movements also display emotions. These movements are often diffuse, otherwise meaningless, and often idiosyncratic (peculiar to individuals).[17] Hand movements especially convey the level of excitement of a speaker: hands waving, clutching each other, straining. Anxious speakers often show such nonverbal signs that are not intended to communicate, and attempts are often made to conceal them.

Gestures, especially hand movements, may reveal feelings and emotional states that persons don't intend to reveal.[18] Many of these feelings or attitudes are directed toward oneself.[19] Self-directed gestures may include covering the eyes, touching or covering part of the face, and other hand movements designed to groom or hide parts of one's body. Such movements are frequently indicative of shame or embarrassment.[20] One research team asked subjects to view a film and then to *honestly* describe their feelings in one interview, and *dishonestly* in another. Observers were able to identify *twice as many* self-directed motions when the subjects gave *dishonest* reports; further, they rated the dishonest reports significantly lower in credibility.[21]

On the other hand, many people are quite aware that small, unobtrusive movements may reveal more of their emotions or feelings than they wish to reveal. To compensate, they may be fairly clever at deliberately using other movements to convey a contradictory impression; for example, artifices may be used to show confidence in order to conceal real anxiety. In such a case, gestures that can usually be taken as *indexical* (the result of an inner emotional state) are being faked; such gestures should be interpreted only with considerable care.

Your postures and gestures, like your eye contact, should show your listeners that you are concerned about them and their understanding of what you say. If you are communicating responsibly, most of your gestures will communicate the urgency and importance of how you feel.

You should be concentrating on your message rather than on yourself. You should be concerned with "how clear is my message?" rather than "how do they see me?" If your topic is truly important to you, and important for your audience to hear, then your bodily actions will reflect this urgency.

The most important consideration is the composite of the various message cues that a speaker sends and is received as an impression by the listener. We like one author's description of former first lady Rosalyn Carter as a public figure and public speaker:

> *Her collectedness gives her authority. Her voice does not. It is small, thin, lacking the drama of volume change or pauses for effect. There is no verbal underlining for important phrases. This woman does not depend on theatrics. She probably does not know how to use them. She relies, instead, on directness. She listens thoughtfully, considers, then begins an answer that may grope for words and change verb in mid-sentence, that must struggle in order to say exactly what she means. She is not naturally articulate, and not even close to glib. Her vocabulary is rudimentary, but her simplicity inspires belief. She is*

Figure 8-2 Factors of Good Bodily Communication

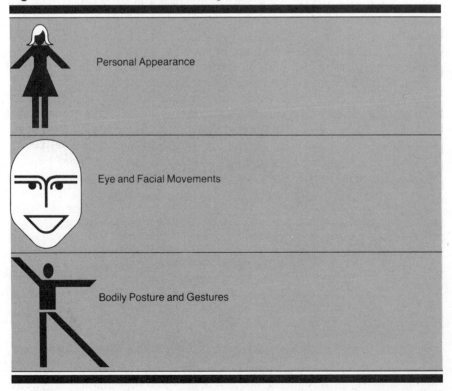

Personal Appearance

Eye and Facial Movements

Bodily Posture and Gestures

forthright, and she is confident. She dresses herself as simply as she does her conversation—without flair but with certainty. She does not appear to operate on many levels. She does not conjecture; she dislikes hypotheticals. She concentrates her energies on what she cares about and what she knows. [22]

We think that this appraisal shows the importance of directness, simplicity, and confidence for the public speaker.

PREPARING FOR THE SPEAKING SITUATION

As you prepare for the presentation of your speech, we have suggested a number of choices that you must make. Additional choices are required, depending upon your physical environment, your method of delivery, and the type and amount of practice. Consider the pros and cons of these choices.

Adapting to Your Physical Environment

Usually, you don't have the opportunity to choose *where* you are going to speak. Your speech class, for example, meets in a specified classroom and you have been assigned to speak on a given day. What choices, then, are available to you?

You must decide your physical relationship to the audience. Some speakers may stand behind a lectern that holds their notes, others will stand behind a table, while others will stand in front of the table directly before the audience. While there is no right or wrong answer, the choice that you make will affect how the audience perceives you. To stand apart from the audience may give the impression that you place yourself above them, that you will be lecturing to them rather than speaking with them. Additionally, standing behind a large lectern or other piece of furniture places a physical barrier between you and your audience that produces a negative psychological impact. The goal of speakers should always be to reduce or eliminate barriers between themselves and their listeners. Consider your own reactions to teachers and how they position themselves in the front of classes.

Can you be easily heard by everyone present? You may have to choose whether or not to use electronic amplification. The number of people present, the acoustics of the room, and your personal abilities to project your voice will be some of the considerations. In exchange for being able to be more easily heard by a large number of people, you will give up some of your personal contact with the audience and will be limited in movement because of your reliance or proximity to the microphone. In any case, being heard should be the prime requisite. If you plan to use amplification, be certain to test it beforehand and practice using it, if possible. You may have to learn to ignore the echoes and reduce your pace if your own voice returns to you. We are different people as we move from one environment to another. If the surroundings are known to us and we feel comfortable in them, we may be more confident and feel more at ease. Teachers who teach in a variety of classrooms can attest to how each room has a character of its own, and in some ways influences the communication that takes place. With practice, the speaker learns his or her capabilities in various surroundings and the extent of adaption that is necessary.

Your Method and Style of Delivery

There are four widely used methods of delivering a speech:

1. *Impromptu*—A speech given without prior knowledge or preparation. Such "talking off the cuff" forces you literally to "think on your feet." The key to success in such situations is to determine quickly the point or points that you wish to make and try to recall supporting materials that will help you. Parliamentary sessions and business meetings call for such skills, and you should seek opportunities to try such speeches in your speech classroom.

2. *Manuscript*—A speech that will be subjected to scrutiny and that must be recorded for history should likely be written and read. Professional conventions and research programs often expect the closely-reasoned thought reflected in a manuscript ready for publication. The speaker can feel confident in reading such a speech that has been polished

Figure 8-3   Method and Style of Delivering a Speech

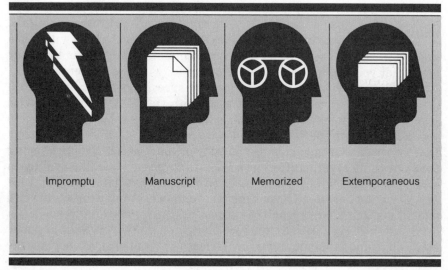

| Impromptu | Manuscript | Memorized | Extemporaneous |

in grammar, precision, and exactness. Such a speech, however, takes a long time to prepare, and limits the opportunity to adjust to the audience and the occasion. Many speakers lose contact with the audience if they are reading from a manuscript.

   3. *Memorized*—This method of speaking combines the advantages of the manuscript speech with the opportunity to develop greater contact with the audience. This method is rarely used, however, because of its inherent disadvantages: preparation time is extremely long; very little adaptation is possible; delivery has a tendency to sound rote and mechanical; and there is the constant fear that the memory will slip and the speaker will be left wordless.

   4. *Extemporaneous*—This speech is planned in advance, carefully outlined, and even practiced. However, the actual choice of words will be left to the moment of speaking. Such extemporaneous speaking allows for greater spontaneous interaction with the audience and is the most frequently used of the four methods. The basic focus of this book is on the development of this method of delivery.

   Since extemporaneous speaking will be the most likely method for your delivery of most public speeches, we shall consider the practice sessions and the need for directness in your presentation.

Practicing Your Delivery

Practice, practice, practice! If there is a roommate or a member of your family willing to listen to your speech, you will find their reactions helpful. But even if you must rehearse aloud by yourself, by all means do it and do it repeatedly. Oral practice is the means of fixing your ideas well enough in mind that you will be confident of them and of yourself when you speak before your audience. Although you are not memorizing the speech, you are significantly reducing the possibility that you will be at a loss for words on the platform, and consequently so dependent on your notes that you fail to make adequate contact with the audience.

   Prepare yourself by rehearsing the speech aloud, in front of a full-length mirror, if possible. Speak as though you were conversing with several of your friends. Using your outline in early rehearsals will help you to remember the content and sequencing of ideas in your speech. Don't worry about memorizing the body of your speech. Practice saying the same thing several different ways so that you won't be "thrown" by an inability to remember some exact word order. A vital part of your practice is not only to help your memory and to exercise your use of voice and action, but also to practice expressing the message in words.

   Rehearsing with a tape recorder can help you learn to vary your rate, pitch, and intensity. If you are concerned about projection, place the microphone far enough away from you so that you remember to raise the volume of your voice. Listen to the tape with a friend and make note of grammatical errors, mispronounced words, clichés, or disfluencies.

Your attitude during practice is extremely important. Think positively about your opportunity to speak and how rewarded you will feel in being able to communicate your ideas to your intended audience. Remind yourself of the importance of your topic. You must make your listeners feel that what you have to say is important to them as well as to you.

The practice time should make you familiar enough with your topic and the ideas that you wish to communicate so that you will not have to grope for words. At the time of presentation, you will want your listeners to feel what you feel, to understand your thinking, and to enjoy and share a memorable experience with you. You should be free to be audience-centered, rather than self-centered. Your attention can be directed toward maximizing the opportunities for interaction with the audience.

Public speaking should be for communication, not for exhibition. Undoubtedly you have heard speakers attempt to use public speeches to "show-off": "See how much I know," "Doesn't my voice sound nice?" "See how big a vocabulary I have." We think that about the most condemnatory thing that someone can say about a speaker is, "Oh, that speaker has been studying public speaking." No one in the audience should be forced to pay attention to your delivery for delivery's sake. Talking with the audience in a direct conversational manner should be your goal. As you gain more and more experience in public speaking, you will be more conscious of joining in conversation with members of the audience. If you have a message that is truly important to you and your listeners, the delivery will tend to take care of itself. If, however, you are poorly prepared, self-conscious, and fearful of how the audience will react, you can be certain that these factors will be communicated. You can achieve the directness you seek through a comfortable speaking stance, eye contact, and an enthusiasm for your subject. This will convey to your listeners an attitude of confidence—confidence in your message and in yourself.

BUILDING YOUR SELF-CONFIDENCE

Everyone feels anxiety before giving a public speech. In fact, a poll reported by the *Book of Lists* shows that Americans' greatest fear is speaking in public. A person who feels no anxiety may be so unconcerned about self and audience that everybody's time is wasted. We are anxious because we want to be well-received and have our message understood and accepted. The key to success is when anxiety spurs us to a greater effort rather than serves to distract from our capabilities to communicate.

The Normality of Anxiety

The focus of this chapter has been directed toward preparing in a way that reduces unnecessary tension or "stage-fright." If you consider yourself generally a shy person, Philip Zimbardo's book, *Shyness*, provides valuable advice for overcoming shyness and developing your social skills.[23] Properly controlled and utilized, nervous energy is a friend to be welcomed, not an enemy to be feared and resisted. Just as the successful athlete is "keyed up" and "feels butterflies" before a game, so the effective speaker is emotionally charged to meet the requisites of the speaking situation. Your goal should not be to eliminate tension, but to temper and regulate it so that it works for you rather than against you. If your initial tension causes you discomfort, face up to it and determine to live with it. As a rule, the progress of the typical student in controlling anxiety is proportional to the frequency of successful public speaking experiences.

Inasmuch as the beginning student is usually more apprehensive about the possibility of unfavorable listener reaction than about the act of speaking, the audience is the focal point of fear. Students sometimes claim that listeners look bored and "poker-faced," seem to smirk, and in other ways noticeably indicate their disapproval. Such negative judgments usually represent students' errors in interpreting the feedback from the audience. Unless hearers are actively hostile to you or your subject, they are unlikely to show overt signs of disapproval, particularly in a speech class where active, empathic listening skills are emphasized. As for audience criticism of your speech, we suggest that you heed the advice of Zimbardo: "Don't allow others to criticize *you* as a person; it is your *specific actions* that are open for evaluation and available for improvement—accept such constructive feedback graciously if it will help you."[24]

Steps to Achieving Self-Confidence

Immediately before the speech, consciously focus on your desire to communicate. Think positively, because fear of failure can become a self-fulfilling prophecy. Say to yourself: "Here's my opportunity to share my thinking. I think I can gain their attention and make them understand." If you possess keen interest in your subject and have prepared thoroughly, you know more about the subject than your audience does, and the audience will tend to respect you accordingly. Breathe deeply and regularly to relax muscle tension. Think about your opening statement, but not your entire speech; focus your feelings on the desire to communicate. When called upon, walk calmly and deliberately to the platform or front of the room. Pause a moment before speaking, arrange yourself and your notes, look at your audience for another moment, and then start in!

During your speech, consciously "eliminate the negative" and "accentuate the positive" in the following ways:

Do not's:

1. Do not focus inward; that is, avoid being overly concerned about how you feel, look, or sound.
2. Do not concentrate on how well you're doing or on whether the listeners like you personally, think you are nervous, or consider you an ineffectual speaker.
3. Do not try to camouflage nervousness by applying more tension. For example, avoid adopting a sarcastic, belligerent, or aloof manner to mask uncertainty.

Do's:

1. Concentrate upon the process of communicating your ideas to the listeners. Forget yourself and concentrate on transmitting your ideas from your mind to their minds.
2. Think positively. If you act as if you are confident, you will begin to feel more confident. If you expect your initial nervousness to subside, it is more likely to do so.
3. Look at the individual people in the audience, and talk directly to them. Consider them receptive persons who are pulling for you to do well.
4. Think about whether or not members of the audience are comprehending you. From the facial expressions and body sets of your listeners, attempt to read clues as to the reception your ideas are getting. If some persons look perplexed, perhaps you need to amplify your examples; if some listeners seem to be straining to hear, increase your volume.
5. Attempt to convert nervous energy into appropriate outlets of animated vocal and physical delivery. Without going to extremes, move around. Use the gestures that you practiced; they should be a natural outcome of what you are saying.
6. Instead of permitting tension to restrict your voice, divert the nervous energy into increased vocal emphasis and greater variety of rate, pitch, and force. Try to maintain the lively, flexible vocal and physical delivery of conversation, expanded to fit the needs of the speaking situation.

An opportunity to speak to an audience presents a real challenge. The skills and abilities to present yourself and your ideas can only be developed with practice and feedback from a caring audience. Hopefully your speech class will provide the opportunity for such development.

You cannot be *trained* to be a public speaker; you must learn it yourself. You can receive help from others in eliminating undesirable behavior patterns, but that is about as far as instruction can go. Your messages must arise from the meaning that is within you. When you are congruent—when your actions match your words—and able to focus your energy, you will be able to communicate effectively with the audience.

It is reasonable and predictable that you will approach a speaking event and start your speech with a certain amount of nervous concern for what you are about to do. The objective now is to translate this nervous energy into positive, purposeful, and animated speaking. A feeling of being prepared, a sincere desire to communicate ideas, and a direct speaking manner will all combine to use this energy to the best advantage.

SUMMARY

In this chapter we have emphasized the importance of congruence between your vocal communication and your actions. If you have a message that you sincerely want to communicate, and feel good will toward your audience, your words and actions will likely be congruent.

If your voice is to retain the attention of your listeners, variety is needed in loudness, time, pitch, and quality. Variety in these vocal attributes will help you avoid monotony. Good diction and correct pronunciation are important if we are to be understood and respected. Practice will be necessary for you to feel comfortable and fluent in front of a group of people.

In discussing your bodily communication we suggested that you have choices to make under three categories: (1) personal appearance, (2) eye and facial movements, and (3) bodily postures and gestures. Your appearance reflects both how you think about yourself and what you want others to think of you. Your bodily communication should reinforce and add emphasis to your spoken words.

As you prepare for the speaking situation you have a number of choices to make. Through practice you will be able to become familiar enough with your topic and the ideas that you wish to communicate that you will be free to be audience-centered rather than self-centered. We have discussed the normality of anxiety and have suggested some ways in which you can increase your self-confidence. You will be able to convert your nervous energy into positive speaking attributes.

LEARNING EXPERIENCES

Objectives

After studying this chapter, you should be able to *do* the following:

1. Try to make your verbal messages and nonverbal behavior *congruent.*

2. Avoid distracting verbalisms such as, "You know," etc.
3. Use pronunciation and diction that are intelligible but not distracting.
4. Speak with fluency and clarity.
5. Use your voice in an attractive way that varies in pitch, timing, loudness, and quality.
6. Present an attractive personal appearance that is not distracting from your message.
7. Use bodily postures and gestures that are natural to you, congruent with your message, and emphasize your intended meaning.
8. Accept your anxiety as a normal feeling.
9. Focus on your message as you deliver it, not on what your listeners are thinking about you.
10. Practice your presentation with growing self-confidence.

Exercises

1. Using an audio-recorder, tape the introduction to a speech that you have prepared. In groups with your classmates, listen to the recordings and give honest feedback to each other. If you have not heard your own voice before, you may be surprised because you are accustomed to hearing yourself through your inner cavities. Listen particularly for articulation or diction problems or distracting verbalisms ("you know," "er-uh," "see") that call attention to themselves.
2. After the critiques and practice, record the introduction again. Work for enthusiasm and variety in your speech. Compare the two recordings for improvement.
3. Prepare and deliver a short speech of demonstration. For example, explain and demonstrate the proper technique of the golf swing. Do not use notes.
4. Prepare and present a short "chalk talk" in which you explain some phenomenon through the use of chalkboard drawings. Do not use notes.
5. If videotaping equipment is available, arrange to record your speech. Treat the camera as if it is a prominent member of your audience. Evaluate your bodily communication and the congruence between your vocal and visual messages.
6. Volunteer to help your classmates by giving them constructive feedback and help in improving their delivery. In return, ask for their help. Your instructor will be available with exercises and expert help if special problems are noted.

NOTES

[1]I. A. Richards, "The Future of Poetry," *The Screens and Other Poems.* New York: Harcourt Brace and World, 1960, p. 122.

[2]Edward Hall and Mildred Hall, "The Sounds of Silence," *Interpersonal Communication in Action*, Bobby R. Patton and Kim Giffin, Eds. New York: Harper and Row, 1976, p. 213.

[3]See for example, Leonard Zunin and Natalie Zunin, *Contact: The First Four Minutes.* New York: Ballantine, 1973, pp. 6-10.

[4]Roger Barker, "The Social Interrelationships of Strangers and Acquaintances," *Sociometry*, vol. 5 (1942), pp. 169-179.

[5]Lewis R. Aiken, "The Relationship of Dress to Selected Measures of Personality in Undergraduate Women," *Journal of Social Psychology*, 54 (1963), pp. 119-128.

[6]Norman Compton, "Personal Attributes of Color and Design Preferences in Clothing Fabrics," *Journal of Psychology*, vol. 54 (1962), pp. 191-195.

[7]R. A. Hoult, "Experimental Measurement of Clothing as a Factor in Some Social Ratings of Selected American Men," *American Sociological Review*, vol. 19 (1954), pp. 324-328.

[8]Monroe R. Lefkowitz et al., "Status Factors in Pedestrian Violation of Traffic Signals," *Journal of Abnormal and Social Psychology*, vol. 51 (1955), pp. 704-706.

[9]Wilbert J. McKeachie, "Lipstick as a Determiner of First Impressions of Personality," *Journal of Social Psychology*, vol. 35 (1952), pp. 241-244.

[10]George C. Thornton, "The Effect of Wearing Glasses Upon Judgments of Personality Traits of Persons Seen Briefly," *Journal of Applied Psychology*, vol. 28 (1944), pp. 203-207.

[11]Kenneth M. Goldstein, "The Smiling of the Infant and the Problems of Understanding the 'Other,'" *Journal of Psychology*, vol. 44 (1957), pp. 175-191.

[12]George Simmel, "Sociology of the Senses: Visual Interaction," in *Introduction to the Science of Sociology*, R. Parks and E. Burgess, Eds. Chicago: University of Chicago Press, 1921, p. 350.

[13]Paul Ekman and Wallace Friesen, "Nonverbal Leakage and Clues to Deception," *Psychiatry*, 1969, pp. 32, 80-106.

[14]Albert Mehrabian and M. Williams, "Nonverbal Concomitants of Perceived and Intended Persuasiveness," *Journal of Personality and Social Psychology*, 1969, pp. 13, 37-58.

[15]Jean Graham and Michael Argyle, "A Cross-Cultural Study of the Communication of Extra-Verbal Meaning by Gestures," *International Journal of Psychology*, vol. 24 (1975), pp. 21-31.

[16]James C. Baxter et al., "Gestural Behavior during a Brief Interview as a Function of Cognitive Variables," *Journal of Personality and Social Psychology*, vol. 8 (1968), pp. 303-307.

[17]Paul Ekman and Wallace Friesen, "Nonverbal Behavior in Psychotherapy Research," *Research in Psychotherapy*, vol. 3, (1968), pp. 179-216.

[18]Maria Rudden, "A Critical and Empirical Analysis of Albert Mehrabian's Three-Dimensional Theoretical Framework for Nonverbal Communication," Ph.D. Dissertation, Pennsylvania State University, 1974, pp. 12-22.

[19]Norbert Freedman and Stanley P. Hoffman, "Kinetic Behavior in Altered Clinical States: Approach to Objective Analysis of Motor Behavior during Clinical Interviews," *Perceptual and Motor Skills*, vol. 24 (1967), pp. 527-539.

[20]Paul Ekman and Wallace Friesen, "The Repertoire of Nonverbal Behavior: Categories, Origins, Usage and Coding," *Semiotics*, vol. 1 (1969), pp. 49-98.

[21]Paul Ekman and Wallace Friesen, "Hand Movements," *Journal of Communication*, vol. 22 (1972), pp. 353-374.

[22]Sherrye Henry, "The Real Rosalyn Carter," *Vogue News*, July 1979, p. 163.

[23]Philip G. Zimbardo, *Shyness*. Reading, Massachusetts: Addison-Wesley, 1977.

[24]Zimbardo, p. 159.

9

Presenting Your Message: Language and Visual Aids

The ability to speak in clear, understandable language is a prerequisite for achieving your communication goals. Your ideas must be translated into the kind of verbal communication that accomplishes your objectives. This means your words must be clear, your message easy to follow, and your language reflective of your personal style. The words you use to convey your meaning say much about you to the audience. Sometimes a speaker speaks "down" to an audience, making listeners feel that the speaker is trying to manipulate them in some way, or, at the very least, has a low regard for them. An audience, like the speaker, wants to be respected. Speakers, thus, should realize that to a certain extent how listeners will perceive them depends upon the wording of the speech. Hence, we will begin with a discussion of verbal communication in terms of the impact of language upon public speaking. Then we will examine visual communication with particular attention to visual aids.

YOUR VERBAL COMMUNICATION

In the first place, people view facts, events, and ideas from different experiences, from different frames of reference. Someone who lives in Alaska certainly has a different reference for the words "winter" and "snow" than someone born and raised in Texas. In other words, through associating a word to the world around them, and what they feel inside as a result, individuals produce particular meanings. People see the world not as it is, but *as they are.* Their opinions, interests, motives, and attitudes differ from those of their neighbors. The total of their

experience, thinking, and feeling gives them unique abilities to conceive and grasp an idea. No two people witnessing the same automobile accident will give identical testimony about it. A mountain means different things to a ski enthusiast, a lumberman, a miner, and a forest ranger. Ask twenty adults to define the word *happiness* and you will get vastly different definitions. People vary widely in life experiences related to culture, religion, race, politics, morals, and family backgrounds. They also differ greatly in personality and character, which affects their mental and emotional reaction to words.

Language scholars point out that people attach denotative and connotative value to words. *Denotative* meanings are logical, objective, and extensional. A denotative meaning points beyond a person's mind to the reality of the outside world. Denotation has an explicit referent, like the section on a map that represents a definite territory. We can, for example, point to the state of Nebraska as a geographical entity. We often associate denotative meanings with concrete or *name* words, such as "chair," "bar," or "wall." Yet the terms *denotative* and *concrete* are not the same because an individual's frame of reference will determine whether words have implications beyond the naming of a real object. Clearly, to a prison inmate, *wall* and *bar* will have meanings related to their particular environment.

Words also have associative value and thus we say that *connotative* meanings are emotive, subjective, and intensional. To someone from West Virginia, the mention of Nebraska probably will produce in that person's mind only the denotation of a western plains state. However, to a person strongly identified with Nebraska, the word "Nebraska" may well generate intense feelings about the Nebraska Cornhuskers football team and pride in the outstanding beef cattle produced in the state.

Intensity of experience produces connotative meanings. The word *mother*, for most people, is a supercharged value term because of the positive connotations we attach to it. Conversely, any term that is in direct and strong conflict with our basic values will have a potent negative connotation; for instance, the word *dictator*. Connotation is the affective quality of a word, and this affective value may have great influence on a person's life. People may, for example, experience inner emotional turmoil because of a habit of using affective, self-deprecating words about themselves.

It should be easy to see how these concepts apply to public speaking. A speaker should always strive to be aware of what words, if any, are likely to have strong connotations for a listening audience on the subject being discussed. Lack of such awareness oftentimes will produce an unexpected negative response among audience members, whereas the use of words with strong positive connotations should help the speaker's cause.

Second, people spend their lives giving names to things. The coffee you drink is labeled as strong, hot, or black. People may designate society as heartless, unchanging, indifferent, or responsive. They may feel that other people are essentially selfish, generous, hostile, or friendly. This naming process is the basis of all kinds of prejudices. We all carry in our minds a long list of labels—emotion-laden words and phrases that act as filters to our minds. Some people fail to see the true qualities of a person of another race, for example, because they have categorized the person with a label.

The audience will to a certain extent form their impressions of public speakers by how they label things. Labeling migrant workers as "shiftless aliens" certainly provides a different image than if one referred to them as "oppressed farm workers." Responsible speakers are characterized by fairness and openness and will always be prudent about what labels they use for things. Remember, good will is essential to responsibility.

Finally, words, like thoughts and conceptions, vary in abstraction. We use symbols that indicate a total class of things ("animals"), to a particular class ("dogs"), to a specific member of that class ("my dog 'Pepper'"). To cite other examples, "justice" is abstract; "trial by jury" is concrete. "Democracy" is abstract; "voting at election time" is concrete.

When dealing with concrete words that have denotative referents —such as "book," "tree," or "typewriter"—we have generally agreed-on referents; highly abstract terms such as "justice," "obscenity," and "truth" are less likely to have common referents. The more abstract the word, the greater the ambiguity and the greater the chances of misunderstanding. High-level abstractions are quite useful in that they allow us to talk about things in general. In fact, the more sophisticated our minds become, the greater our ability to deal with abstractions. Keep the following suggestions about language in mind as you get ready to present your speech.

Strive for Clarity of Thought

Throughout this book we have emphasized the importance of helping listeners understand new information and helping them to reach sound decisions. To fulfill this objective, a responsible speaker will always attempt to use language that is clear to the audience. When you speak of abstract matters such as "truth," "justice," or "public welfare," be sure to appreciate that listeners will attach their own meanings to those terms unless you tell them quite clearly what you have in mind. Definition and the use of example are in order. Numbers, like words, may also be abstract. For example, a student speaker was describing the size of her home state of Alaska and said that it contained over 590,000 square miles. How large is this? This abstract number meant little to those of us in the audience until she explained that this area equalled the size of the original thirteen states plus Florida, Tennessee, and Mississippi. She then placed a cutout map of Alaska over the whole of central Europe to demonstrate visually the bigness of the state.

The speech by the native American student that was cited in the previous chapters paints a vivid word picture of the problems of the native American:

These are unpleasant facts. It's so much easier to consider all Indian schools comparable to those of the Carlisle's whose Indians made glorious gridiron history! And it's so comforting to deafen our ears to the flogging of innocent Indian children, to forget that they are fed dried fruit which is filthy with worms. Let these conditions exist on the reservations until the race is dead and there are no more Indians. Nice, silent, anonymous Indians. On and on this sordid citation of examples could go, incidents where the Indian has been robbed of his lands, rights, and life and then handed a piece of paper, soiled and dirtied by a lie. He has seen 26 reforms and no improvements. He walks away when the agent mentions the word "reform." He now endures in proud silence, too tired and dispirited to protest against a life of hopeless drudgery and a diet of horsemeat and contaminated flour. It seems ironical that in an era when this nation is attempting to hold aloft the principles of democracy for the world to witness, that we have failed to hear the call of 350,000 loyal native Americans.

Use Understandable Terms

When military people speak of a "blue goose" assignment, the rest of us may suspect that they are not preparing to go goose hunting but beyond that we have little idea as to what they might mean. The use of jargon, or technical language, abounds in today's world. The area of study in which you are a specialist, such as your academic major, has a specialized language known only to those inside the field. If you are to be understood, you must use terms that are meaningful to your listeners. Complex and significant ideas don't have to be presented in erudite language. One analyst noted that in the Gettysburg Address, of the 266 words that Lincoln used, 190 were of one syllable, 56 had two, and only 20 had more than two.[1]

The problem resulting from the failure to use understandable terms is illustrated in this frequently told story:

> *A plumber wrote the U.S. Bureau of Standards about using hydrochloric acid to clean drain pipes. . . . Several days later he received this reply: "The efficacy of hydrochloric acid is indisputable, but the corrosive residue is incompatible with metallic permanence." Confused, he wrote again and asked if the acid "is okay to use or not."*
>
> *A second letter advised him, "We cannot assume responsibility for the production of toxic and noxious residue, and suggest that you use an alternative procedure."*
>
> *Still baffled, he wrote, "Do you mean it's okay to use hydrochloric acid?"*
>
> *A final letter resolved the question, "Don't use hydrochloric acid. It eats the hell out of pipes."[2]*

Paint Word Pictures

Words that call up, through their meanings and sounds, sensory impressions, emotions, and sounds are words that produce mental images. Such imagery makes us see, hear, and feel the ideas a speaker is presenting. Imaginative expressions and sufficient detail of sight, sound, movement, and the like, are essential for vivid imagery. Most great historical addresses contain striking word pictures. William Jennings Bryan electrified a Democratic Convention with the phrase, "You shall not press upon the brow of labor this crown of thorns. You shall not crucify mankind upon a cross of gold." Patrick Henry warned his fellow Virginians, "There is no retreat but in submission and slavery! Our chains are forged! Their clanking may be heard on the plains of Boston!" Daniel Webster, in his speech "Seventh of March, 1850," told his fellow senators, "Let us not be pygmies in a case that calls for men." And General Douglas MacArthur's moving "Farewell to the Cadets" of West Point made the meaning of the academy's motto, "Duty, Honor, Country," vivid to the cadets through its imagery:

> *From one end of the world to the other, he [the American soldier] has drained deep the chalice of courage. As I listened to those songs, in memory's eye I could see those staggering columns of the First World*

War bending under soggy packs on many a weary march, from dripping dusk to drizzling dawn, slogging ankle-deep through the mire of shell-pocked roads; to form grimly for the attack, blue-lipped, covered with sludge and mud, chilled by the wind and rain, driving home to their objective, and, for many, to the judgment seat of God.

Such imagery is not necessarily reserved to outstanding orators in history. Students are perfectly capable of painting word pictures also. A beginning speech student speaking on the importance of soil conservation, produced the following imagery:

The sun's rays were beginning to lose their luster. What was unusual about that? It was two o'clock in the afternoon in Kansas. The sun gradually turned into a red ball and appeared no longer to possess the needed energy to light the earth. The red spot grew dimmer and dimmer, until it disappeared altogether. The sky became grayish-orange and visibility was limited to a few hundred feet.

The cows turned their noses upward and sniffed the impure, dusty air in a perplexed fashion. The small boy and his older sister, herding the animals, were struck by fear. They placed handkerchiefs over their noses to filter the dust. Leaving the cattle unattended, they started for home, walking rapidly; soon they were trotting, and then they were running. Following the fence line, they reached the farm home safely.

The orange-colored dust grew so intense that night had come in the afternoon. Home alone, with their parents in town, the terror-stricken children huddled in a closet. The boy, in childish naivete, thought that the world was coming to an end. It was the first dust storm he had experienced.

I was that boy. And I recall that dark, dusty day vividly. I think it most ironic that as a lad I should have linked the idea of the world coming to an end with a dust storm—the depleting of our soil upon which we depend for life-giving food.

Speak in the "Here and Now"

As you are talking with your audience, be willing to talk about yourself and the audience in this particular situation. As you are reporting your experiences, your thoughts, your feelings, or your intentions, clearly indicate that you are the owner. Use personal pronouns: I, me, my, and mine. Rather than making you sound as if you are self-centered and selfish, as you might fear, such words put the proper focus on you as the source of the message.

Responsible communication is enhanced by the use of such expressions as "I feel," "My perception is ..." The movement from general ownership ("People usually think . . .") to more specific ownership ("I think . . .") reflects an increase in ownership and in the level of responsibility.

When you are talking about the "there and then," do so in such a way as to make them relevant to the people in this audience. Try to address individuals in your audience specifically, even while you are addressing the entire audience. Constantly strive for contact and attempt to utilize the interaction.

Use Clear Transitions

The coherence and unity of a speech must be shown vocally by the speaker. The listener cannot see the scheme of indention and symbolization on the speaker's notes. The audience may get a few cues from the speaker's pauses and his or her movements, but they depend primarily on words for signals that the speaker is moving on to a new subtopic, or is about to do so.

Just as we use transition words between paragraphs in this book, we must also use them in our speeches. Think about your potential listeners and try to move their thinking along with your thinking. Transitions are difficult to manage well, even for experienced speakers. Practice helps in keeping your attention on the relationship of one part of your speech to the next part, and hence strengthens your grasp of the progression and structure of your ideas. As you complete a point and move on to the next one, let the audience know about it; for example, "Now that we have seen when and why good tennis players rush the net, let's move on to the next aspect of strategy—moving the ball from side to side." Sometimes an internal summary, briefly reviewing what has been covered, helps the listener to follow the speech; for example, "Thus we have seen that the first three dimensions of critical listening involve the problem of meaning, the question of documentation, and the motivation of the speaker to speak. Let's then briefly examine the fourth and final one, 'So what?' or what is the importance of the speaker's argument?"

A special comment should be made about transitions between major points or elements in your outline. As you state a major point, define its first and second terms, show that existing conditions coincide with the definition of your second term, explain, give examples, and illustrate this idea, perhaps with visual aids, you will need to be sure you have not lost your listeners when you move to the next major point. They will need to see how it relates or connects with the prior major point. For example, a speaker on disarmament stated:

> *Weapons do not provide security. By weapons I am referring to our nuclear arsenal, now containing over 50,000 warheads. Security can only exist in a world in which we feel safe from the fear of a nuclear war. If anything we feel more insecure than ever. In 1978 the nations of the world were spending $350 billion each year for military purpose. Now the figure is approaching $600 billion. Military planners now talk about "winning a nuclear war." Have the increased weapon capabilities then promoted security?*

This process of relating or connecting one major point with another gives your presentation coherence. Such a connection must be achieved with optimum clarity. To do this you carefully select connecting words that show the relationship. The following are some of the ways such relationships may be shown:

1. Showing sequential progress: "Previously I have shown . . ." "In the second place . . ."
"At the same time in . . ." "At last . . ."
2. Drawing a conclusion: "Thus we can conclude that . . ." "Under these conditions . . ."
3. Summarizing a point: "We have seen . . ." "To summarize my support of this point . . ." "Briefly, I have suggested . . ."

These are only a few of the ways that you can show that you are concluding the development of one major point and starting the exposition of another one. The function of such transitional phrases is to help your audience follow your thinking, identify material connected with one point and then another, and, overall, to see how your major points together form a logical pattern.

YOUR VISUAL COMMUNICATION

For years people have clung to the idea that "seeing is believing." Note the statement does not say, "hearing is believing." In other words, for most people seeing something with their "own eyes" is the best test of truth. Hearing the same information does not carry as much weight. It so happens that not only are people more likely to believe something that they see with their own eyes, but also they are more likely to remember it. A few years ago, Robert S. Craig reported on some interesting research concerning this topic. His studies showed that when people were merely told something, their recall three hours later was 70 percent, and three days later, only 10 percent. However, when they were shown the same information in a visual presentation, their recall three hours later was not too different—72 percent, but three days later it was more than three times as great—about 35 percent. At the same time, when *hearing and seeing* were combined, the recall three hours later was 85 percent, and three days later, 65 percent. A marked improvement indeed! This research certainly emphasizes that a combination of stimuli in informative presentations—seeing and hearing, or speech and pictures—greatly increases recall ability.[3]

Seldom should an informative speech be given without visual aids. Yet, far too often speakers do just that. One of the authors recalls listening to a fifty-minute classroom lecture on the critical importance of visual aids without the use of visual aids. This is roughly akin to giving a travelogue without accompanying pictures. We think that responsible speakers will be more considerate of their listeners.

What about persuasive speeches? Should visual aids be used on those occasions? Absolutely, if appropriate. Suppose you told people that you had seen a flying saucer parked on the ground. How many do you think would believe you? But what if you were able to show them a photo of yourself standing next to a flying saucer parked on the ground? Then how many would believe you? Certainly a lot more. Visual aids can also be used to dramatize discourse. A chart, for example, showing a phenomenal increase in sales during the last quarter of the year, will have greater impact than words alone.

The subject matter of the speech should tell you what type of visual aid to use. A report on a trip to an "island paradise" seems to call for slides, or at least, photographs, as does a report on some strange and unusual birds found in a certain region of the world. At the same time, a year-end financial report of an organization invites the use of charts and graphs—displayed either through the use of an overhead projector, posters or flip charts on an easel, or carefully typed handouts. The question to answer at all times is: How can I achieve maximum vividness so that listeners will both comprehend and remember my information?

The use of slides, or an opaque projector which allows you to reflect a page from a book on a screen, is relatively simple. All you need to do is check to see that the equipment is functioning properly, that you know how to use it, and then use it skillfully in conjunction with your verbal message. We can hardly overstress the importance of checking out the equipment. One of the authors once planned to give an hour-and-twenty-minute lecture that was based entirely on photos to be shown by an opaque projector only to have the bulb blow out when he switched it on and there was no replacement bulb available. For want of a spare bulb the hour was lost.

Visuals we make ourselves warrant greater attention. First of all, almost anyone can prepare effective visuals. To be sure, artistic talent is helpful, for it allows you to be more elaborate and more imaginative, but it is not essential. Therefore, we will explore a few principles concerning the production of visual aids that will aid you in preparing your own. Typical examples of visual aids are illustrated in Figure 9-1. (See pp. 140–41.)

Let's suppose you want to make a bar graph for a speech. Four criteria can be employed: the graph should be *clear, easily read, attractive,* and *imaginative.* In the first place, what each of the bars represents should be clear and the numbers should be readable.

Pie graphs should be similarly treated. A pie graph can be used to depict what happened to a company's gross income; different colors or graduated shades of the same color represent the pieces of the pie. Colors or shadings make the pieces easier to discern, make the pie more attractive, and give added impact to the statistics. A variation on the pie graph shows "What Happened to Each $1 of Sales" and utilizes a divided dollar bill for the pie. Although this visual may require some artistic skill to prepare, it nevertheless illustrates what student speakers can do if challenged.

Visual aids need not be limited to a display of numbers. Key terms or topics can often be effectively displayed on a poster or chart. The flip chart is an especially useful device when several visual aids are to be used. A flip chart is a large tablet, the pages of which can be turned for purposes of moving from one visual to another. The same effect can be achieved by using posters and fastening them in the upper corners with rings. The flip chart allows you to use a lot of visuals, giving a strong visual dimension to your speech. It provides a side benefit as well. The visuals can serve as the notes for your speech. Instead of writing notes on a small card or a sheet of paper placed on the lectern, you have the equivalent of notes placed on the flip chart and can display them to the audience as you speak on each topic.

One word of advice: whenever you expect to use posters or flip charts make certain that you can display them effectively. If you expect to use an easel, be sure one will be present. Some experienced speakers take no chances—they bring their own. Compact, lightweight aluminum easels are now available at a relatively low price.

The presentation of technical data, such as a financial report, may require handouts. The only problem with handouts, as compared to a poster, is that the speaker has little control over what items listeners are focusing on. It is often easy for audience members to lose track of what the speaker is saying because they get too engrossed in the handout. Some speakers, therefore, prefer to display data on a screen, or on a poster, and then provide the audience with appropriate handouts after the speech.

Finally, real objects, or models of real objects, make effective visuals. If you were to try to explain how to fill out the federal income tax short form, it would be most useful to display it, perhaps on an opaque projector, while showing how to complete the form. If you were to demonstrate the proper use of a crutch, having a crutch as a visual would certainly be helpful. An address on different varieties of roses could make effective use of pictures or slides—but better yet, show several types of real roses. A talk on how a carburetor functions would certainly be helped by the display of an actual carburetor. A demonstration of guitar picking seems to call for a guitar. At the same time, models can be equally effective. Anyone wishing to explain the functioning of the inner ear might do this through a model showing the parts of the inner ear.

Whatever the form of visual aid, remember that the visual device used is designed to enhance and clarify the message; such aids should support your ideas. In displays, such as in museums, the objects alone are the messages. But that is not true of a speech. Always remember that the overriding purpose of the visual aid is to help you communicate *your ideas* to this audience.

Figure 9-1   Examples of Visual Aids

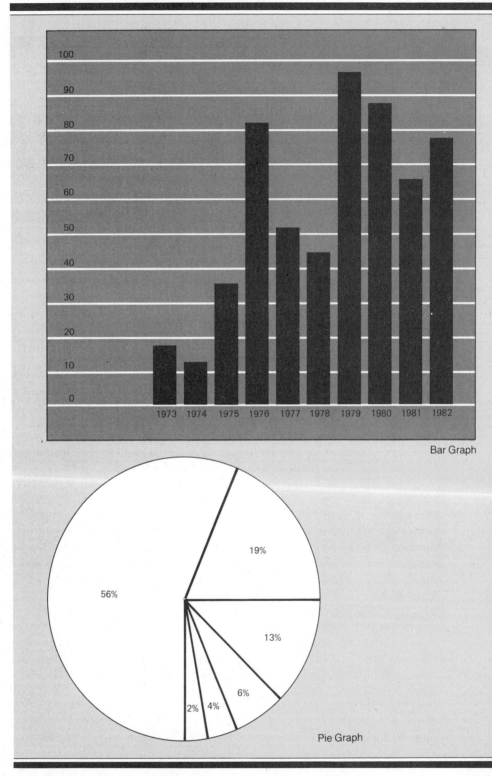

Bar Graph

Pie Graph

Expenditure Breakdown

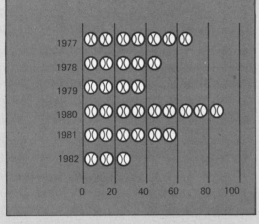

Chart

Poster

SUMMARY

People who make up your audience came to you with different experiences, different frames of reference, and with different labels for phenomena. In order to use language effectively, we made five suggestions: (1) Strive for clarity of thought; (2) Use understandable terms; (3) Paint word pictures; (4) Speak in the "here and now"; and (5) Use clear transitions. The language of your speeches should be clear, interesting, and correct.

We have pointed out the difference between denotative and connotative meanings of words. You must strive to be aware of what words are likely to have strong connotations for your audience. You should always be fair and open as you apply labels and choose your words.

In terms of visual communication, we have cited ways in which visual aids can truly *aid* your presentation. Audiences like to see as well as hear and remember better when the vocal message is reinforced with visual support. We have suggested several principles concerning the production of visual aids that will aid you in preparing your own. Bar graphs should be clear and easily read. Pie graphs allow you to show the relationships of pieces of the whole. If you use posters or flip charts, you must make certain to display them effectively. Practice with visual aids is an important preparation for presentation.

LEARNING EXPERIENCES

Objectives

After studying this chapter, you should be able to *do* the following:

1. Explain the difference between denotative and connotative definitions of words.
2. Cite examples of levels of abstraction of words you commonly use.
3. Make greater use of personal pronouns as you speak in the "here and now."
4. Make coherent transitions between major ideas.
5. State the values of visual aids.
6. Differentiate between the types of visual support available and cite pros and cons about them.

Exercises

1. Prepare a one-point speech in which you concentrate on your use of language. Record the speech and check yourself on the suggestions made in this chapter.

2. Analyze a written speech in a source such as *Vital Speeches of the Day* (or one of the speeches in the *Speeches for Analysis and Study*) and evaluate the use of language.
3. Present a one-point speech supported by a visual aid. Seek constructive feedback from your classmates.
4. Analyze a speaker on television in terms of the visual support provided.

NOTES

[1]J. Jeffrey Auer, *Brigance's Speech Communication.* New York: Appleton-Century-Crofts, 1967, p. 112.
[2]Bobby R. Patton and Kim Giffin, *Interpersonal Communication.* New York: Harper & Row, 1974, p. 8.
[3]Conwell Carson, "Best Memory by Eye and the Ear," *The Kansas City Times*, April 19, 1967, p. 13-A.

Arthur Grace/Stock Boston

Part 3

Preparing Specific Speeches

The foundations have now been laid. You are ready to begin the process of putting all the ingredients together and developing well-prepared speeches. The challenge will be to integrate the skills of preparation as you attempt to share information with an audience or help them reach decisions in a responsible manner.

In previous chapters we have presented techniques of preparing speeches; many of these techniques were described in brief fashion so that you could begin to use them in early speeches in your classroom experience.

In Part 3 we will present a focused discussion of approaches to preparing informative and persuasive speeches, and consider examples of such speeches by students who went through similar stages of preparation. We believe that you can learn by working through the experiences of others, and thus put the "finishing touches" on your public speaking skills.

10

Helping Listeners Understand: The Informative Presentation

Have you ever had a mechanic try to tell you how to start a car when the carburetor was flooded? Or a teacher try to explain a procedure for working an algebra problem? Or a friend try to demonstrate how to cut out the material to make a dress? Have you ever started working on a new job and had someone attempt to explain to you what part of your pay is withheld and for what reasons? If you have experienced any of these conditions, you have participated in a situation where a speaker was trying to help you understand. Such situations call for an informative presentation.

To the extent that you are becoming informed, trained, educated, or experienced, to that extent you are likely to have information or insights that are important to others. Any time you have the attention of a few listeners who need the benefit of your experience, you will need to present your information in a responsible, efficient manner. The situation may not be very formal; your listeners may not sit in rows—they may not even sit. You may have no lectern and you might not use notes. But if you try to help your listeners understand, you are giving an informative presentation.

DETERMINING YOUR QUALIFICATIONS

Our daily lives are filled with important communication events. Remember when someone tried to tell you how to enroll "late"? Or what happened when you were poorly informed about playing a "six no-trump" hand in bridge? Or when you were told how to find the Registrar's office

146

and that you "couldn't miss it"? The responses to such information are dependent upon the qualifications of the sources of the messages. The key question is: "Who do you trust?"

Checking Your Perceptions

The accuracy of our perceptions and the ideas generated by them are less than perfect for a number of reasons. First, we tend to see best what we want to see most. We pay attention more to those aspects of events or conditions that our prior experience has led us to think will be important.[1] Sometimes this behavior is called selective inattention. A second obstacle is that we tend to think we see or hear what we want to see or expect to see. We tend to take note of items and sources of information that please us in a process of selective exposure to such.[2] For example, if you own a new Ford, you will tend to pay more attention to things people say that are favorable (including advertising) about new Fords.

Evaluating Your Information

There are other obstacles to achieving accurate perception, such as lack of experience required to understand various possible meanings or interpretations of an event or situation. The point is clear: We often need help in understanding the significance of events and conditions even when we are "right there." In addition, much of the information we need to meet life's requirements is not available directly to us through our own experience, but can only be gained from reports of experiences of other persons. The presentation of such information is very important, and your ability to discern "the facts" and to interpret them carefully are very valuable qualifications. A large part of this chapter will be devoted to exploring tests of these qualifications.

Informing others should only be attempted by a speaker who has information that is needed or desired by listeners. The purpose of the speaker is to help the listeners understand. This understanding may involve nothing more technical than insight into a process, for example, the way that payment of student fees entitles you to obtain football game tickets. Or the needed understanding may involve precise data: how many credit hours are needed for a major, what courses are required, what limitations are put on choice of electives, and when such courses are taught.

Your listeners may need information of special kinds in order to do their jobs, achieve their goals, or make appropriate adjustments to changes in their surroundings. In addition, they may need information to confirm their perceptions of events and situations. People with normal common sense and ordinary sources of information tend to act as if they have adequate understanding of their world and its events; their predictions of common events often work fairly well. Even so, they often check their perceptions with their friends and acquaintances.[3] How often have you heard one of your friends say, "Did you see that?" or "Am I right in thinking that . . .?" or "What do you think of . . .?"

Much of what people "know" or opinions they hold or even actions they take are influenced by what they hear from others, including you. The meanings of many events we observe firsthand are mediated by people with whom we interact. Much of what we hear from others is screened or distorted by their less than accurate perceptions; some of it is not very dependable. Even so, we still are interested in comparing our ideas with theirs because we know our perceptions are also not thoroughly dependable.

You must determine what items of information are relevant to your listeners' needs or interests. And you must use your time and your listeners' time efficiently. In addition, you will need to present these items in a reasonably ordered fashion. You will need to organize your thoughts, think ahead, preview your material, and present it in a form that is most easily comprehended.[4]

If you are to be successful, your audience must be willing to listen. Our presumption in this chapter is that they need or desire the information you possess. In some cases, you may face people who (you think) ought to want such information (at least, that is the way you see it), but they apparently are unaware that they need it. For this chapter, however, we will presume that you have willing listeners.

Even with willing listeners, you must make certain that members of the audience are aware of your unique qualifications to speak on a topic. The implicit identification of your background on the topic and any specific biases you hold will help your listeners evaluate your information. Consider, for example, your reactions to this introduction from a speech presented in the 1979 Interstate Oratorical Association contest:

> As I start this presentation, I would only ask that each of you give careful consideration to the question I am about to ask, before attempting to answer it. The question is, "Are we, the citizens of the United States, either through our general lack of knowledge, and/or apathy, responsible for creating the CAREER CRIMINAL?"
>
> My name is Darryl Moore, and I am an ex-convict. I was sentenced to an indeterminate to six-year sentence at a State Penitentiary, on a charge of possession and conspiracy to distribute narcotics, that narcotic was Marijuana. My subsequent incarceration in the Maximum Security Unit, as well as later being housed at an Honor Facility, and eventually in a Community Placement Center, have made me keenly aware of the problems that exist within our Penal Institutions today. Residivism, which is nothing more than the number of times an ex-offender recommits a crime, and is re-incarcerated, is at an all time high. The national average indicates that residivism is 67 percent throughout the nation. That figure is taken from a research project, conducted by the Catholic University of America, by Professors Paul Hanly Furfey, and Rev. Thomas Joseph Harte.[5]

The speaker's qualifications as a credible source of firsthand information were established with his listeners and he established the groundwork for his opinions with the facts that he discovered through his research.

MEETING YOUR LISTENERS' NEEDS AND INTERESTS

As you try to help others to understand, you must carefully identify ideas that you believe are facts from those which make up your opinions. However, we will first take up the problem that becomes your major concern: What do you need to do to be sure you meet your listeners' needs and interests?

The essential elements in an informative speaking situation are: (1) You have knowledge of a certain phenomenon, event, or process, and (2) your listeners need or desire that information. You must know something that they want to know.

Many times speakers such as teachers, parents, politicians, and salespeople misjudge this; they think you or someone else wants to know something they know—or something they think they know. And you really don't care to listen. No doubt you have experienced such a situation, probably with teachers who presumed that you wanted to know what they knew.

Recall how you felt and see if you can agree with this suggestion: If you are going to try to inform people, you should first find out if they want your information, and just how much of it they want.

Even though you may be quite convinced that someone wants information you possess, it is wise to check out this assumption. Suppose, for example, you work in the Student Union; three new employees are hired, and it is your responsibility to explain to them who will work which hours of the day. You can expect them to want this information. Even so, before you have them sit down and deliver a four-minute exposition, you might ask if they want to listen to you—particularly, right now. As professors, we have found that we teach best when students ask questions; often when a question is raised, we will ask for an indication (raised hands) of all students who want it answered, and make a little agreement with the class that we will together spend four or five minutes going over that issue. It has been highly rewarding to our students and to us to share our knowledge *when it is desired.* On the other hand, we have had to make a special effort to train ourselves to be quiet when students don't want to listen—making special arrangements to meet with a few at a time who are interested in some item or topic. In like manner we encourage you to determine what your listeners want to hear from you before you presume they are interested.

There are two types of listener needs that you may meet by presenting information: insight and data. In some cases listeners have plenty of factual data of their own but need help in interpreting their data; they lack insight into relationships that exist among the data. For example, much of the counseling done with students and parents takes the form of going over items already known but requiring interpretation or explanation.

Enhancing Listeners' Insights

Insight that other people sometimes need may pertain to events, processes, or principles. In each case the desire is met by careful explanation. An event may be recounted; for example, a female friend may have missed geometry class last time it met, and may need to know what happened in class. As you describe that event, you soon begin to realize that not every little thing that happened is of interest to your friend—only those happenings that she has to do something about will hold her attention. Perhaps she will say: "Did anything happen that I need to know about?" She is really asking you to make a judgment regarding her needs as a student. You must make a critical selection from the detailed list of events that transpired. Thus you recount whatever she needs to know in order to carry on as a member of the class. Literally, she is asking for an *interpretation* of the event and an explanation of details that have some special meaning to her. Even when you describe a single event to a listener, you must take his or her needs into consideration and explain the meaning of various parts of the event in terms of those needs as you perceive them.

Even more important are the listeners' needs when you try to explain a process. The amount of detail covered in explaining various parts of the process should be chosen according to their needs. In addition, the order in which various procedures occur will be important to an understanding of the process.[6] For example, suppose you have occasion to explain to a group of friends how you trained your dog to "heel." Some of them will be very interested in considerable detail so they can try to train their own dogs. Order of events and attention to details will help to meet their needs. On the other hand, for those who are only interested for the sake of their store of general information, you can quickly give an overview and go on to something else. Depth of detail in portraying a process can vary a great deal. So, indeed, can a person's interest. You will need to match them as carefully as possible if you are going to be proficient in helping listeners to understand to the extent that they desire.

The most difficult need to satisfy in helping a listener to understand is that involving explanation of a system. In essence, a system involves relationships between two or more things (events, objects or procedures) in which one (or more) influences the other(s). Sometimes such systems are explained in terms of a principle or general rule or series of rules. For example, the human respiratory system may involve the principle of capillary action. Not only the depth of detail must be decided in terms of needs of your listeners, but the degree of complexity of interrelationships among the components of the system must also be considered. You may be able to overview the components of a system of mail delivery to the various university dormitories; it may be relatively easy to meet your listeners' needs for understanding of this system. On the other hand, if you are building your own high-fidelity recording and tape-playing system you may have considerable difficulty explaining the relationships among the various components of the system—even to a very interested, intelligent, experienced friend.

Supplying Relevant Data

A second type of need your listeners may have is for data. They may already have an adequate understanding of an event, process, or system, but lack specific information. For example, they may have a good understanding of enrollment procedures but need to know which instructors teach various sections of a certain course.

In the presentation of data you must pay careful attention to the capability of your listeners to receive, store, and use such information. Quantity of data, degree of complexity, logical order or progression, and depth of detail must all be considered in terms of your listeners' needs and capabilities. Complex sets of numerical data, such as a list of your classmates' telephone numbers, are best portrayed visually as well as orally. Probably such numerical lists should be typewritten, mimeographed, and distributed to your listeners. Lists of addresses, calendar dates, and rules and regulations most likely should be handled in similar fashion.

If specific data are really needed by your listeners you should not shortchange them by poor presentation. Such data should be transmitted with care so that they can use well what they really need. Numerical data in rows and columns should be given special care; the rows and columns must be clearly identified, and their relationships clearly expressed. For example, tables of insurance rates, tax assessments, football records, used car values, relationships of chest, waist, and inseam measurements in children's clothing—all such complex collections of data need to be presented clearly, if at all. Usability of data by your listeners should be your primary goal if they really need such information.

THE BASIC ISSUE: WHAT ARE THE FACTS?

You are faced with a problem: your listeners want information and presumably you have it. What do they need when they want "information"? Are you at liberty to tell them just anything that pops into your head? If not, what is the nature of quality information? What are the "facts" when we say, "The facts are these . . ."? What are "opinions"? How can our listeners be sure we have made careful and useful distinctions?

For optimum credibility you will need to carefully distinguish elements in your beliefs that you see as being *factual* from those that are your *opinions*. If your listeners hear what appear to them to be opinions presented by you as if they are facts, they will begin to doubt your good will and/or competence as a speaker who wishes to help them to understand better the world in which you live.[7]

Identifying Your Beliefs and Opinions

We cannot be too careful about seeking to be a responsible speaker—credible in our own eyes as well as in the perceptions of others. We should be careful to tell our listeners which of our statements we perceive as factual and which we are presenting as our personal opinions. How do we determine the difference?

Begin by asking: Is it possible for you to observe an automobile accident firsthand, recount the "facts" you observed, and have another firsthand observer report the "facts" as being different from your set of "facts"? Is someone necessarily lying? If not, think about this question:

When the facts of an event, situation, or condition are being presented, does it make any difference "whose facts" are reported? If so, what makes the difference? Even more important is this question: How responsible do you wish to be as a person? As a speaker? These questions are important because they directly involve your credibility—the basis for your listeners' being willing to believe you when you offer an informative presentation.[8]

A *belief* is any statement claiming the *existence* of something; or that something is *good or bad;* or that something *should be done.* You may hold a belief with great certainty, or with very little conviction, or with any degree of assurance in-between.[9] For example, you can believe that there are living plants on Mars (a belief that something *is,* and probably held with little conviction). Or you may believe that having ability to play the piano is valuable (an *evaluative* belief, perhaps held with great certainty).

With a little thought you can see that all the things people know or think they know, or even suspect are true, can come under this umbrella-term—*beliefs.* Also, when you think about it, you will see that helping people to understand—presenting information—involves giving them the benefit of your beliefs. If you are to avoid antagonizing them by wasting their time or leading them astray, try to give them beliefs that are dependable, that is, information which will serve them well. You should seek to give them facts whenever you can, and opinions when they want them, if the facts are unavailable. And in so doing, you should be sure they know which of these you are offering.[10]

Facts and opinions should not be viewed as two separate, airtight categories. Rather, they should be viewed as ways of indicating the degree of certainty a person has regarding one of his or her beliefs. You may think of a fact as a belief held with a high degree of certainty, an opinion as a belief held with a lesser amount of conviction, and most of your beliefs ranging somewhere in between.[11] It is vital that your listeners know the degree to which you believe your statements are dependable. It is also essential that you know the limits of reasonable conviction and the way in which most people determine the dependability of what they believe to be true.

Establishing the "Facts"

Ordinarily a "fact" refers to what has "really happened" or a statement that is "the truth." How is such "truth" known? The usual answer to this question is "by actual experience or observation." But we should ask further: "By *whose* observation?"

Such a line of questioning will eventually drive us back to this position: A fact is a belief that can be supported by empirical data. More specifically, a fact is an object, event, or situation about which persons *in whom we have confidence* agree in their reports regarding its existence, occurrence, or causality. This seems to pin down most of the relevant essentials. But there is a loophole: Suppose these persons agree somewhat but not fully? And there is another loophole: On what do you base your confidence in "certain people"—how are they selected?

We can answer these questions as follows: A fact is a purported object, event, or situation, regarding which there is a high degree of agreement in reports of its existence or condition, on the part of persons in whom you have confidence regarding their ability to observe, and to report honestly and accurately their observations. You now can see that there is plenty of room for difficulty in getting at "the facts" and that you probably are fortunate if you can be absolutely certain about anything. Even so, many times each day you have to act as if you have adequate factual information, so you do the best you can with what you have. Otherwise, you would hardly be able to get past breakfast. And yet, you should be careful to understand each criterion employed in the above definition of a fact. Each criterion deserves our special attention.

When you make an informative presentation to your listeners, only rarely will you be showing them the actual event or situation that is at issue. Ordinarily you will either be (1) reporting your own firsthand observations, or (2) reporting on the reports of others. In either case, you will be using factual statements.

Degree of Agreement.   In the first place, you must be aware of the need to compare conclusions you draw from your observations with conclusions reported by other people. To what extent are your statements generally in agreement with those of persons in whom you have confidence? This *extent of agreement* must be checked to your own satisfaction; you need to know the way in which dependable people view the statement. Your general life experiences may give ample proof for many of your beliefs. Even so, you need to be careful that you don't present to others statements that your experiences have not shown to be acceptable to other responsible people. When you are tempted to make such statements, simply stop, wait, and actively check the accuracy of beliefs with selected others.

Degree of Confidence.   How should you choose these "selected others"? *In whom should you have confidence* about making judgments on the validity of purported facts? They should be persons who routinely test the validity of information by evaluating the source of such information to observe carefully and to report honestly and accurately. Such testing requires that the exact source of an alleged factual statement must be specified. To say that "It was in the paper" or "I heard it from one of my friends" automatically blocks this testing process.

To determine the ability of a person to make accurate observations we ask first, *was the person "there"*—that is, did he or she really have the *opportunity* to see, hear, count, or measure the essential factors of the reported object, event, or situation? Next, we ask if the observer has had *sufficient training or experience to identify specific variables in question.* For example, does a sports personality advocating that we use a particular product have any unique training that allows this judgment?

Ability to Observe. Does your observer *have an open mind?* This question is our third criterion and a very serious one. In his book, *The Open and Closed Mind*, Milton Rokeach reviews ten years of careful research and concludes that some people are actually unable to see events or conditions that are incongruent with their general beliefs.[12] Other research verifies this principle. In a well publicized experiment, for example, Allport and Postman found that persons who held a stereotype associating black people with violence actually believed they had seen a razor in the hand of a black person in an experiment even though in that situation the person holding a razor was actually white.[13] Other experiments have demonstrated that ordinarily persons *do not* hear clearly *nor remember well* information that contradicted their prior beliefs.[14] In general, research has shown that people tend to read and listen to information that agrees with their prior views, to misunderstand information that contradicts these views, and quickly to forget that tending to force them to change their beliefs.[15] When checking your beliefs against those of persons in whom you have confidence, take care to guard against personal bias by noting the general belief systems of such persons; are they generally open-minded and dependable in their orientation toward the type of event or situation involved? Along with Rokeach, we believe that some persons, the closed-minded, are prone to distort selectively their perceptions; also, with Rokeach, we reject the conclusion that they do so because they want to.[16] Instead, we believe *they do so only to the extent that they cannot help it.* So far as we know most people try hard to discern reality accurately. Some persons are less capable than others in seeing reality that is incongruent with their prior personal beliefs.

Ability to Report Honestly and Accurately. The fourth criterion for selecting persons with whom you should check your observations is the ability to report their observations honestly and accurately. Lack of desired honesty may derive from social pressure or from gaining some personal advantage in not telling the truth. In some cases people who are willing and ready to tell what they have seen or observed do so with the deliberate purpose of shading or distorting the truth. It is often easy enough to discern that informants are personally involved in some way. In many other cases, however, it is difficult to discern a personal investment, but you should do so if at all possible. You will need to check on the following factors: Do the observers favor some particular movement or program? Are they sponsored or supported by some action group? Are they in any way likely to gain in social or economic status if their beliefs are accepted? If you believe any of these factors to be true you should view such observers with a measure of skepticism.

Inaccuracies in reporting can come from lack of ability to express oneself clearly. It is difficult to achieve agreement among witnesses concerning the existence of events or conditions if their *reports* are ambiguous or unclear. Such reports must comply with appropriate grammatical, linguistic, and semantic requirements. You will be seeking to determine the degree of agreement with such reports by people in whom you have some confidence; likely these people will be persons who seem to use good judgment and practical wisdom. Probably they will be at least fairly well educated and have fair ability in making and evaluating such reports. If the statements to be judged are garbled, confused, or do not make sense, such people are not likely to concur. It must be possible for such persons to discern and agree upon the apparent meaning of such reports; there should not be too many possibly varying interpretations. Such reports should, so far as possible, refer to specific objects, events, or situations that can readily be *identified* rather than to high-order abstractions that have no common referent. For example, a statement such as, "Our teachers don't have any time for poor students" may be unacceptable as factual because of lack of clarity, too many possible meanings, and the difficulty of identifying a referent for "poor students" (i.e., financially poor, ignorant, having low grades, not interested, lacking in self-esteem, not very bright). In any case, accuracy of such reports is enhanced by specificity. In every case it is important that you check, insofar as possible, the factuality of statements you propose to present to others in terms of the relative amount of agreement on the part of other people in whom you have confidence.

Qualifying Your Sources of Information

You are likely to find that your listeners are interested in information that you have obtained from other people who made firsthand observations when you were not in any position to do so yourself. In such a case, instead of your listeners evaluating you as a source, you and they together will need to evaluate these other sources. However, since you are the one believed to have better access to such sources (that is, you are the one doing the informing) you will carry the primary burden.

It should be apparent that you and your listeners will need to evaluate these outside sources in the same way we have suggested that you check the reliability of your own observations. You will need to apply the following criteria:

1. Are the exact sources identified?
2. Are they capable of observing precisely?

3. Were they where they could see, hear, measure, count, etc.?
4. Do they have sufficient training to identify and quantify relevant factors?
5. Are they open-minded; is there any suggestion of observer bias?
6. Do they have a reputation for being honest?
7. Is there any possible personal advantage in their being less than perfectly honest?
8. Do they express themselves clearly, in appropriate grammatical, linguistic, and semantic style?
9. Are they in agreement with other qualified sources?

The last criterion is critical and, in essence, points up the importance of all the others. If more than one source meets all of these requirements and if they are in complete agreement with each other, we tend to think we have "a bit of a handle on reality." If there are more than two sources and no indication at all of dissension, we tend to think we are getting at the truth. In qualifying your sources of information for your listeners, you should be careful to point out to them the relative amount of agreement. Do so, but be honest; unfounded claims may later be exposed to them, and live to haunt you. You cannot afford to diminish your own credibility in any way.

When you have not personally observed something about which you are informing your listeners and you are relying upon other people as your sources of information, make this clear to your listeners before it becomes apparent to them. In no way can you afford to let them conclude that you were less than honest. As you indicate your information sources, identify them specifically and give their qualifications insofar as your listeners want such information. Research on the value of citing and qualifying such sources is not entirely in agreement; some studies have found it helpful and some have not.[17] The guiding principle is this: *You must satisfy the question of the reliability of your information in the minds of your listeners*, whatever their various needs may be. If they are unsatisfied, you must meet this need if you can. Don't bore them needlessly, but meet their need. If you are unclear as to what they need, ask them. Then satisfy them if you can.

Establishing Your Personal Credibility

It would be satisfying in terms of orderliness of thinking if we could make a clearcut distinction between the theme of this chapter and that of the one which deals with persuasion. In the present chapter we have focused on helping our listeners to understand selected parts of their world by providing information they desire—meeting their need to know—and in the chapter on advocacy we focus on persuading them that they should have certain beliefs as to certain things that they presently do not believe or do. It is really not possible to make such a neat distinction because the reality of our lives does not provide situations that fall into these discrete compartments. Life presents three kinds of situations that tend to blend into each other. First, there are situations where our listeners need information that we have and they are quite willing to accept the idea that we know what we are talking about. This is the ideal setting for us to make an informative presentation; for the most part this kind of situation has been presumed in the present chapter. Secondly, to the extent that our listeners are unwilling to believe that we know what we are talking about, (if we are convinced that they really need the information we possess, and if we are convinced that our information is accurate and reliable), we are faced with the problem of convincing them that we have such information. To the extent that our listeners are not ready and willing to believe we know what we think we know, to that extent we are faced with a problem of persuasion—trying to convince them that we have dependable information that they should also possess and utilize. The degree of difference may be small or great; listeners may be entirely willing to accept our information as accurate, or they may be almost willing, or somewhat willing, or quite unwilling, or not willing at all.

A third kind of situation occurs in our lives when we believe for reasons that seem sound to us that our listeners should do something they are not now doing or don't ordinarily do. This clearly is a situation that poses problems of persuasion, and is the major theme of Chapter 12.

The point is that you may think your listeners are ready and willing to accept you as a source of valid information, but such may not be the case, at least for some of your listeners. To the extent that listeners are not ready to accept you as a reliable information source, you will need to give them reasons to believe in you. In other words, you must establish your own credibility. This will be especially true when you try to convince your listeners that they should do something different from their present practices. But it is also critical if you are trying to convince listeners that your information is valid. Thus, this section of the present chapter is also essential to the problem of persuading them to adopt policies or behaviors that appear to you to be necessary.

THE INFORMATION PARADIGM

We have presented an extensive treatment of the problems you face as you seek to inform your listeners. We would like to review this material for you by offering five specific suggestions. They cover the essential principles discussed in this chapter; together they comprise the essential features of any good informative presentation:

1. *Identify your listeners' needs.* Determine what, in their minds, they need to know or want to know that you know well.

2. *Establish the "facts."* A "fact" is an object, event, or situation regarding which there is a high degree of agreement in reports of its existence or condition by persons in whom we have confidence regarding their ability to observe and to report honestly and accurately their observations.

3. *Qualify your sources.* Show that they were capable of reporting honestly and accurately to a high degree. Report their qualifications to your listeners.

4. *Indicate your beliefs and opinions.* When you *believe* that a situation or condition exists but this belief or opinion cannot be supported, either by your own observations or by reports of persons in whom you have confidence, admit this clearly to your listeners.

5. *Establish your personal credibility.* Try to demonstrate to your listeners that you are responsible and have personal integrity.

SUMMARY

In helping listeners to understand their environment, job requirements, opportunities for pleasure and achievement, there are numerous occasions when you need to make informative talks. These may be relatively informal or formal, but the crux of such situations is that you have information that is needed and wanted by your listeners. To be successful, you will need to make special efforts to identify your listeners' particular needs and interests and select relevant items from your store of experience and knowledge.

You may meet your listeners' needs and interests in one of two ways: by sharing insight or interpretation of data they already have or by providing specific items of data they need or want.

Your listeners will need to know the degree of dependability of your data. They will need to know what you regard as factual and why. Factuality is determined by the relative amount of agreement on the part of observers in whom you have confidence regarding their ability to observe and to report the observations honestly and accurately.

You will need to analyze your beliefs carefully to produce highly factual statements when needed by your listeners. If you are depending upon observations and opinions of persons other than yourself, you will need to qualify specifically your sources to the satisfaction of your listeners, as they see fit.

We have said a factual statement is one about a purported object, event, or situation regarding which (1) there is a high degree of agreement in reports of its existence or condition, (2) on the part of persons in whom you have a high degree of confidence, (3) regarding their ability to observe, and (4) to report honestly and accurately.

In all of your efforts to be helpful to others in meeting their needs for insights or data, your most valuable attribute will be your credibility. Use it wisely and protect it with great care.

LEARNING EXPERIENCES

Objectives

After studying this chapter, you should be able to *do* the following:

1. Identify information a potential audience might want to hear.
2. Select data that you can share that meets these listeners' needs and interests.
3. Identify factual information as such.
4. Identify beliefs and opinions as such.
5. Qualify the sources of your information.
6. Know the process of establishing your personal credibility.

Exercises

1. You are now fully ready to embark on the preparation of an informative speech. Evaluate your learning to this point. Select the topic that you feel most comfortable developing into a major speech. Review your credentials and knowledge on the topic.
2. Analyze your potential audience. Determine how much your classmates already know about your topic and the information that you plan to share. What are the needs that you will be meeting?
3. Research your topic utilizing all the available sources. Differentiate in your own mind what is fact and what is opinion. Analyze your own beliefs on the topic.
4. Apply the criteria cited in this chapter to the sources that you will be using. As an exercise, prepare answers to the questions on two of your sources to be shared with your instructor.

NOTES

[1] For an interesting discussion of this phenomenon see Louis P. Bucklin, "The Information Role in Advertising," *Journal of Advertising Research*, 5 (1965), pp. 11-15.

[2] For a detailed explication of selective exposure to information sources see Milton Rokeach, *The Open and Closed Mind*. New York: Basic Books, 1960, pp. 400-401.

[3] For a more detailed discussion of this need for confirmation see Kim Giffin and Bobby R. Patton, *Fundamentals of Interpersonal Communication*, 2nd ed. New York: Harper & Row, 1976, pp. 72-76.

[4]For a review of research supporting this principle see Wayne N. Thompson, *Quantitative Research in Public Address and Communication*. New York: Random House, 1967, pp. 65-72.

[5]Darryl Moore, "No Win System," *Winning Orations of the Interstate Oratorical Association*. Mankato, Minnesota: Interstate Oratorical Association, 1979, p. 1.

[6]For a review of related research see James C. McCroskey, *An Introduction to Rhetorical Communication*. Englewood Cliffs, NJ: Prentice-Hall, 1968, pp. 154-157.

[7]See research findings summarized by R. Samuel Mehrley and James C. McCroskey, "Opinionated Statements and Attitude Intensity as Predictors of Attitude Change and Source Credibility," *Speech Monographs*, 37 (1970), pp. 42-52.

[8]For a report of relevant research findings see Gerald R. Miller and John Basehart, "Source Trustworthiness, Opinionated Statements, and Response to Persuasive Communication," *Speech Monographs*, 36 (1969), pp. 1-7.

[9]Milton Rokeach, *Beliefs, Attitudes, and Values*. San Francisco: Jossey-Bass, 1968, p. 113.

[10]Marvin E. Shaw and William T. Penrod, Jr., "Validity of Information, Attempted Influence, and Quality of Group Decisions," *Psychological Reports*, 10 (1962), pp. 19-23.

[11]See Daniel J. Boorstin, *Democracy and Its Discontents*. New York: Random House, 1974, p. 13.

[12]Rokeach, *The Open and Closed Mind*, pp. 395-396.

[13]Gordon W. Allport and Leo J. Postman, "The Basic Psychology of Rumor," *Trans. New York Academy of Science*, Series II, 8, pp. 61-81.

[14]William S. Watson and G. W. Hartmann, "The Rigidity of a Basic Attitudinal Frame," *Journal of Abnormal and Social Psychology*, 34 (1939), pp. 314-335; see also Max M. Levine and Gardner Murphy, "The Learning and Forgetting of Controversial Material," *Journal of Abnormal and Social Psychology*, 38 (1943), pp. 507-517.

[15]For an excellent summary and critical evaluation of relevant research see Joseph T. Klapper, *The Effects of Mass Communication*. New York: Free Press, 1960.

[16]Rokeach, *The Open and Closed Mind*, pp. 400-401.

[17]For a summary of research on this issue see Robert N. Bostrom and Raymond K. Tucker, "Evidence, Personality and Attitude Change," *Speech Monographs*, 36 (1969), pp. 22-27.

11

Developing the Informative Speech

The last fifty years have produced a remarkable information explosion. If this vast wealth of knowledge is to be properly disseminated, people must possess proficiency in expository writing and speaking. It is hard to escape the informative oral presentation in most professions. The doctor explains a remedy to the patient, the tax lawyer clarifies tax laws for a client, and the sales manager explains sales techniques to the staff. Informative discourse also flourishes in the classroom, in the lecture hall, in the Armed Service Training Center, in industrial training centers, in civic clubs, at women's club meetings, and on guided tours of all sorts.

The most basic of all informative presentations is a one-point speech. We are often called upon to explain single ideas. One of the authors, for example, is frequently asked to explain the process of presenting a motion in a parliamentary meeting. Hence in our discussion of developing an informative presentation, we will begin with a speech that has a single point. This procedure has the added advantage of allowing us to explain the process of developing a point—which will be useful in developing the points of a longer speech. In this chapter we will follow the practice of using an illustrative speech, interspersing analytical comments as appropriate. Our remarks are intended to be instructional, and we will simply try to highlight important speech techniques.

THE ONE-POINT SPEECH

A one-point speech involves four steps: (1) stating the point to be developed; (2) defining and explaining the point; (3) supporting it with clarifying materials; and (4) terminating the discussion. At all times the

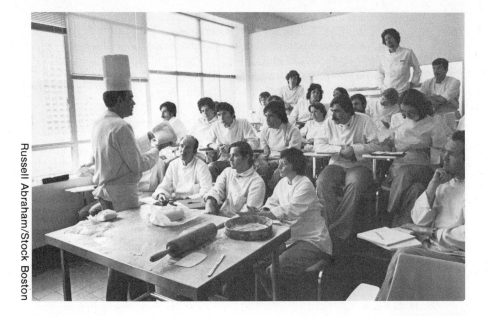

point to be developed should be clearly stated at the outset. For example, the speaker may begin by saying, "I want to take five minutes to explain as concisely as I can the problem the chair has in dealing with a main motion in a parliamentary meeting." The speaker may then proceed by asking, "Just what do we mean by a main motion? Before getting into a discussion of the problem of dealing with a motion, let's be sure that we all understand what a main motion is." After defining the main motion, the speaker will then proceed to explain how to receive such a motion from the floor, present it to the assembly, call for a second, ask for discussion, ask for a vote, and give the result of the voting. In order to make the point as vivid as possible for the audience—a critical objective of informative discourse—the speaker will then illustrate the point with an example. Inexperienced speakers oftentimes end such a discussion by leaving it dangling, without bringing it to a definite ending. A good speaker, on the other hand, will specifically terminate the point with a definite conclusion.

Example of a One-Point Speech

On page 164 is a one-point speech given by a student in a beginning speech class. Read it carefully and see how Russ Hodge, the speaker, unfolds his single idea.*

"Do You See What You Expect to See" by Russell E. Hodge.

I'd like to demonstrate today that your expectations can influence what you see. And by that I don't mean that your mind somehow influences the thing you are looking at itself, but rather, if you and I are sitting in a room and I asked you about something you saw, like five minutes ago, your mind, your expectations, will influence what you think you saw.

In this brief opening section to his speech, Russ Hodge states explicitly the idea he is going to develop and then quickly and succinctly attempts to tell you what he means by his topic. Since the point may still be somewhat unclear to the average listener, Russ follows this opening statement with an example that helps clarify what he has in mind.

There are some good examples of this. One of them is a very old psychological study. It's quoted in the book, *Psychology and Life*, used in a number of classes here at the University of Kansas. In this text, a teacher had two men run into a classroom. One of them had a red handkerchief, and the other had a banana. The two men ran to the front of the class and the one with the banana pointed at the other man and said, "Bang, bang." The other man waited, then they both ran out of the room. The teacher told the students, "Without communicating to each other, I want you to write down what you saw." There are a number of interesting results. One of them was that people said that they heard guns going off, they saw blood, they saw three people or five people or one person—all different sorts of things. So what happened? The students in the class saw what they expected to see in this kind of an event, and they indicated what they thought they saw. In all such cases, your mind sort of fills in what you expect to see, what you think you saw.

This example should make the concept Russ Hodge is trying to explain much clearer to the average listener. However, how credible is the concept? Hodge seems to anticipate this question and turns to B. F. Skinner for support.

B. F. Skinner, a famous behaviorist, says that you tend to see what you are reinforced for seeing, that is, your past has an influence on your present vision.

The thought that the past has an influence on your present vision is a slightly new twist to the topic, and so the speaker finds it useful to again turn to an example. This time the example is a personal illustration.

A good example is, I remember the first few days I came to the KU campus. I was wandering around without my glasses on and I thought I recognized just about everybody—you see, my vision isn't that good. And, I expected to see people that I knew, so I'd walk up to someone and speak to him, only to be embarrassed because the person didn't know who I was and I didn't know him. Since I was hoping so strongly to encounter someone I knew, I actually thought I was seeing people that I knew.

In order to prove his point directly to his listeners, Russ involves them in a simple experiment.

Another way of showing this perhaps is through the old optical illusion that I'm sure you've all seen. Now when I show you this I'd like you to raise your hands in response to my questions. Looking at this card, how many of you think that the top line is longer than the bottom line? Raise your hands. [No one responded] How many of you think that the bottom line is longer than the top line? [No one responded] How many of you think that they are the same? [All raised their hands] Well, I have to confess that I pulled a little trick on you. I assumed that you had all seen this before—you know, perception illusions that lead you to believe one line is longer than another but it really is not—so I drew the bottom line three quarters of an inch longer than the top line. I was certain that your expectations, based upon past experiences with this sort of thing, would influence what you thought you saw.

   It thus would seem correct to say that your expectations can and do influence what you think you see.

An outline of Russ Hodge's presentation might look like this:

I. Your expectations can influence what you see.
   A. Brief explanatory statement of how our expectations influence our perceptions.

1. Example from *Psychology and Life.*
2. Tie example back to original statement.
   B. Cite B. F. Skinner to the effect that one's past influences one's present vision.
   1. Example of first few days at K.U.
   2. Visual perception example.
   C. Terminate by restating main point.

Criteria for Evaluating Your One-Point Speech

1. Is the point stated clearly and meaningfully?

2. Are key terms defined and is the concept adequately explained?

3. Is the point adequately illustrated and supported?

4. Is the point effectively terminated?

A DEFINITIONAL SPEECH

Definition is vital to most informative discourse. Sometimes we are even called upon to give a short presentation which has as its sole mission the definition and explication of a single term embodying a large concept. For example, what is meant by "behaviorism"? What is meant by "pragmatism"? What is "poetry"? What is meant by a "liberal" education? And so on. We will therefore briefly elaborate definitions and then give an example of a short definitional speech. Every speaker should realize that a good definition commonly involves more than a dictionary definition, especially since one is likely to encounter dictionary definitions such as: "Communication: the art of communicating." The following are some definitional techniques that you will want to use to supplement your dictionary definition for an audience.

By Classification. Place a term within a class. For example: "Chimpanzees are one of the great apes." "Poetry is an art form." Classification helps the listener to visualize the term being discussed since it narrows what it might be. If you do not know what an *aardvark* is, knowing that it is a mammal is useful information. At least that tells you that it is not a reptile, a fowl, or a fish.

By Comparison. "Chimpanzees are smaller than gorillas." Such a statement narrows the nature of chimpanzees even further than the simple classification as a great ape. Oftentimes comparison occurs in the form of an extended contrast of concepts. Observe how Kathy Weisensel uses this technique in a classroom speech on mental retardation:

> . . . *let's extend that definition with a series of contrasts. Mental retardation is always permanent; mental illness is usually temporary.*

Mental retardation is subnormal intelligence; mental illness is distorted intelligence. Mental retardation involves deficient cognitive abilities; mental illness involves emotional impairment of cognitive abilities. Mental retardation is manifested early; mental illness may occur any time in life. The mentally retarded person is behaviorally stable; it is the mentally ill person who is given to erratic behavior. The extremely mentally retarded person is submissive and mute; the extremely mentally ill person may be violent and criminally dangerous. Thus retarded people are retarded, and no more.[1]

By Negation. Saying what a thing or concept *is not* is extremely useful because it differentiates between concepts that may seem similar. "Chimpanzees are not ordinarily included in the group of hominids." "Mere rhyming of lines is not necessarily poetry." "Mental retardation is not mental illness."

By Authority. A quotation from an authority helps to give credibility to the speaker's definition. For example, "Bertrand Russell defines 'matter' as something occupying space and incapable of thought or consciousness." Kathy Weisensel employed authority in her attempt to develop a clear understanding of mental retardation: "According to Dr. E. Milo Pritchett, 'Mental retardation is a condition of impaired, incomplete, or inadequate mental development.'"

By Operation. Sometimes *operational* definitions describe the *function* of something. For example, "Cable cars are vehicles pulled by cables in which people ride." An operational definition recognizes that "ultimate" definitions are seldom possible. As a consequence, the speaker will tell the audience how he or she is going to use the term for purposes of avoiding misunderstanding during the course of the speech.

By Etymology. Occasionally it is useful to give the historical derivation of a word. For example, a speaker may say: "In our effort to define *communication*, it may be useful to look at its historical derivation. Etymologically, the word communication stems from the Latin *communicare*, meaning to commune or to share."

By Necessary Conditions. Often the best way to clarify a term is by enumerating those conditions that must be met if the term is to apply. For example, "A 'monopoly' exists only if there is exclusive control of any given commodity in any given market."

Each one or any combination of these types of definitions may be used, and the nature of the concept involved will determine which type you will choose. To a great extent, an operational definition will most often be of greatest use to you.

Example of a Definitional Speech

For an example, we will analyze a definitional speech given by Lauralee Peters on the question, "What is Totalitarianism?"[3]

Her first paragraph functions as a brief introduction to the speech, and is designed to give importance to the term about to be defined and explained. The fact that the term *totalitarianism* enjoys widespread current usage should make the average person want to know what it means. The last sentence of the introduction clearly states the topic of the speech.

In the early 1930s a new word was coined in the language of the political scientist. Used at first to describe the changes occurring in Hitler's Germany and Stalin's Russia, the term *totalitarianism* soon enjoyed widespread usage. As with any complex term, however, its usage by laymen and newsmen looking for a convenient label has led to a dilution in its meaning. In the American press, for example, the term *totalitarianism* is applied to virtually anything which doesn't reek of democracy. Dictators, communists, strong military leaders and the like are all labelled totalitarian. In view of the present easy use, if not misuse, of this term, it is my purpose to attempt to arrive at some understanding of what the term *totalitarianism* actually means.

The speaker begins her definition in the second paragraph by stating what it is not. She ends the paragraph by raising the question, "What then does it mean?" She forecasts that she is going to search for unique features of totalitarianism that distinguish it from other forms of government. She finds it strategic to begin by citing an authority, J. A. Piekalkiewicz, a political science professor. Read the next two paragraphs and observe how Lauralee attempts to clarify the term she is dealing with.

To begin with, totalitarianism does not mean simply any government which is not democratic in nature. To employ such a definition for the term would render it completely meaningless, for to be sure there are many forms of nondemocratic rule in our present-day world. Nor does the term *totalitarianism* denote any dictatorship. The dictatorships, for example, of most of South America and South East Asia, overthrown with great regularity as they are, reflect, not a totalitarian state, but a situation of intensified political struggle among the members of the power elite of the nation. What then does it mean?

To understand totalitarianism it is necessary for us to understand the unique aspects of a totalitarian state which make it different from other forms of government. J. A. Piekalkiewicz, professor of political science at the University of Kansas, has devoted considerable research and writing to the problem of defining totalitarianism. It is, he says, a system in which the group or party in control claims to have a complete and comprehensive plan or idea to answer all problems of a political, social, and economic nature in a given society. They claim to have, that is, a monopoly on truth and their

---

monopoly includes the exclusion of all alternative solutions and all differing points of view. The solutions they have are total and comprehensive and the control they exercise over the people and the institutions of society is total and complete.

In the next paragraph Peters focuses upon the "necessary conditions" of totalitarianism. She uses specific examples to clarify the necessary conditions she cites: Arthur Koestler's novel, *Darkness at Noon;* Hitler's Germany; Mussolini's Italy; and modern-day Paraguay.

In a brief paragraph that follows she uses an authority to pinpoint the basis of totalitarianism, thereby giving further insight as to what is involved in the concept.

This definition, I think, helps us understand the unusual nature of the totalitarian state. Totalitarianism, for its existence, demands not only concentration of power in the hands of the government, but that this power be unlimited. Governmental power must be unlimited in two respects. First, it means complete government control of school curricula, newspapers, magazines, public and private utterances of individuals, in short, all aspects of social and intellectual life. This control is maintained through extensive police forces with the power to eliminate any deviation or suspected deviation from the "official line." Second, there must be present a single-minded ideology which is all-encompassing in nature and to which devotion can be demanded of the people. The devotion is demanded not only to the ultimate ends of the society, but also to any means which the regime might employ. This is illustrated aptly by Arthur Koestler in his novel, *Darkness at Noon,* in which the central character is liquidated, not because he disagreed with the *end* of the Russian state under Stalin, but with certain minor aspects of the *means* being employed.
Modern-day examples of the existence of such conditions include Hitler's Germany, Mussolini's Italy, and the Communist regime, particularly under Stalin. Another example of the totalitarian state which points to these characteristics is that of Paraguay under the rule of the Jesuits. Here was a state in which unlimited power was given to a government which possessed an all-encompassing ideology, in the form of the church, which demanded allegiance of the people.
N. A. Berdyaev, an early Marxist philosopher, wrote that at the basis of totalitarianism lies a reaction against fragmentation of human life and automatization of its various aspects. Thus the totalitarian state attempts to achieve a unity through the absolutization of the state, thereby hoping to achieve a unity of thought and purpose.

In the next section of the speech, Peters attempts to determine whether or not contemporary conditions are compatible with totalitarianism.

At this point we must ask the question, "Is totalitarianism compatible with modern technology and universal literacy?" Samuel Hendel in his book, *The Soviet Crucible,* says that it is an illusion to hold that totalitarianism is incompatible with these factors. Hendel notes that "It is precisely modern technology with its all-embracing means of communication, its high-speed transmission of commands and reports and armed force to any point in a country, its mass-communication and mass-conditioning techniques and the like, which for the first time makes it possible for total (undivided) power to aspire to be totalist (all-embracing) power." It is, in fact, at this point that some political scientists distinguish between a totalitarian state and the absolute monarchy. According to one theorist, "It isn't that Louis the Fourteenth didn't try, he just didn't have the means available." Indeed this dependence on technology seems to be what Alexander Herzen, a nineteenth-century Russian liberal, foreboded when he wrote: "Some day Genghis Khan will return with the telegraph."

It is a fallacy to rely on universal literacy as a bulwark against totalitarianism. We need only to turn to modern Germany to see an example of one of the most highly literate and technologically trained peoples in the history of man adopting totalitarianism. Modern totalitarianism, in fact, requires that the people be able to read so that they can all be made to read the same thing at the same time. It is not the ability to read, but the ability to choose between alternative types of reading which is a potential—and only a potential—liberating element.

The final two paragraphs conclude the speech. The first paragraph summarizes the essence of totalitarianism. The final paragraph tries to illustrate this summary through an example—George Orwell's novel *1984*. The last two sentences of the paragraph bring the speech to a definite ending. The final sentence succinctly restates what might be considered Peters' definition of totalitarianism.

"Totalitarianism," then, describes, not every strong-arm regime, but rather a particular political system. This system depends on promulgating a single ideology through the undivided and all-encompassing power of the state. Attempts at establishing totalitarian states have met with varying success throughout history, but modern technology and methods of mass communication have given such attempts special impetus.

Perhaps the best description to date of the perfected totalitarian system is provided by George Orwell's novel *1984*. Orwell describes for us a state which has assumed almost infinite power over the lives of its people. Two-way telescreens placed in all public and private places enable the state to observe and listen to the citizens at all times; the Ministry of Truth rewrites history to agree with the party line and, using the telescreens, invades the lives of the people constantly with official propaganda; and finally a state language, Newspeak, is adopted, whose vocabulary expresses only those concepts the state deems desirable. Here we see the ultimate end of the totalitarian state. The utilization of *all* possible means of control to establish the ultimate supremacy of the state in *all* aspects of the people's lives.

A skeleton outline of the body of Lauralee Peters' speech would be:

1. What is not totalitarianism?
2. What is totalitarianism?
3. What are the necessary conditions for totalitarianism to prosper?
4. Do these conditions exist today?

Criteria for Evaluating Your Definitional Speech

1. Is the definition clearly stated?

2. Is the definition made meaningful to the audience through the use of appropriate definitional devices?

3. Is the definition given credibility through the proper use of authority?

THE PERSONAL EXPERIENCE SPEECH

Probably the type of informative speech most familiar to all of us is the one that tells a story, a narrative of a chronological sequence of events— our childhood experiences of "Once upon a time." Suppose you want to tell your friends about your trip to Lake Turkana. It seems logical to deal with major events of the trip in the order in which they happened. So your problem of outlining such a presentation appears to be rather simple and straightforward. You need to decide what events were major items. For example, you might list as item one a description of the fun (or problems) of getting ready for the trip. However, Lake Turkana is not just any old lake.

Consideration of the current possible thinking of your listeners regarding your topic may raise these questions: What is Lake Turkana? Where is it? Why choose to visit a lake eight thousand miles away from home? Early in your presentation you may need to explain that Lake Turkana is a very ancient lake in northern Kenya, Africa; it is the site of important discoveries of traces of mankind three million years old. You would need to share with your listeners your special reasons for being interested in such prehistoric records, your excitement in seeing sites of ancient peoples and events, along with accounts of Richard E. Leakey's discoveries that have made this lake famous. In the long run, your principal problem with this topic might consist of deciding what events and incidents will be of interest to your friends and not bore them too much. You may soon find that travelogues are of most interest to fellow travelers who have also been there or to a somewhat similar place. "War stories" tend to be of most interest to warriors.

Example of a Personal Experience Speech

Personal experience speeches tend to be meaningful to the speaker and can have considerable impact upon the audience. To illustrate this, we have chosen a personal narrative by a Japanese-American who, after World War II, related his experiences as an American flyer during the war. Ben Kuroki, a Nebraska farm boy, delivered this speech at the opening session of the annual New York *Herald Tribune* Forum in New York City in 1945. By that time he had won two medals in fifty-eight missions flown over Europe and Japan despite the racial bigotry he encountered.

E. B. White, the author, once wrote, "Don't talk about man; talk about *a* man." In other words, talk about a person with a name, place, and personal traits; people can more readily identify with a specific person than with a generalized example. Ben Kuroki in his introduction to his speech, "Nebraska Boy Over Japan,"[4] utilizes this principle—he himself is *the man* talked about. He opens his speech by setting the scene—rural and small town America in the Platte River Valley of western Nebraska. As the central character in the story, Kuroki makes his entrance by telling you of his family and his parents' farm. He develops character for himself, and his kind, with the line, "Dirt farming isn't a very easy life, but it suits us fine." From the rural locale of Hershey, Kuroki moves the story outward: North Platte, Colorado, Chicago, New York, and finally Tokyo. The dramatic quality of the introduction intensifies when he tells his listeners, "Japan is the land of my ancestors, but I never had any desire to go there. And yet, one morning like a lot of American boys, I started out down the road from my house and I was headed for Tokyo." The scene is now set for the event that precipitates Kuroki's story: the Japanese attack on Pearl Harbor. As a response to this attack Kuroki and his kid brother "piled into the Chevrolet" (again the kind of specificity with which the average American can identify) and traveled to Grand Island to join the Army. As a Japanese-American, Kuroki quickly encountered the prejudice that ultimately gave rise to this speech. By the end of his introduction, the speaker has developed interest in two ways: (1) by casting himself as a typical American living in western Nebraska, and (2) by previewing his harsh encounter with prejudice. Read the first four paragraphs of the speech below and note how the speaker draws his listeners into his story.

The town I came from is called Hershey, Nebraska. It's near the Platte River, between Cozad and Ogallala, about twelve miles down the road from North Platte. We've got a farm there—my father and mother and my brother George and I. We raise sugar beets and seed potatoes. Dirt farming isn't a very easy life, but it suits us fine.

I never traveled much. I'd go down to North Platte for feed, or go fishing up in the mountains over in Colorado or down to Chicago to see my sister. I figured some day I'd get to New York, but I didn't plan on visiting Tokyo. Japan is the land of my ancestors, but I never had any desire to go there. And yet, one morning like a lot of other American boys, I started out down the road from my house and I was headed for Tokyo. And like a lot of other American boys, I got there the hard way.

The day after Pearl Harbor my kid brother and I piled in the Chevrolet and drove 150 miles down to Grand Island and enlisted. I remember, after we were sworn in and before we got our uniforms, we were on a train headed for camp. There were some people on the train and they stared at me and said, "What's that Jap doing in the Army?" They said it good and loud, so I'd hear. It just knocked me off my feet. After coming from a town where I knew everybody, I suddenly realized that no matter where I was born or what was in my heart, to these people I was an alien. All the way to camp people kept looking at me, staring at me. I'll never forget that train ride.

I went into the air force and applied for flying. Somehow my papers got lost; they always seemed to be lost, or held up somewhere or going through channels. When I finally got overseas it was as a clerk with the 93rd Bomb Group. It was quite an outfit—the newspapers called it Ted Timberlake's Flying Circus.

The first main point of Kuroki's speech—what we might call Scene One of his personal drama (counting the introduction as a Prologue)—relates his details of his European tour of duty. In this section of the speech Kuroki sketches critical experiences in Europe, ranging from how he became a tail gunner to how another gunner, an Irishman from Wisconsin, saved his life by holding a mask to his face after flak had ripped off his oxygen mask. Kuroki moves the story quickly, utilizing the tools of the novelist—*specificity, concreteness, action,* and *detail.*

Those were the early days in England and things weren't going so good. Liberators were getting knocked off like flies, and there was a shortage of gunners. I remember one day in England, I picked up a magazine and read about an organization called the Native Sons and

Daughters of the Golden West. They had a plan to isolate all Japanese-Americans down in the swampland somewhere. I kind of blew my stack when I read the article. I volunteered for gunner. I had five days of training, and then the outfit pulled out for Africa.

I flew my first bombing mission over Bizerte. Our tail gunner got it on that mission and I moved back to the tail turret and that's where I stayed. We tagged some rough missions those days—Naples, Wiener-Neustadt, Rome. We had a saying, "On the way to the target, you're flying for Uncle Sam. On the way back, you're flying for yourself."

My twenty-fourth mission was to Romania, to a place called Ploesti. It was the first low-level raid on that target. It was murder. Two out of nine planes in my squadron came back.

I finished my tour of missions and our outfit was set to go home, but I volunteered to stick around and fly five more. My kid brother still wasn't overseas and so I figured I'd just check off five missions for him.

The last mission was Muenster, where flak ripped open my turret, the plexiglass cut my face, and the blast ripped off my oxygen mask. A gunner named O'Connel from Superior, Wisconsin, got a mask and held it to my face and everything came out okay.

The second act of the drama opens back in the United States, back in Nebraska. Kuroki came home a hero to friends and kinfolk. People along the Platte River appreciated his wartime heroics. (These people are the "true Americans" in this story.) But when Kuroki reported back to the Army in California, he once more encountered prejudice. He had been asked to appear on a radio program as a bonafide hero of the war in Europe, but an hour before air time he was asked to drop from the program because as a Japanese-American he was a controversial issue. From this experience, the speaker turns to a *human interest story* about Ed Bates, with whom he had flown dangerous missions in Europe and whom he encountered in California. Ed Bates had just received the news that his younger brother had been killed in the Pacific. This tragedy spurs Kuroki to continue fighting—only this time in the Pacific against the Japanese, his ancestors. His motto became, "Tokyo or bust."

Then I came back to the States, back to Nebraska. I felt like a kid on Christmas morning. Everybody looked at my ribbons and shook my hand. It was wonderful to know that people appreciated what I'd done and respected me for it.

When I reported back to the Army in California, they asked me to go on a radio program. That was still pretty early, when returned veterans were something special. I really felt like a big wheel. I invited some of my buddies to see the show, and they all sat there in the front row. And then an hour before we were to start, word came through that I couldn't go on. They didn't object to my being a tail gunner. They didn't mind my having two D.F.C.'s. But it seemed I was a Japanese-American and that made it a controversial issue.

In California I met a boy I'd flown with in Europe, Ed Bates, a kind of rough-and-tumble kid. He'd had his fingers frozen off on a mission. It didn't seem to bother him. Nothing bothered Bates, except his brother. His brother had just been killed in the Pacific. He went half crazy when he heard the news. Bates wanted another tour in the Pacific, but they wouldn't let him go on account of his hand. Maybe that was when I first got the idea I wasn't through with this war. And when I got to Denver, that cinched it. I started to get into a taxicab with somebody, and he said he wouldn't ride with "no lousy Jap." I was wearing my wings and all my ribbons, but it didn't matter. I almost cried, I was so mad.

The third and climactic act of Ben Kuroki's personal drama tells of his tour of duty in the Pacific. He begins it with a strong transition. "After that, it was Tokyo or bust," However, once more he encountered barriers because of his race. He begins this section of the speech therefore by telling about the problem he had and how there were true Americans willing to help him. *Specificity* is achieved by naming those who came to his assistance.

Then comes a moment of high drama. Just before leaving for the Pacific, Kuroki receives the news that his boyhood friend back in Hershey, Gordon Jergeson, was killed in the Solomon Islands. Kuroki, a Japanese-American, went to console Gordon Jergeson's mother. Once more he *humanizes* the story through recalling *details* about when he and Gordon used to go duck hunting and how he would come by at three in the morning, "honk the horn and wake everybody up."

From this emotional human interest story, Kuroki quickly comes to the climax of his story: Kuroki's bomber, the "Honorable Sad-Saki," bombed Yokohama, his mother's hometown.

After that, it was Tokyo or bust. I wanted to fly in a B-29 and for about three months I listened to people tell me, no, it was impossible; there were regulations against it. But I also ran into some people who were willing to go to bat for me—Dr. Deutsch, vice-president of the University of California; Chester Rowell, of the San Francisco *Chronicle,* and Ray Lyman Wilbur, of Stanford University—a lot of people all over the country who believed my record earned me the right to be trusted. A Congressman from Nebraska, a former commander of the American Legion from Wisconsin, the head of the War Relocation Authority—they all put up a holler, and the next thing I knew I was training for B-29's. It gave me a little courage to meet people everywhere who didn't judge a man by his grandfather's nationality or the color of his skin.

It was just before I left for the Pacific I heard about Gorden

Jergeson. I guess he was the closest friend I ever had. Back in Hershey we played together since we were kids. We were on the basketball team. In high school he was president of the class and I was vice-president. I got a pass and went to see his folks. We sat there and his mother remembered how we used to go duck hunting and I'd come by at 3:00 in the morning and honk the horn and wake everybody up. Gorden was killed in the Solomon Islands. That was another reason for going to Tokyo.

We flew out of an airfield on Tinian in the Marianas. The name of our bomber was "Honorable Sad-Saki." I flew twenty-eight missions in the Pacific, over Kobe and Osaka and finally Tokyo. I even had a crack at my mother's home town—Yokohama.

When the boys in my outfit found out I'd flown a tour over Europe they figured I had holes in my head for volunteering again. I used to kid around and tell them that communications were all cut off from Japan and that this was the only way I could visit my Uncle Nagasaki. I never talked much about my real reason for being over there.

The last sentence of the paragraph above begins a transition to the equivalent of an epilogue in which Kuroki explains why he fought in the war. He notes that he fought side by side with a lot of different men— Polish, Jewish, German, and Dakota Indian. Then he states the message of his speech: "I saw men wounded, and whatever land their grandfathers came from, their blood was always the same color. And whatever church they went to, the screams of pain sounded just the same."

Not only did I go to war to fight the fascist ideas of Germany and Japan, but also to fight against a very few Americans who fail to understand the principles of freedom and equality upon which this country was founded.

I'm no authority; I'm not an expert or a big wheel. I don't know anything that any boy from Nebraska couldn't tell you. But I know this: I fought with a lot of men in this war, all kinds—a Polish gunner, a Jewish engineer, a German bombardier and even a full-blooded Dakota Indian. I saw men wounded, and whatever land their grandfathers came from, their blood was always the same color. And whatever church they went to, the screams of pain sounded just about the same.

The last two paragraphs constitute Kuroki's conclusion. He begins by referring to himself in the here and now—he is tired, his hands are shaking, and many nights he can't sleep. His foremost desire is to retreat to the idyllic life of western Nebraska and "lie under a tree somewhere and take it easy." But, for people such as himself, there is still a war to be fought—the battle against prejudice. By *analogy* with planting a seed on his parents' farm—when you planted a seed it was certain to produce a plant—he *illustrates* his disillusionment, because he felt he had planted a large seed during the war but the yield seemed uncertain. That summarizes what he tried to do in the war: plant a seed "to bring in a crop of decency and peace for our families and our children."

Kuroki ends his personal experience talk by relating back to his introduction. Once more he refers to his "old home town" where people believe that "freedom isn't color but a way of life, and all men are created equal until they prove otherwise." The final sentence ends the speech on the same note with which it began: "Hershey, Nebraska, just down the highway from Cozad, which is near North Platte."

I've had fifty-eight bombing missions now, and I'm still tired enough so my hands shake, and plenty of nights I don't sleep so good. I'd like to go home to Nebraska and forget the war, and just lie under a tree somewhere and take it easy. It's hard to realize that the war is not over for me. Not for a lot of us, Jewish-Americans, Italian-Americans, Negro-Americans, Japanese-Americans. While there is still hatred and prejudice, our fight goes on. Back in Nebraska on our farm, when I planted a seed, I knew that after a while I'd get a crop. That's the way it was with a lot of us in this war: we went to plant the seeds to bring in a crop of decency and peace for our families and our children.

Back in high school in Nebraska, one of the things they taught me was that America is a land where it isn't race or religion that makes free men. That's why I went to Tokyo. I went to fight for my country, where freedom isn't color but a way of life, and all men are created equal until they prove otherwise. That's an old idea we have in Hershey, Nebraska, just down the highway from Cozad, which is near North Platte.

A common mistake beginning speakers make with a personal experience speech is that they neglect to prepare an outline: after all, they are only going to tell a story. This practice usually leads to a lack of coherence, a lot of "Oh, I should have mentioned a little while ago when talking about..." and a lack of clear and meaningful progression of thought. We have identified above the main points of Ben Kuroki's speech; you may want to complete the outline by relating the subpoints and supporting materials to these main topics.

Criteria For Evaluating Your Personal Experience Speech

1. Does the experience embody enough meaningful information to make it worthwhile to a group of listeners?

2. Is the experience interesting to listeners?

3. Is the experience unfolded in a logical and coherent manner?

4. Does the speaker use enough descriptive detail, dialogue, and interesting anecdotes to make the experience come to life?

5. Does the introduction create interest in the experience to be related?

6. Does the conclusion effectively terminate the discussion?

7. Is the lesson (or lessons) to be learned from the personal experience made sufficiently clear to the audience?

THE PROCESS OR "HOW TO" SPEECH

In filling out your enrollment card be sure to note that there are three sections to the card asking for different kinds of information. At the top of the card you are to place personal information such as your name, address, and phone number. The main part of the card asks you to list the courses you have chosen to take, and the bottom of the card asks you to make a grid of what hours you are taking courses so as to avoid duplication of times. Be sure to fill out the top of the card first.

Recently one of your authors made this "how to" speech to a new freshman student going through the enrollment *process.* When you stop to think a minute, you can probably recall listening to many similar presentations, either formal or casual. One of the most common forms of communication in which we engage is to tell someone how to do something. In the classroom such speeches are often called demonstration speeches explaining a process. Think, for instance, of the master mechanic explaining how a new carburetor works; an executive demonstrating how to read an annual financial report of a corporation, a music critic describing how to enjoy an opera; or a police officer on the street corner telling a motorist how to get to the ballpark. In every case the speaker is explaining a process.

Speeches dealing with a process or procedure frequently have a logical starting point and pattern of events; one cannot be described until another has been presented. For example, a description of training procedures for flying light aircraft normally would start with principles learned in "ground school" because that is what happens first, and making practice landings is not ordinarily practical until other skills and principles are mastered.

Not all process-oriented speeches tell "how to do" something.

Oftentimes they simply explain what happens. For example, a scientist might explain the process of how the earth relates to the rest of the solar system. Or a teacher might inform students about the process of how a collection of people form a talk-oriented group.

Outline of a Process Speech

We will use as an example an outline of a speech delivered extemporaneously on "How to Conduct a Meeting." Explanatory and analytical comments will be placed in brackets in the outline itself.

How to Conduct a Meeting

Introduction

I. [Gaining attention, trying to get listeners mentally involved with the topic] Most of you have probably had the experience of sitting through meetings of various sorts, such as a house meeting or a club meeting, that were extremely chaotic. Everybody seemed to talk at once and no particular order prevailed. Perhaps you have even had to chair such meetings and were very frustrated by the experience. I have.

   A. [Reinforcing favorable attitudes] Anyone who has had such an experience, I am sure, would agree that the orderly conduct of meetings is not only useful, but essential, to the conduct of business.

   B. [Establishing credentials] For some time now I have had at least a passing interest in parliamentary law, and recently I have taken a very good course in parliamentary procedure. Because of this, I have read and studied *Robert's Rules of Order*, Alice Sturgis' *Standard Code of Parliamentary Procedure*, and one or two lesser writings on the subject.

   C. [Eliciting a fair hearing] I know that I am only a student like you are—I certainly am no licensed parliamentarian, but I think I have learned a few things about conducting a meeting that I think should be useful for you to know. I know that you may also think: "Parliamentary procedure? My, how dull." But I'll promise you that if you will just be a little bit patient and stick with me, I'll try to make it as interesting as possible.

   II. [Focusing on the topic] What I want to do is to provide you with just a few basics about conducting successful meetings. I will in no sense try to cover all the rules of procedure. What I will cover should be easy to remember and should prove helpful to anyone who ever has to conduct a meeting.

Body

I. The first thing that you should know is that there is a standard agenda to follow. Being sure of what comes first and what comes next will give you the kind of demeanor that will gain respect from the group's members.

    A. First, call the meeting to order in a very definite manner. Simply say firmly and clearly, "Will the meeting please come to order!"

    B. If you have minutes of previous meetings, the second thing to do is to ask the secretary to read the minutes of the last meeting.

        1. After the secretary has read the minutes, ask if there are any questions about the minutes, any additions or corrections.

        2. If there are corrections, ask the secretary to make them. Hearing none, simply state that since there are no corrections the minutes will stand approved as read.

    C. If you have a treasurer, the third thing you want to do is ask the treasurer to make a report on the organization's finances.

        1. Afterwards, ask if there are any questions about the treasurer's report.

        2. If there are, ask the treasurer to answer the questions. Otherwise, simply state that the treasurer's report has been received and accepted.

    D. Next, you will want to call for committee reports, if there are any.

        1. If there are, hear the reports and ask for questions.

        2. If a committee report involves business, the reporter should be asked to make a motion to that end.

            a. You will then, of course, have to deal with the motion.

            b. I won't go into how to do this at this time because I will cover this later.

    E. After all committee reports, you should then ask if there is any old or unfinished business from the last meeting.

        1. If there is, resume discussion of this business.

        2. If not, go directly on to new business.

    F. If you follow this agenda for your business meetings, you will already have brought some order to your meetings.

II. New business is conducted through main motions. Main motions are introduced and received by the chair in the following manner:

    A. Chair recognizes a speaker: "Mr. John."

        1. Mr. John introduces the motion thus: "Mr. Chairman. I move that we hold our annual picnic May 3 at 1:30 in the afternoon."

        2. The chair then states: "A motion has been made that we hold our annual picnic this year on May 3 at 1:30 in the afternoon. Is there a second to the motion?"

        3. Ms. Jones: "I second the motion."

        4. The chair then submits the motion to the assembly. "It

has been moved and seconded that we hold our annual picnic May 3 at 1:30 in the afternoon. Is there any discussion?"

B. At this point debate may occur on the motion. It is useful to remember the following basic principles about debating a motion.

    1. No one should be allowed to speak without first being recognized by the chair.

    2. If the motion is controversial, the chair should try to alternate pro and con speakers.

    3. No one should be allowed to speak twice before everyone else has had a chance to speak.

    4. Each speaker is under a ten-minute time limit.

    5. Whatever you do, do not allow any talking except from individuals you have recognized as having the floor. Do everything possible to avoid private conversations that disturb the meeting. Ask any such individuals to please save their comments and direct them to the chair when they have the floor.

    6. When it seems that everyone has had a chance to speak and the discussion is completed, ask the assembly if they are ready to vote. If so, proceed to the vote.

C. Before the vote be sure to restate the motion: "All those in favor of holding our annual picnic at 1:30 in the afternoon on May 3rd, please say, 'Aye.' All those opposed say, 'No.'" Announce the motion in favor of the side having the most voices, such as, "The ayes have it. The motion carries. Is there any other new business?"

D. If there is no further business, ask for a motion to adjourn.

Conclusion

I. These are the basics of conducting any meeting. There, of course, are a lot of other motions, such as amendments, refer to committee, and so on, but time does not allow me to cover all these things at this time.

A. [Summary] But whatever you do, remember first of all to follow an orderly agenda and then be sure to insist upon an orderly process of presenting and receiving motions. Finally, control debate on the motion carefully.

B. [Ending note] If you do these things, you will have orderly meetings, and you and the membership of your group will be much happier about your meetings. Parliamentary procedure is designed to expedite business, not to impede it. Keep that thought in mind, and be sure that everyone else understands this. If you do, you are likely to get few complaints as to how you conduct your meetings.

We have refrained from commenting upon the body of this speech because it is a routine outline of information. Perhaps the primary failing of this speech on "How to Conduct a Meeting" is its relative lack of interest materials. Can you think of a way of making this speech more interesting? Use your imagination.

> Criteria for Evaluating Your Process or "How To" Speech
>
> 1. Is there a logical progression of ideas?
> 2. Is each point presented clearly?
> 3. Is each point either illustrated or demonstrated?

THE ORAL REPORT

Perhaps the most common speech form is the oral report in which the speaker presents data or principles, or in a general sense, imparts knowledge, to an audience. The ten-minute report, or briefing, is common in the business world. The lecture in education usually is a presentation of data or principles: the historian describes westward

Figure 11-1 Types of Informative Speeches

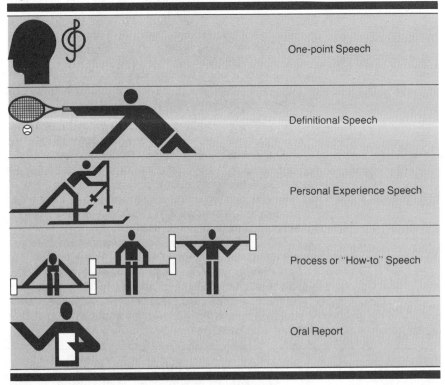

One-point Speech

Definitional Speech

Personal Experience Speech

Process or "How-to" Speech

Oral Report

migration in American history; the communication teacher discusses principles of small group discussion. In most meetings, someone will make a brief report, such as a committee report. We think, therefore, that this speech is one of the most important ones you will give in your class.

Since clarity, leading to comprehension, is essential to a report, good organization of ideas is vital. An oral report should be carefully structured, transitions made clear, and ideas carefully related. Effective definition and meaingful explanation tend to be critical to success in imparting knowledge; visual aids often are a must.

Example of an Oral Report

The speech we have chosen as an example was given by Stephen Gibbs, when he was an undergraduate in a public speaking class.* "Valuable Junk" is a report on Steve's hobby—the collecting of Coca-Cola memorabilia. Class response was excellent, due to the high degree of interest Steve generated in his subject and due to his personal credibility. Prior to his speech, Steve arranged a display of unusual Coke memorabilia on a table next to the speaker's lectern. The class responded so favorably and with such interest that the rest of the class hour was consumed by questions from the audience.

Steve initiated his speech by displaying various Coke items and by asking the audience questions about them. This technique generated a high degree of interest. The visuals made the discussion authentic.

If someone were to walk up to you and hand you these matches, [displays Coke matchbook] what would you do with them? Most likely you would use them or toss them. How about this Coca-Cola pen? [Displays Coca-Cola pen] Being a studious college student, I'm sure you would use it and then throw it away when the ink ran out. And what about this Coca-Cola bottle? [Displays Coca-Cola bottle] If I were to give this twelve-ounce bottle to you as a gift would you keep it or take it back for the deposit?

That is what most of you would do. But by a show of hands, how many of you would take this bottle to a bank and put it in a safety deposit box? That is no surprise, since like 99 percent of the general public, you are unaware that this bottle is worth hundreds of dollars!

Having caught the interest of the audience, Steve turns quickly to the subject of his speech—antique collecting. He establishes his credentials by revealing that his family collects Coke memorabilia—in fact,

*"Valuable Junk" by Stephen Gibbs

they have collected 5,000 relics. Moreover, his mother was president of the national group for two years and Steve is now the national Newsletter Editor. Steve at this point had provided the audience with the "authentic sign."

Antique collecting has been around for years. The collecting of Coca-Cola advertising memorabilia is relatively new, however. There are some 5,000 people across the nation who belong to the Cola Clan, a group for Coke collectors. My mother was president of the national group for two years and I am now the national Newsletter Editor. While my family and I are becoming fairly knowledgeable about the history of the Coca-Cola Company and its advertising, our collection—of some 5,000 relics—is relatively small compared to many of the finer collections around the country.

This completes Steve's introduction and the next sentence is a transition to the body of the speech.

If in fact you DO run across a Coke item someday while rummaging through an antique store, should you buy it? Let me try to help. . . .

Steve's first point deals with reproductions of Coke items. He makes the audience aware that a number of famous reproductions exist and informs them how they can tell such reproductions from authentic originals. Throughout, he relates his family to the discussion. He then tells the audience about a *specific example*—the Johnny Weismuller tray.[5] This example is used to inform the audience about ways of detecting reproductions. The Johnny Weismuller example, of course, functions as a strong interest factor as well.

Be sure to observe how effectively Steve concludes and rounds off his first point. He warns the audience about possible frauds and advises them to consult a Coke-collectors book before buying anything. He skillfully ends the point by utilizing the Coke slogan of the 1970s: the Coke collector is looking for "the real thing."

The majority of collectors, like my family, got their start five years ago when the Coca-Cola Company came out with the "Bring back the good old trays" promotion as part of which they reproduced six of their old trays and gave them away in the grocery stores, and many, like ourselves, picked up the trays because they were "cute." While these reproduction trays are authentic in that they were produced by Coke, they are not worth more than a couple of dollars.

The way to tell an official reproduction is to look here on the lip of the tray and it tells you that it is a 1976 reproduction. [Points to the lip of a tray he is holding]

There is one other type of reproduction to look for. A few years back, a Texan found the Johnny Weismuller tray at an antique store for $100. The tray normally goes for $400 so he bought the tray. Meanwhile, this same tray was showing up all over the country and unsuspecting buyers like the Texan were shelling out hundreds of dollars for this "rare" Weismuller. It took awhile, but someone got smart, turned the tray over, and noticed the backing on the tray was white, whereas the Company's trays for 90 years had had black backs.

This is the most famous example of fraud, but there are others. All I can do is warn you to use good judgment and to get advice from a Coke-collector's book if you should indeed run across an expensive item you consider buying. Keep in mind, a collector is looking for "the real thing."

Steve clearly indicates the beginning of his second point with the expression, "The second thing . . ." In this point Steve enumerates for his listeners specific ways of telling the age of an item. In each case he reinforces his point by displaying an item and pointing to tell-tale signs. His use of the three prominent Coke slogans gives interest to the point. He ends his second point succinctly, in effect restating the essence of the point.

The second thing to look for in determining whether or not to buy an item is the age. Usually, the older an item is and the better its condition, the more valuable it will be. There are a couple of ways to tell age: First, some items bear the date right on them, like on the lip of a tray. [Displays tray] Second, look for the "Trademark." If it is below the words Coca-Cola, the item is post 1940s. [Displays item and points to trademark] If Trademark Registered is in the tail of the "C," then it is pre-40s. [Points to example] Third, look for clothing styles worn if you are dealing with a tray, sign, or poster. [Displays and points to example] Fourth, the slogan is a dead giveaway. "It's the real thing" is 1970s. "Things go better with Coke" is 1960s. "Delicious and Refreshing" is OLD. Remember that rare items have value, and old items are rare.

Steve's third point is brief. It simply tells the audience that where you find the Coke item tends to be an indicator of its authenticity. He ends the point with zest when he tells the audience if they ever find something in their grandmother's attic, "steal it," thereby indicating that it will probably have great value.

> The third thing to look at if you are considering a Coke piece is where you find it. If you're in an antique store, the item is probably legitimate, but it will also be expensive. A garage sale or bazaar will usually offer good bargains, but you just need to keep an eye open for the '76 reproduction trays. If you find a Coke item in your grandmother's attic, steal it!!!

As a final point, Steve suggests that if the three criteria he has just given don't help, the listener should seek assistance from a book—Shelley Goldstein's *Coca-Cola Collectibles*. This reference should not only be helpful to the audience but also the mention of it enhances Steve's personal credibility. Once more, Steve ends a point with a *slogan:* "Things go better with Coke" collecting if you know what you are doing.

> If these three tips don't help and you are still interested in buying the item, go to the library and look it up in Shelley Goldstein's *Coca-Cola Collectibles*. It lists the going rates of thousands of items, but the going rates used are a little outdated, so *double* the price in the book to find out the probable worth of your find. "Things go better with Coke" collecting if you know what you are doing, and oftentimes a little research will help you to know what you are doing.

Steve's conclusion is brief. He begins by calling attention to the fact that he is "someone who has been there," a thought which once more, in an inoffensive manner, calls attention to his credibility. He appropriately ends his speech by warning his listeners that they might get "hooked" on collecting "valuable junk", if they ever get started. The audience was amused by the ending and felt that concluding on a light note was appropriate.

> Take one last piece of advice from "someone who has been there." When you are standing in that garage sale or antique store, contemplating buying your first Coke piece, just keep in mind that it probably won't be your last. In fact, don't be surprised if the following weekend you find yourself wandering around garage sales, flea markets, and antique stores looking for MORE of this unique, valuable, precious JUNK!

Criteria for Evaluating Your Oral Report

1. Is the subject clearly and effectively disclosed at the beginning of the speech?

2. Are ideas clear? Are there sufficient illustrations? Is the explanation effective? Are adequate definitions given?

3. Does the speaker help the listeners understand why this is important to them?

4. Does the body of the speech have coherence and a clear thought progression? Are transitions effective?

5. Are points properly supported with visual aids? Are the visual aids effective?

6. Does the speaker effectively tie materials together at the end of the speech?

7. Is the information worth knowing?

SUMMARY

We have gone through the stages of preparing five types of commonly presented speeches. The speeches are all attempts to present data in an unbiased, objective fashion that will be clearly understood by the audience.

The examples cited—the one-point speech, the definitional speech, the personal experience speech, the process or "how to" speech, and the oral report—were all presented by beginning speakers like yourself who drew from their personal experiences and insights. Their examples, we hope, will stimulate your thinking toward topics and plans of presentation appropriate to you.

The one-point speech characteristically involves four steps: (1) stating the point to be developed; (2) defining and explaining the point; (3) supporting it with clarifying material; and (4) terminating discussion. The speech by Russ Hodge illustrated these steps in his speech on perception.

A definitional analysis speech usually contains some of the following techniques of definition: clarification, comparison, negation, authority, operation, etymology, and necessary conditions. The speech by Lauralee Peters uses several of these techniques.

A personal experience speech must contain meaningful information that will be interesting to your listeners. As a speaker you must present it in a logical and coherent manner and use enough descriptive detail and interesting examples to make the experience come to life. The speech by Ben Kuroki illustrates these criteria effectively.

The process or "how-to" speech must contain a logical progression of ideas in which each point is presented clearly and illustrated and demonstrated. The outline of the speech on parliamentary procedure illustrates an emphasis upon the key ideas.

The oral report places emphasis upon the clarity of ideas that are often supported by visual aids. Frequent examples, illustrations, and organizational clarity are important. The speech on collecting Coca-Cola memorabilia by Steve Gibbs illustrates these factors.

LEARNING EXPERIENCES

Objectives

After studying this chapter, you should be able to *do* the following:

1. Explain and differentiate between the five styles of informative speeches.

2. Define terms clearly using the seven techniques cited.

3. Critique the five speeches presented as examples.

4. Develop a full informative speech integrating the principles cited in the previous chapter.

5. Provide constructive feedback to the presentations of your classmates.

Exercises

1. Prepare a one-point speech that is based upon your experiences and expertise. Apply the criteria suggested in this chapter.

2. Define a term that is germane to your major or future plans. Strive to make the presentation as interesting and clear as possible.

3. Prepare and present either a personal experience speech or a process ("how to") speech. In small groups, discuss your preparation efforts and any special problems that you perceive.

4. Elicit feedback from your instructor and classmates on possible improvement. What would you do differently if you were to give the same speech again?

5. Prepare and present an oral report.

NOTES

[1]Kathy Weisensel, "David: And a Whole Lot of Other Neat People," in *Contemporary American Speeches*, 5th ed., Wil A. Linkugel, R. R. Allen, and Richard L. Johannesen, Eds. Dubuque, Iowa: Kendall/Hunt, 1978, pp. 72-73.

[2]Weisensel, *Contemporary American Speeches*, 5th ed., p. 71.

[3]Lauralee Peters, "What Is Totalitarianism?," in *Contemporary American Speeches*, Wil A. Linkugel, R. R. Allen, and Richard L. Johannesen, Eds. Belmont, CA: Wadsworth Publishing Co., 1965, pp. 69-72.

[4]Ben Kuroki, "Nebraska Boy Over Japan," in Robert T. Oliver and Rupert L. Cortright, *New Training for Effective Speech*, Revised Edition. New York: The Dryden Press, 1951, pp. 25-29.

[5]Johnny Weismuller at one time was Tarzan in the motion pictures.

12

Helping Others Reach Decisions: The Persuasive Speech

The need to become an advocate rises from living with other people. The very word *community* implies cooperation, and from time to time we need to solicit that cooperation through the spoken word. At times we seek only to influence one or two people—members of our family, or our close friends or associates. At other moments we perceive that a problem and its solution will require the concerted effort of a group, such as our swimming team. As we grow older and take more responsibility for our broader surroundings, we may see a need for a change in values in our community, for example, to try to persuade our community to value the arts by diverting funds from recreational activities to supporting an arts center. Eventually we learn to perceive social questions that demand the attention of a larger part of society, perhaps a state, or the nation—even the entire world. Advocacy, as such, is not to be equated with guilefully imposing your will on others; enlightened speakers, imbued with good will for their audiences, can use the tools of persuasion in a way that recognizes responsibility to themselves and to their listeners. If you have an idea that you believe will improve the human condition, you will assume the responsibility of trying to enlighten your fellow citizens through some form of persuasive presentation.

ASSESSING YOUR QUALIFICATIONS FOR SPEAKING

Before you, as a student or as a citizen, attempt to help others reach decisions, you should carefully evaluate your qualifications for being an advocate. You should determine (1) your own beliefs, (2) your true motives, and (3) your credibility on the topic.

Michael Sullivan

Evaluating Your Own Beliefs

The first problem that you must confront as an advocate is one that originates with yourself. Why do you believe that you must persuade others? Who are you to tell them what they should believe or do? You will need to compare carefully your perceptions with theirs; insofar as possible you should do this without bias or prejudice. Look at their beliefs with an open mind, seeking to *understand* what they believe; this consideration includes an objective evaluation of *why* they believe it. In order to do this well, you will need to understand the basis of their beliefs. In effect, you should ask them to *inform* you, that is, to *help you understand* the basis for their beliefs. As they do this, you should apply to their presentation the criteria for credibility that we have asked you to apply to yourself. You may be surprised to find that you and others do not really see things very differently—you only thought you did. Or you may find that their view is more credible than yours. Be careful: Do not reject their views simply on the basis of your own personal biases; also, do not accept their views as better than yours unless you really become convinced that they are based on stronger foundations.

Examining Your Motives

Suppose, however, that others' beliefs are, in your judgment, incredible; you have sought to understand what they believe, and why, and you have determined that it fails to meet the tests of credibility. Suppose also, that you are convinced that you should try to help them adopt a different view—yours. You will need to look at your own motives. Is it just your ego or pride that makes you want to influence others? Do you want to "straighten them out," just to show that you are "better" in some way? Or are you motivated by a sense of responsibility—a desire to help them have a more useful view? Do you believe that changing their view can make their lives, as well as yours, more satisfying? It may bother you to recognize that how they act may influence your own happiness; perhaps you should recognize that you feel more psychologically comfortable if people that you care about, or persons in close association with you, act as you do. This may very likely be the case, and you may need to recognize that your motives are mixed or complex—that you are (1) somewhat concerned about their happiness, and (2) also moved somewhat by concern for your own. Few of us do things for single, simple motives; fewer still do things for the pure benefit of others.

If you have been trying to convince people that your beliefs are right and their beliefs are wrong without checking out your own motives and bases for your beliefs, you were trying to be an advocate before you were ready. But let's say that you are not operating that way—you are certain that the bases of your beliefs are credible and that your motives include some consideration of the needs of your listeners. You are now ready to be a responsible advocate.

Assessing Your Credibility

The major problem you must confront as an advocate is to gain your listeners' respect for your ability to perceive and to understand the situation in question. This is clearly a problem of credibility—yours. Are you a person whom your listeners would select as one in whom they have confidence concerning the ability to make (relevant) observations and to report them honestly and accurately? If you really do not meet these criteria, can you correct your behavior? If so, do so. However, more often than not, you actually do meet the credibility requirements, but your listeners do not realize this. Essentially, then, your problem is to establish your credibility *in their* eyes. We have previously called your attention to the three factors of personal credibility: expertness, trustworthiness, and good will (see Chapter 1, p. 5). Your goal is to present yourself and your message so that your listeners view you as a credible source. How do you do this?

Let's begin with expertness. Recall that when we discussed speech introductions we noted that as a speaker you should reveal your credentials or qualifications for speaking on the topic early in the speech. Perhaps through a personal illustration, you can reveal past relationships with the topic. You may also state directly what experiences you have had with the subject—why you feel qualified to address the audience on this topic. You will also enhance your expertness through a careful examination of evidence supporting your points. After all, experts are supposed to know the "facts" of the case, so make sure that you bring out the most important facts. The way you handle your evidence also makes a difference. For example, you will appear more expert if you are careful to cite your sources. Finally, experts do not guess; they are specific. Take the time to verify information so that you can be authoritative.

If you use evidence carefully, you also will have started to demonstrate your trustworthiness and your good will. To increase this trust, you will do well to display character traits the audience holds in high esteem. Usually this means a degree of humility and an expression of warmth, friendliness, tact, and diplomacy. A genuine regard for the listeners' customs and manners, as well as for the occasion, will contribute to your trustworthiness. Good will can be demonstrated in various ways. For example, it is helpful to keep checking with listeners if they understand what you are saying, or if they have questions about your information. You can do this by carefully observing nonverbal feedback, and from time to time even asking them if they understand what you have been saying, and, if not, invite them to raise questions. You can also tell your listeners how they can get additional information on the topic of your speech, and especially, how they can get information on the other side of the proposition you are upholding. Good will in a persuasive speaking situation is always a matter of demonstrating concern that the audience will reach the best possible decision.

Dynamism is mostly a matter of effective delivery. It implies activity, energy, and force. The listener should perceive you as a person of action, someone who gets things done. As a general rule, people respond more favorably to active personalities than they do to passive ones.

INTEGRATING YOUR THINKING WITH THAT OF THE AUDIENCE

As you prepare to influence the beliefs and actions of others, no matter how careful and valid your thinking has been about your speech topic, you must consider how your thoughts will be received by your listeners. Very likely they have done some thinking of their own. They may have come to certain conclusions (perhaps on information that is different from yours); some of them have prejudices, vested interests, or prior commitments. You must familiarize yourself with their thinking, their feelings, their primary concerns, biases, and "blind spots." You must think as they think, because, as you seek to influence the actions and beliefs of others, in effect, you are seeking to do their thinking for them—at least, in part. The objective is to *integrate* your thinking with theirs, to think like they do, and then add your information and reasoning to theirs—not an easy task. How do you proceed?

Begin by discussing the problem with as many people as you can; ask for their opinions; read their published sources of information. Do not *adopt* any data or conclusions with which you honestly disagree; do not "find where your listeners want to go and run out in front" just to be accepted or approved. If you are not straightforward and sincere in dealing with your audience you will most likely be found out and lose the respect of your listeners. Make sure you understand their thinking, accept what is credible to you, integrate it with your thinking, and present the composite to them, hoping that they will do the same for you. In the long run, however, *you must satisfy the demands of your own logic and conscience.* Then you must, as honestly and clearly as you can, offer to them the essence of your thinking.

The suggestions for your proposed attempt to influence others are beginning to take the following shape: (1) Tell your listeners what you believe, (2) indicate the reasons why your belief is credible, (3) make sure that they realize that you clearly understand what they believe and that you have carefully evaluated its bases, (4) show them why your belief is credible, and (5) tell them *why* you want them to change their beliefs. Do not be afraid to reveal that your motives are mixed—some satisfaction for you and some advantages for them. Be as clear and honest as you can. It will work best for you in the long run.[1]

CHANGING YOUR LISTENERS' ATTITUDES

Attitude may be defined as a predisposition to behave in a particular way under a specified set of conditions. Some people who have a definite belief in God feel strongly about the value of prayer in our public schools. Yet others, who also believe in God, are opposed to prayer in public schools because they cling firmly to their belief that church and state should in all instances be kept separate. Atheists, on the other hand, may be opposed to prayer in public schools as a general principle. As can readily be seen, our beliefs, from which our attitudes arise, tend to govern what perspective we bring to problems and what we think the proper course of action or policy should be in dealing with that problem. Knowledge of listeners' attitudes thus is of vital concern to any advocate.

In a general way, you can assess people's attitudes by observing their behavior. However, you must be careful; studies have shown that such behavior may be deceptive.[2]

Attitudes are *not always consistent* with observable behavior.[3] The verbal expression of an attitude is called an opinion. It is also somewhat risky to infer an attitude (predisposition to act) from an expressed opinion because many circumstances can cause a person to express an opinion inconsistent with a real attitude. Your best bet is to determine if any of the following circumstances are present: (1) pressure from groups or organizations of which the person is a member, or (2) influence of status persons who hear the opinion. If one or both of these factors appear to be present, you need to discount an expression of opinion. Even so, *behavior and expressed opinions do tend to reflect attitudes of your potential listeners.*[4]

The development of their attitudes has been influenced by their experiences, including the attachments they formed for other people in work groups, teams, churches, and so forth. In an intensive four-year study of the entire student body of Bennington College, Theodore Newcomb found that roommates and other "reference groups" influenced changes in students' attitudes.[5]

The amount of information individuals have about a subject may influence their reaction to your effort to change their viewpoint. When people are well-informed they tend to have more intensive, less change-able attitudes, either for or against that about which they are well-informed.[6] Such information about your listeners can be helpful as you seek to present your thinking to them.

Some of you may have read some studies of attitude change that reflected easy, successful experiences in influencing people. Indeed, you may have had such an experience yourself. In one way or another you may have formed the notion that there are tricks and formulas for manipulating people easily. In some instances this seems to be the case, but for the most part, once a person has formed an attitude, it is not easily changed; attitudes tend to persist over long periods of time. You will need to be aware of certain factors that cause their retention. The most important one appears to be a tendency of people to seek out information consistent with their currently held attitudes; this practice has been called *selective exposure.* People tend to form friendships, join organizations, and subscribe to newspapers and magazines that reinforce previously obtained attitudes.[7] When people cannot avoid information inconsistent with their attitudes, they tend to pay more attention to available information with which they can agree.[8] Some of your listeners may try to avoid hearing information that is inconsistent with their present attitudes.[9] Often they will distort their perceptions of the *nature* or substance of such information.[10] In some cases, if such undesired information cannot be ignored, or distorted, they will simply derogate or attempt to discredit the source (you), perceiving you as dishonest.[11]

All of these tendencies for an existing attitude to persist (once acquired) have direct bearing on your task as an advocate. They must be considered as you attempt to gain the support of your listeners.

A concept that has been of considerable value in explaining the dynamics of attitude change and has generated considerable research is generally known as attitude *consistency* theory. The essential premise of consistency theory is that people tend to seek a reduction of feelings of dissonance[12] when they perceive their attitudes toward related conditions or events as inconsistent. They tend to seek congruence[13] or a balance[14] between related attitude objects. For example, "I like to drive a very comfortable automobile," and "Large cars use too much gasoline" might be two attitudes held by a person; and these might be perceived as inconsistent and dissonance-producing. If such dissonance is not reduced, psychological tension persists, and this person will seek to change one or both attitudes until a sense of "balance" is achieved.[15]

Listeners appear to have an area or latitude of acceptance around a currently held attitude, a range of positions that are near their own, different to some degree, but still tolerable to them.[16] They also appear to have a similar "latitude" of rejection, a range of positions more distant from theirs which they find more-to-less objectionable. In essence, your listeners may be quite tolerant of your position if it is perceived by them as relatively close to their own.

Now suppose you advocate your solution to a problem; suppose a group of listeners has earlier perceived you as (probably) standing for a position relatively near their own; but suppose they now see your attitude as significantly different from theirs. In such a case, not only are they likely not to change their attitudes (in spite of your persuasive efforts); they are likely to be even *more* negative or opposed to you than before.[17] Indeed, you must beware of an additional factor: if your listeners perceive your position as being within their latitude of rejection, they are likely to see it as *much more extreme* than will those who see it as within their range of possible acceptance.[18] This is an important factor because it can sometimes explain a very disconcerting attack upon you by someone whom you thought to be only mildly opposed to your position.

If your position is seen by your listeners as different from their own, you must be careful not to present your message in its most extreme form. In such a case, proceed with care. To the extent that you can show that your position is similar to that of your listeners, do so. Show them elements of similarity, placing less stress on those areas of disagreement. In no case, however, should you be dishonest or leave out a significant part of your reasoning supporting your position. Be completely clear, honest, and forthright, and stress areas of agreement between yourself and your listeners.

HELPING LISTENERS DECIDE QUESTIONS OF POLICY

There are many situations in life where you can perceive that you and other people have a mutual problem—but they don't see it. Perhaps you and your classmates are working on a project; all of you wish to see it completed in good fashion, but you believe that following procedures you have adopted, the project will not be finished by the agreed-upon deadline. You see the problem, but the other members of your group do not. Or perhaps you ride to work in a car pool. All of the riders know that you have a problem of ordinarily using a highway that is undergoing construction. The others are content to negotiate this tortuous route, but you are convinced that a smoother but longer road would be a wiser choice. In cases such as this, you have done some thinking along problem-solving lines. You would hope your associates would realize the value of your thinking. In fact, you would like to have them change their behavior—cooperate with you—to help you and them solve a problem that is, as you see it, of mutual interest.

A situation in which you and others have a mutual problem is one in which you should, if at all possible, encourage them to work with you in a problem-solving group.[19] Some of them may be interested, some may not; you should try to work with those who are interested. You should seek to arrange face-to-face meetings where your thinking and theirs is fully expressed and mutually evaluated. In these meetings use standard problem-solving procedures: carefully identify the problem, clarify the degree of individual concern, describe the desired goal, compare the desired condition with the present circumstances, and obtain information relevant to adequate analysis of the problem. Then identify all reasonable approaches to solving the problem (both your favored approach as well as those favored by the others), and evaluate these various proposals by predicting probable outcomes of each. You should hope to do this by forecasting outcomes on the basis of past experiences of yourself and others. You and your group should then implement, if possible, the decision chosen by the group.

At any point along this series of procedures you may find yourself in disagreement with others; in such cases you will need to express your thinking in clear and credible ways so that others will agree with you, unless, as is very often the case, you see enough value in their viewpoint so that you wish to modify or change your own. However, if you have carefully considered your views and theirs and you still believe yours is more defensible, you should continue to try to show the superior value of your position. Thus you should be an advocate.

In essence, you are seeking to think for other people, to identify problems and achieve their solutions for others who are affected by the problems but who are uninformed about important things in their environment. Your own thinking must be done with care, and then it must be presented to them with accuracy. What should be the guidelines for such careful thinking and accurate presentation? They should include procedures for analyzing a problem and choosing the most reasonable solution. Speech teachers have developed "stock issues" for assisting students in this process. These issues, in question form, are three in number: (1) Is there a need for a change? (2) Will the proposed solution meet the need identified? (3) Will the proposed solution introduce inherent disadvantages? Consideration of the first stock issue involves a three-step process explained below.

Stock Issue 1: Is There a Need for a Change?

How did you arrive at your decision that something should be done? How did you reach the conclusion that a particular proposal should be adopted? Very likely you started with a feeling of concern about a certain part of your environment. Some of the things around you—situations, conditions, or ways in which people behaved—bothered you. You sensed that, in some way, things were not the way they could be and perhaps ought to be.

Step 1: Carefully compare the existing condition that seems to bother you with the condition you desire. This process of comparison is the first step in analyzing a problem and should be the first step in getting yourself ready to influence the action of others. By definition, a problem is an undesirable situation. For example, you may have a part-time job that demands more of your time than your health will allow. Or perhaps a local custom exists, such as the practice of racial discrimination in the use of local recreation facilities; you believe that such a custom is not what *ought* to exist. In such a case, it is first desirable to identify very clearly the condition that exists, making certain that you have a good hold on reality. You should verify that what you think exists is, in fact, true. Then you should state clearly what you think should exist in its place. Don't settle for such thoughts as "there ought to be a law," "they ought to know better," or "they ought to want to do right."

Describe very specifically the condition or situation that you want to see brought about. If you cannot do this, you are not prepared to try to explain what you would like to see brought about; if you aim at nothing in particular, you are likely to hit it, and nothing more.

Analysis of a problem essentially consists of determining the *difference* between what exists and what you wish would exist. However, the determination of this precise difference is a fairly complex process. The essential issue is this: Is there a realistic *need* for people to change what they are doing? Does their current behavior constitute a clear and present deterrent or danger to a desirable common cause? Is this desired goal realistic? Is it within the realm of reasonable achievement? Is it a practical goal, not too idealistic or ethereal? Can you state this desired condition in specific terms? All of these questions must be answered in your thinking when you have adequately identified the problem your proposed change of actions of others is to meet.

Step 2: Analyze the nature of the problem. You must carefully consider the field of forces that are inherent in it. You must gain a perspective of it in terms of its environmental conditions. Specifically, this means that you should identify two kinds of forces that are at work in the situation: impelling forces and constraining forces.

Impelling forces are conditions that show a change is needed. For example, your goal may be recreational facilities for teenagers in your community. Impelling forces in such a situation might be youngsters playing in the streets, constituting a hazard to traffic and to themselves; misuse of parks, causing their deterioration; vandalism of public school playgrounds; pre-delinquent behavior by youngsters having little opportunity for excitement other than petty theft, fighting, or wanton destruction. A careful consideration of all such conditions pointing to a need for a change in terms of opportunity for teenage recreation can help you gain needed perspectives on the nature of the problem you hope to resolve.

Constraining forces are conditions that keep a desired change from happening. When you stop to think about it, if such a change is as desirable as you think it is, why doesn't it just come about of its own accord? Some practices, needs, or attitudes must be acting in *constraint* of such change. The idea that any particular situation is the way it is at any given moment because of counterbalancing forces was develped by Kurt Lewin; he borrowed the concept from the physical sciences and offered it as a way of understanding social problems.[20] Analyzing impelling and constraining forces inherent in a problem is often called "force-field analysis." Such analysis is necessary to be certain that you have carefully understood a problem before attempting to resolve it. For example, possible constraining forces for the problem of teenage recreation facilities might include extremely poor economic resources in the community (a sharecroppers' village, perhaps); highly temporary or transient employment (an Alaskan pipeline boomtown); or a preponderance of retired persons in the community (a decaying western plains farm community).

Both the impelling and constraining forces must be carefully considered as you approach the next logical step in your thinking: What are the various possible alternative ways that the problem might be resolved? As you consider various approaches, you need to be sure that you don't miss any; you must carefully evaluate all possible approaches before you are ready to advocate change of other people's behavior. You cannot afford to take a position of advocacy favoring one particular line of action only to have one of your listeners point out to you and your audience a better way, one that you have utterly ignored in your thinking.

Step 3: Carefully identify all possible significant approaches to solving the problem you have analyzed. Adequate consideration of impelling and restraining forces (as we have just described this procedure) can be very valuable in preparing you for this third step. For example, you may become aware that a major restraining force to providing opportunities for teenage recreation in your community is an assumption that all boys and girls work after school and on weekends (a common assumption in many traditional farming communities). However, let us say that your town has been growing, becoming more urbanized, and that there are now over four hundred teenagers whose parents work on jobs where youngsters cannot be expected to help. Changing the existing, erroneous assumption may be a reasonably viable approach to the problem. Similarly, identification of impelling forces may suggest possible ways of approaching the problem. For example, to find that petty crime and vandalism by young people has rapidly increased in your community may suggest the need to provide facilities for more constructive use of the time of teenagers—perhaps by development of science fairs, athletic programs, swimming pools, and part-time employment programs.

All possible solutions to the identified problem should be considered; none should be missed or ignored. Only by giving fair consideration to all viable approaches can you be sure that your proposed solution will be worthy of your time and effort as a responsible advocate.

Stock Issue 2: Will the Proposed Solution Meet the Need Identified?

Once you have determined that a change is called for, you are ready to advance a proposal that you feel provides the best solution to the problem.

Carefully evaluate the probable workability of each of the optional approaches you have identified. Remember that your objective is to influence the action of others. In order to do this, you must advocate a plan of action that will stand the criticism of your listeners. Careful analysis of practical experiences have made students of advocacy aware of a basic criterion that can be used to test any proposed plan of action: Will this proposal produce the desired changes in the current situation?

To determine the degree to which any proposal or approach to a policy problem meets this criteria, you must go back to the results of your problem analysis. Compare the impelling and constraining forces in your force-field analysis with the actual changes indicated by various proposed action plans. Does one or another proposal actually change one or more of the existing impelling or constraining forces? Which proposal does the most? Is it the one you intuitively favored? Or have you been influenced somewhat by prejudice, or limited examination of relationships to impelling and constraining forces? It should never be too late to change your mind about the plan of action you will advocate if a new approach is, in your own estimation, better able to achieve the change you desire. *Note that each possible approach or proposal should be evaluated in terms of its probable effect on each of the impelling and constraining forces earlier identified.* Thus, the quality of work you have done earlier in identifying these factors inherent in the problem situation will directly affect the quality of the proposal you eventually choose to advocate. The basic issue involved is: Will your chosen plan really work?

Stock Issue 3: Will the Proposed Solution Introduce Inherent Disadvantages?

As you consider the third stock issue, you will need to consider this criterion: *Avoid serious disadvantages in a proposed plan of action.* You may agree that many times we could think of a proposal that really would produce a desired change but would also cost too much, perhaps in terms of money, effort, or even severe loss of human liberty. For example, small children *can* be made to be quiet in church—by taping their mouths and tying their hands and legs; the cost of such a plan would be too severe and it does not really achieve the desired goal—a worshipful demeanor. Disadvantages inherent in a proposal usually consist of risks that your listeners cannot afford. Costs are probably judged to be too severe if they are greater than the benefits likely to be achieved. They are also judged to be too severe if they are greater than the costs of other proposals that can also achieve the desired results. Once again, before you decide that you will advocate a particular proposal, you should evaluate all possible plans of action against this criterion; for each alternate plan, what will likely be the cost—in money, time, effort, or loss of human values.

Prediction of Future Events

In our discussion of the second and third stock issues, we have been suggesting that you determine the degree to which various possible approaches to a problem will both work and avoid undesirable consequences. How can you decide the degree to which any proposal meets these criteria? The answer to this question is not simple, but the principle involved is used by all of us: the prediction of future events on the basis of our knowledge of *similar* (as we see them) events in the past. It involves a voyage from the known to the unknown—an intellectual leap into the dark. This leap may seem rather risky—but we do it every day. When we decide to eat at our favorite restaurant we are predicting on the basis of past experience that our needs *probably* will be satisfied better than if we were to go elsewhere.

The prediction of the nature of future events involves reasoning, that is, identifying reasons for believing that such types of events will occur. The act of identifying and evaluating such reasons requires a knowledge of *relevant* or *similar* past events and the circumstances that may have influenced or caused them. From this knowledge, we can predict the *probability* of a similar event occurring under similar conditions in the future.

The essential core of this reasoning process is the identification of relevant similarities between various events and their surrounding conditions. This process first involves a classification of past events according to a pertinent set of characteristics. Do blondes have more fun? To test this generalization about such events, one must be able readily to distinguish "blondes." The reasoning process also requires observation of events, either by you or by someone else, with special attention to selected similar circumstances. Concerning blondes, it might be possible to determine that people with hair lighter in color than a carefully identified shade have more fun on dates. However, having "fun" may be rather difficult to determine unless it can be defined accurately.

As you attempt to evaluate various proposed plans of action, including the one you happen to favor at the moment, you should raise certain questions:

1. Has a *similar* proposal been tried elsewhere? If so, were pertinent *conditions similar?*
2. Were such trials, if any, successful? Did they meet a *need that is similar* to the one that you have identified?
3. Were there any costs or dangers that are not similar to those your listeners can accept?

In this list of questions, the importance of identifying relevant similarities between observed past events and the result desired from adopting a particular plan of action should be obvious. However, this principle is important, and an illustrative example may be useful. Suppose you are helping a friend with pre-enrollment for next semester. You need to know in advance which courses are interesting and valuable. You have had three courses with Professor Smith. Other students have commented on finding courses with Professor Smith highly interesting and valuable. From your experience and reports of other students you begin to form a *generalization:* Professor Smith's courses are interesting and valuable to students.

Forming generalizations covering selected characteristics of events and conditions is called *induction;* this process is basic to critical thinking or the scientific method. It is the process by which we establish reliable knowledge about our world, physical and social. As we use it we must be careful that we observe as many relevant similar events and conditions as possible. The particular characteristic in question (in the example given above, interesting and valuable) must be noted with great care; it is most helpful if some method of quantification can be devised to measure such characteristics. (How much of interest was offered in Professor Smith's courses, or how valuable were they?)

The primary question in reasoning can be seen as one of relevant similarity: Is the unknown future event one of a set covered by the generalization we have formulated? In our example, will Professor Smith's course next semester be similar (in ways that matter to us—interesting and valuable) to those he has previously offered? We look carefully for information about these characteristics: Is next semester's course numbered and described the same as one previously offered? Does Professor Smith tell us it is similar, that he plans to teach it the same way and cover the same material? In all relevant ways we try to make certain that the future event in question will be one of a set about which we have formed our generalization. Traditional scholars of logic have called this process *deduction.* They usually illustrate this part of the reasoning process as follows: All of Professor Smith's courses are interesting; course 530 is one of Professor Smith's courses, therefore course 530 is interesting. This paradigm is called a *syllogism;* we suspect that you have previously seen deductive reasoning illustrated this way. Actually, in this simplified approach the key issue of relevant similarity is neglected. What such reasoning can actually provide is this: Courses previously offered by Professor Smith have been interesting.

Next semester Professor Smith will offer a course that appears to be essentially similar to a selected number of courses he has previously offered. Next semester's course with Professor Smith *probably* will be interesting.

In this paradigm the issue of relevant similarity is clearly exposed. If the future event cannot be judged to be similar in relevant ways to those events over which the generalization has been made, then one's predictions regarding that future event will not be reliable. The practical application is this: As you try to evaluate various proposals to solve a problem, you must test the predicted results of each proposal (including the one you favor) in terms of its relevant similarity to previous experiences with such approaches.

Structured Logic

A contemporary British philosopher, Stephen Toulmin, has devised a structural model of reasoning that focuses on the comparison of relevant similarities between past observed events and and a future one about which a prediction is desired.[21] His model is composed of three elements: relevant *data*, a *claim*, and a *warrant* supporting the claim. (See Figure 12-1.)[22] The *data* consist of verifiable relevant facts (events, conditions). The *claim* is an assertion about a future or unobserved event or condition; it is a statement of belief about the unknown. The *warrant* is an assertion

Figure 12-1 Toulmin's Model of Reasoning

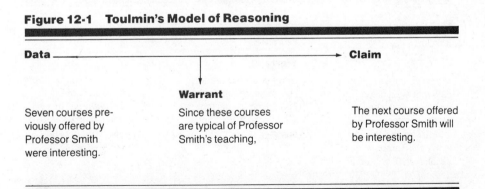

Data ───▶ Claim

Warrant

| Seven courses previously offered by Professor Smith were interesting. | Since these courses are typical of Professor Smith's teaching, | The next course offered by Professor Smith will be interesting. |

of a relationship between the unknown and known events or conditions; it is the connecting link, the inferential bridge between past and future, known and unknown. The *warrant* is a statement of belief that, from data provided, people (readers or listeners) are entitled to draw a particular conclusion; it focuses on *relevant similarities* between the known and the unknown, and is the central core of the reasoning process.

There are few warrants that are universally accurate in simple terms. Generalizations that are valuable in reasoning can seldom state that *all* events or conditions in a selected set have uniform characteristics. Warrants that you will be using in supporting a proposed plan of action ordinarily will need to be qualified; for example, observations of courses offered are likely to show that *many* or *most* of them are interesting, but *not all of them*. Toulmin was aware of this problem; in his analysis he provided for a *qualifier*, thus restricting or limiting the warrant. Such a qualifier identifies exceptions or special conditions that may restrict the claim (see Figure 12-2).

In some cases when you attempt to evaluate proposed plans of action on the bases of past experience, you will be able to determine specific restrictions or reservations on the warrant you use; in some cases you will only know that the experiential data are contradictory without any available explanation (for example, a Youth Center worked very well in Yankton but only moderately well in Clay Center). In most cases the best you will be able to do will be to discover fairly stable patterns among events that are essentially similar. Your available data will produce a warrant that supports a claim of this type: "The next course offered by Professor Smith *probably* will be interesting." (See the *Claim* in Figure 12-2.)

Figure 12-2 Toulmin's Model of Reasoning Including a Reservation and a Probability

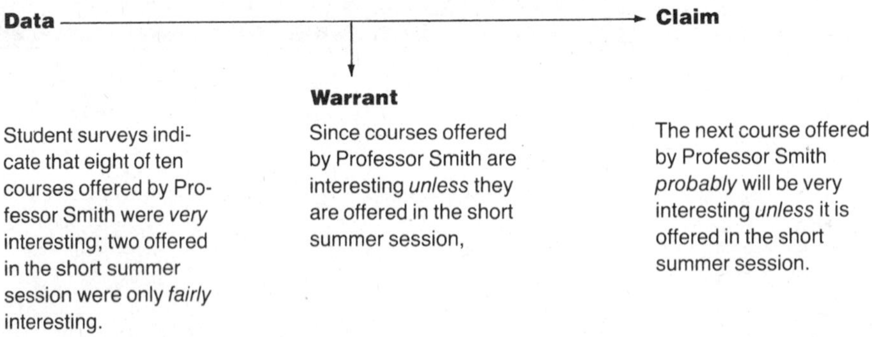

Data ──→ Claim		
	↓	
	Warrant	
Student surveys indicate that eight of ten courses offered by Professor Smith were *very* interesting; two offered in the short summer session were only *fairly* interesting.	Since courses offered by Professor Smith are interesting *unless* they are offered in the short summer session,	The next course offered by Professor Smith *probably* will be very interesting *unless* it is offered in the short summer session.

As an advocate, your ability to predict with high credibility the outcome of a plan of action will be vital. However, a warrant that produces probability cannot support a claim that has certainty. To maintain your credibility, to be an authentic advocate, you must admit probability and not claim certainty when it is not warranted. To the best of your ability you determine for yourself and then tell your listeners the *degree of probability* that your proposed plan of action will produce the desired results.

Developing a Plan of Action

The final step is critical for evaluating your own thinking about a problem and making certain your ideas warrant you to become an advocate, that is, attempting to influence the actions of others. *Develop in detail the plan of action which you have determined will best meet the need without entailing serious disadvantages.*

There are five major issues to be resolved in developing a plan of action: (1) *What* should be done? (2) *At what time* should each action be taken (in what order)? (3) *Where* should each event take place? (4) *Who* should do what? (5) *What resources* (tools, finances, expertise, skills, legal rights, etc.) will each of these persons (or groups, institutions, agencies, etc.) need if the plan is to work?

You will need to make certain that people (agencies, institutions, groups, or organizations) have the opportunity, capability, willingness, and resources to implement the plan you intend to advocate. Most of these issues should be resolved as you are comparing the relative workability of various possible approaches or proposals. If you cannot provide such detailed information for the plan you choose to advocate, then you are not ready. If you do not have such information in hand, you are not ready to be an effective advocate. You can too easily be contradicted on legitimate grounds by a listener who disagrees with you. Such a person may show that he or she knows more about your topic than you do. To be an effective source of influence upon the actions of others, you not only must know *how* your proposed plan of action can work, but you must be able to convince them that it *will* work because the necessary persons are able and willing and that the required resources are available. This may seem to you to be a heavy responsibility, but it is the required preparation of an effective advocate. It is no more than you would like to expect of a used car salesman.

In the practical affairs of the world, any one of the considerations detailed in this chapter may be the limit to which you can analyze a problem; that is, you may not be able to do valid thinking beyond the second step in consideration of the first stock issue: *Analysis of the nature of the problem*—identification of the impelling and restraining forces involved. Presentation to others of your thinking through Steps One and Two can be an authentic presentation that can make a significant contribution. Perhaps you have not been able to identify thoroughly all possible alternative ways of solving this problem. Any presentation should reflect your thinking, starting with Step One: Comparison of existing conditions with the conditions you believe ought to exist or are desirable; and covering, in order, each of the stock issues, so far as you can go on the basis of your careful, informed thinking. Many credible presentations have been given by speakers who clearly analyzed a problem and concluded their presentation by an appeal to their listeners to help them search for a solution. However, it is likely that if your thinking has been well done the second and third stock issues: *the workability and potential disadvantages of all possible optional approaches to solving the problem,* you will then want to cover the final step in advocacy: *Description of a detailed plan of action that you have determined to be the best solution.* Remember, however, that a presentation that covers all stock issues is rather rare and reflects the thinking of a very thoughtful and well-informed investigator.

THE PERSUASION PARADIGM

At this point you may feel that we have presented an extensive treatment of the problems you face as an advocate of policies without giving you adequate instructions on how to proceed. For this reason we offer four specific suggestions. They cover, in essence, the principles discussed in this chapter.

    1. *Show shared concern.* Show that you share the concerns of your listeners, that you and they have basic cares in common, that there is common ground.

    2. *Demonstrate need for change.* This should be *their* need as well as yours. Point to the condition that is dangerous, intolerable, or undesirable. Compare what *is* with what *ought* to be or is desirable.

    3. *Compare alternatives.* Identify alternative approaches or actions. Show why you have chosen one over the others. Give reasons backed by facts.

    4. *Paint a picture of your plan in action.* Describe how your listener will look, act, and feel living under your new program. Paint a word picture; "romance the product," as experienced salespeople say. As you conclude, your listeners should know how it will feel to enjoy the situation or condition that will be the *result* of your plan being adopted.

SUMMARY

As people make their way through life most of them find ways of cooperating and negotiating with other people. From time to time, however, we find ourselves in situations where we need to have others see the situation as we do, and act accordingly. As we seek to help others reach decisions that agree with our thinking, occasionally we find it appropriate to give speeches of advocacy.

In seeking to let others "know what we know," we must explain to them what we believe and why we believe it. The basis for seeking to influence the beliefs and behavior of others is grounded in our perception of reality. To be sure of our ground we must carefully evaluate our own beliefs. We must examine our motives and our perceptions.

As we seek to influence the *beliefs* of others, we must first gain their attention, then establish our credibility. Nothing will be more important than that our listeners see us as credible speakers. If we have carefully identified our beliefs, examined the bases of our beliefs, and studied conflicting beliefs, we then may want to express concern for a problem to an audience we think can profit from our thinking.

As we seek to influence the *actions* of others by having them act as if they believe as we do, we must review our reasons for believing as we do; if our reasons are sound, they will show that we have done as follows:

1. Compared the existing condition with the condition we desire.
2. Analyzed the nature of impelling and constraining forces inherent in the problem situation.
3. Identified all possible valid ways of solving the problem.
4. Evaluated the workability and potential cost of each approach.
5. Developed a detailed plan of action that we believe should be adopted and implemented.

If we have accomplished well these five steps we are now ready to present our thinking to others. As we do, we will need to familiarize ourselves with our listeners' thinking, "start where they are" and integrate our thinking with theirs.

LEARNING EXPERIENCES

Objectives

After studying this chapter, you should be able to *do* the following:

1. Assess your qualifications for speaking on various topics by determining your beliefs, motives, and credibility.
2. Define and determine audience attitudes toward your topic.
3. Analyze a problem in such a way as to reflect careful thinking and accuracy.
4. Utilize the Toulmin Model of Reasoning for a variety of problems.
5. Adapt the Persuasion Paradigm to a topic for a persuasive speech.

Exercises

1. Obtain a manuscript of a persuasive speech from the media or from *Vital Speeches of the Day*. Analyze it in terms of (a) the speaker's qualifications; (b) methods of audience adaptation; (c) the logical pattern of the speech; and (d) how the speech fits the Persuasion Paradigm.
2. Discuss the analysis with groups of your classmates. Compare the speeches studied and rate them in the four categories above.
3. Using Toulmin's Model of Reasoning, diagram major arguments from the speech you studied. Present your analysis to the class. Are you able to detect logical flaws?
4. For one of the topics that you have selected for a persuasive presentation, analyze the need for a change (impelling and constraining forces) and the capacity of your proposal to meet the needs.
5. Review the stock issues suggested for influencing the actions of others. Check your understanding by explaining these issues to an individual who is not in the class.

NOTES

[1] For a discussion of the relative value of lying or telling the truth to those whom you would convince, see Peter Farb, *Word Play*. New York: Knopf, 1974, p. 137.

[2] For a classical study of relation of attitudes to behavior, see Richard T. LaPiere, "Attitudes vs. Actions," *Social Forces*, 13 (1934), pp. 230-237.

[3] See Bernard Kutnev, Carol Wilkins, and Penny Yarrow, "Verbal Attitudes and Overt Behavior Involving Racial Prejudice," *Journal of Abnormal Social Psychology*, 47 (1952), pp. 649-652.

[4] See for example, Melvin L. DeFleur and Frank R. Westie, "Verbal Attitudes and Overt Acts: An Experiment on the Salience of Attitudes," *American Sociological Review*, 23 (1958), pp. 667-673.

[5] Theodore M. Newcomb, "Attitude Development as a Function of Reference Groups: the Bennington Study," in *Readings in Social Psychology*, Eleanor E. Maccoby, Theodore M. Newcomb, and Eugene L. Hartley, Eds. New York: Holt, Rinehart & Winston, 1958, pp. 265-275.

[6] See for example, Gwynn Nettler, "The Relationships Between Attitudes and Information Concerning the Japanese in America," *American Sociological Review*, 11 (1964), pp. 177-191.

[7] Judson Mills, Elliot Aronson, and Herbert Robinson, "Selectivity in Exposure to Information," *Journal of Abnormal Social Psychology*, 59 (1959), pp. 250-253.

[8] See Lewis K. Canon, "Self-Confidence and Selective Exposure to Information," in *Conflict, Decision and Dissonance*, Leon Festinger, Ed. Stanford, California: Stanford University Press, 1964, pp. 83-95.

[9] For an evaluation of research on this issue, see Charles A. Kiesler,

Barby E. Collins, and Norman Miller, *Attitude Change*. New York: Wiley, 1969, pp. 223-224.

[10]Jonathan L. Freedman and David O. Sears, "Selective Exposure," in *Advances in Experimental Social Psychology*, Leonard Berkowitz, Ed. New York: Academic, 1966, Vol. 1.

[11]See David K. Berlo and Halbert E. Gulley, "Some Determinants of the Effects of Oral Communication in Producing Attitude Change and Learning," *Speech Monographs*, 25 (1957), pp. 10-20.

[12]See Leon Festinger, *A Theory of Cognitive Dissonance*. New York: Row, Peterson, 1957.

[13]See Charles E. Osgood and Percy H. Tannenbaum, "The Principle of Congruity in the Prediction of Attitude Change," *Psychological Review*, 62 (1965), pp. 42-55.

[14]See Fritz Heider, "Attitudes and Cognitive Organization," *Journal of Psychology*, 21 (1946), pp. 107-112.

[15]See the reviews of consistency theories by William J. McGuire, "The Current Status of Cognitive Theories," in *Cognitive Consistency*, Shel Feldman, Ed. New York: Academic, 1966, pp. 1-46; also, Elliot Aronson, "Dissonance Theory: Progress and Problems," in *Theories of Cognitive Consistency*, Robert P. Abelson et al., Eds. Chicago: Rand-McNally, 1968, pp. 5-28.

[16]See Carolyn W. Sherif, Muzafer Sherif, and Roger E. Nebergall, *Attitude and Attitude Change*. Philadelphia: Saunders, 1965.

[17]Empirical support for this principle has been presented by O. J. Harvey and John Rutherford, "Gradual and Absolute Approaches to Attitude Change," *Sociometry*, 21 (1958), pp. 61-68.

[18]See Carl I. Hovland, O. J. Harvey, and Muzafer Sherif, "Assimilation and Contrast Effects in Reactions to Communication and Attitude Change," *Journal of Abnormal Social Psychology*, 55 (1957), pp. 244-252.

[19]For a detailed discussion of problem-solving group procedures, see Bobby R. Patton and Kim Giffin, *Decision-Making Group Interaction*, 2nd Ed., New York: Harper and Row, 1978.

[20]Kurt Lewin, *Field Theory in Social Research*. New York: Harper and Row, 1951; see especially pp. 188-237.

[21]Stephen Toulmin, *The Uses of Argument*. Cambridge, England: Cambridge University Press, 1958.

[22]Toulmin, see especially, the "Introduction" and Essays I, II, and III.

13

Developing the Persuasive Speech

 In the previous chapter we considered factors vital to persuasive communication. An open society that espouses the marketplace-of-ideas concept is satiated with all types of persuasion—in newspapers and magazines, on radio and television, in books and on billboards, in speeches, in conversation. Some persuasion is responsible, some not; some is useful, some useless. But occur it does. It occurs in the political arena, in social gatherings, in religious circles, in industrial settings, and even around the family hearth. Indeed, not only does it occur, it is essential that it occurs. Social control is vital to a society, and although laws may restrain crime and violence, persuasion builds social cohesion. It legislates and implements justice; it also frees people from taboos, makes them aware of important problems, and solidifies social action. For this reason, it is important that you as a student of speech communication learn the art of advocacy and become proficient at developing and delivering responsible persuasive discourse. We will examine two examples of persuasive presentations. The first speech will involve generating awareness of and concern for problems; the second speech involves identifying a problem and then presenting a workable solution.

EXAMPLE OF A PROBLEM SPEECH

The speech we will consider in this section, "Insane or Guilty?," was delivered by Jodie Wallace, an undergraduate, in a public speaking class as her final speech in the spring 1981 semester.*

*"Insane or Guilty?" by Jodie Wallace

The Introduction

Speakers often seek to generate interest and attention by beginning with *startling statements*, statements that cause the average person to say, "My goodness, I didn't know that." This is the technique Jodie Wallace uses to open her speech. She sets the scene by telling the audience that she was casually leafing through a recent issue of *U.S. News & World Report* when suddenly something caught her attention. She was startled to read that John Hinckley, Jr., the man who attempted to assassinate President Reagan, could be back in society in four years if he successfully pleads insanity. This information should startle Jodie's listeners also. She then quickly moves from the specific to the general: According to a recent study by the National Institute of Mental Health only *one third* of those who plead insanity actually ever stand trial. This general statistic is intended to give breadth and scope to the problem she identifies at the outset. The second paragraph of her speech constitutes, in a classical sense, the *narrative*. She begins by naming people who were involved in notorious crimes—which again has strong attention value. She then provides a brief history of what her concern stems from, namely the 1972 *Jackson vs. Indiana* decision. She concludes her introduction by pointing out the problems that have resulted from this decision.

Flipping through a recent *U.S. News & World Report* I came upon a startling fact. Did any of you know that if John Hinckley, Jr., the man allegedly responsible for the assassination attempt upon President Reagan, successfully pleads insanity, as legal authorities expect him to, he could be back in society in four years? If this plea is disallowed, he faces a life sentence. Or, how many of you were aware that, according to a recent study made by the National Institute of Mental Health, only *one third* of those who plead insanity actually stand trial? That leaves a frightening *two thirds* who are never brought to trial.

The plea of insanity has become fairly common in recent years, with Charles Manson, Patty Hearst, and David Berkowitz all attempting to employ its usage. Apparently, the 1972 *Jackson vs. Indiana* decision is largely responsible for the rising popularity of the insanity plea, for the decision states that "a defendent who is not expected to regain competency within a reasonable period of time cannot be detained from treatment" by going to prison. Unfortunately, there are several problems with this decision, all leading to its misuse. First of all, the question of what constitutes a "reasonable period of time" is never answered, and secondly, confusion exists between the terms "incompetency" and "insanity." *Competency* refers to a person's condition *at the time of trial; insanity* refers to the person's condition *at the time of the crime.* Legally, this decision (Jackson vs. Indiana) can only be employed in incompetency cases, yet it is used in insanity pleas as an argument for nonimprisonment as well.

The third paragraph of Jodie's speech reveals her credentials for speaking on this subject and makes a transition to the topic of her speech. Jodie begins by trying to make her listeners appreciate that the problem has the potential to affect not only her but everyone in the room. This thought, she says, led her to research the topic in order to find the best available information. She hopes to establish her credentials by telling the audience, "I want to share with you what I have uncovered." This section of the speech could be strengthened if she gave the listener some idea of the extent of her research. What were her main sources of information, for example?

Jodie concludes the third paragraph with a forecast of the development of her speech, and she leads into the body with the statement: "Let's take a closer look at all three of these areas."

These facts led me to wonder just how often the insanity plea is used by criminals and their lawyers as a way of "beating the rap," and what effect that has on me as a citizen as well as every one of you in this room. I have looked into this matter and I want to share with you what I have uncovered. Whether or not the insanity plea is used seems to depend upon three things: one, the length of the hospitalization versus the length of imprisonment; two, the environment of the hospital versus the environment of the prison; and three, the outcome of the criminal charges after hospitalization. Let's take a closer look at all three of these areas.

The Body of the Speech

After restating the first point to be developed (the length of hospitalization versus the length of imprisonment), Jodie relies heavily upon *significant facts* for support. She makes the factual statement that a hospitalization sentence is almost always shorter than a prison term. To give impact and interest to this idea, she notes that if a person is guilty of an assassination attempt in Washington, D.C., that individual, if ruled insane, could receive four years in a hospital, but if judged guilty of a crime that same person could face life imprisonment. "Small wonder Hinckley will probably plead insanity!" Jodie uses this statement about Hinckley to startle listeners and in that way gives impact to what she is saying. From this she leads into a report of a study concerning the difference between the average length of impoundment for the criminally insane versus the length of sentence for a lesser crime if the person is sent to prison. She follows this by citing another study which generally supports the first one. She, however, fails to mention the source of the second study, which weakens her evidence somewhat.

The next section consists of *examples* intended to make vivid the point she has just developed. She mentions two sensational names and then gives some detail about a person named Joseph Baldi who killed four women in four months after being released from "hospitalization." She relates with the audience on this point by telling them, "these victims could have been any one of us." Jodie terminates the point effectively; she restates her first contention: "Therefore, my findings showed that offenders pleading insanity almost always are going to find themselves with a reduced sentence. . . ."

First, the length of a person's hospital stay after a plea of insanity. From the research I did, I discovered that a hospitalization sentence is almost always shorter than a prison term. In Washington, D.C., for example, a person receives four years in a hospital for the criminally insane, but faces life imprisonment as the other option for an assassination attempt. Small wonder Hinckley will probably plead insanity! In a study done by Henry J. Steadman, director of the Special Projects Research Unit in New York, the average stay for a criminally "insane" offender is 22 weeks in a maximum security hospital and then 19 weeks in a minimum security situation—a total of 41 weeks. Compare this with the sentence for even a supposedly lesser crime, such as robbery—25 years imprisonment. In another study, the length of time was increased to about two and a half years before a criminally insane person was back on the streets, which is still considerably less than a prison term.

Now, of course, offenders such as Charles Manson, or "Son of Sam," would never be returned to society so quickly because of the notoriety of their cases, but what about a supposed "no-name" such as Joseph Baldi? I had never heard of him; have any of you? Baldi was charged with the attempted murder of a police officer in Queens and pleaded incompetency to stand trial. He was hospitalized for four months, and, upon being released, proceeded to stab and kill four women within three months. This is where these cases begin affecting you and me; these victims could have been any one of us. If Baldi had been imprisoned for his original charge of attempted murder, he would never have been back out on the streets so quickly to kill again. Therefore, my findings showed that offenders successfully pleading insanity almost always are going to find themselves with a reduced sentence, thus beating the longer imprisonment term.

The second point of Jodie's speech compares the conditions of mental hospitals with those of prisons. She begins by suggesting that the audience might think that the person who receives the lesser term might have to put up with a worse environment. She responds to this thought in two ways: first, she compares hospitals and prisons in terms of escape possibility; and second, she compares the conditions of the two situations. She supports the escape comparison by referring to "studies" without specifying them by source, a weakness that runs throughout this speech. She gives specificity to the point through quotations about New York hospitals. Finally she uses statistics comparing how inmates in hospitals feel about their conditions compared with that of prisons. She then raises a question about the justice involved in the situation. She acknowledges as a kind of qualifier that not all hospitals have ideal conditions but that they are better than prisons. This acknowledgement helps establish that she is not painting a one-sided picture and is trying to be fair in her comparison. This second point of Jodie's speech is not an "impelling force" for being concerned about the problem, as is the first point. After all, that conditions in hospitals are reasonably desirable is no cause in and of itself for concern. It does serve the purpose, however, of giving greater impact to the problem by establishing that the person who successfully pleads insanity gains in all respects.

Now you might think that the person who spends a lesser amount of time would spend it in a worse environment, a fact which might counteract the advantage of the insanity plea; so let's look at the conditions of the hospitals versus the conditions of the prisons. First of all, studies have shown that if the person is interested in escaping he stands a better chance in a mental institution than in a prison, for authorities adopt the attitude of, "After all, the person is crazy, what can we expect?" A *New York Times* article claims concerning New York hospitals, "There are just as many ways of going out as coming in."

As for the conditions themselves, a study of the various mental hospitals in New York described one as ". . . clear and bright. We were impressed with the freshness and all the space. One of the inmates came running up to me saying he'd rather spend his time here than in prison. Then he went off, dancing and snapping his fingers." Forty-eight percent of the inmates in various hospitals described the conditions as "good" and 82 percent said they'd rather be there than in jail. Even in Matteawan, a maximum security hospital described as "cold and stifled," 75 percent said they'd rather be there than in prison.

Why is it that our justice system advocates sending people who have broken the law and committed atrocious crimes to places they *want* to go? Is this any kind of penalty? Clearly, not all hospitals have ideal conditions and some are downright terrible, but the majority are far better than the criminal should be going to; some are even better than the homes they've come from.

Jodie introduces her third point by stating it explicitly and then raising two thought-provoking questions about it. She turns immediately to the District Attorney's records in three New York boroughs to support her point that in most cases criminals sent to mental hospitals are never prosecuted for their crimes. She employs *statistics* to show that of those who are returned to stand trial only a few are sentenced to additional prison terms. The speaker at this point skillfully anticipates a question the average listener might be raising at this time: "Yes, but is there any reason why those who plead insanity should be brought to trial at the end of their treatment. What happens to them? Do they commit further crimes?" Jodie responds to this thought with statistics: "Forty-five percent are arrested again within eighteen months" of their release—and curiously enough, 60 percent of those are returned to mental institutions. The heavy reliance upon percentages here seems to be essential, because most of us would want factual data as to what happens to these "mental patients" upon their release.

Jodie concludes this point by acknowledging that the Michigan and Indiana courts have found at least a partial solution. In these two states an "insane but guilty" verdict is given; this means that after treatment for mental illness the criminal is brought to trial for the original crime. She ends the point with the thought that unless all of our courts use a more informed approach the problem will continue to plague us.

Still, we must look at what happens to the person hospitalized after treatment. Does he go to court now that he's competent to stand trial? Is he released and metamorphosed into a model citizen? In most cases the answer is a strong "No" to both these questions.

According to the District Attorney's records in three New York boroughs, two thirds of the criminals sent to mental hospitals are never prosecuted. Of those who are returned to stand trial, only 27 percent are sentenced to additional time. That means that not even 9 percent of the criminals sent to mental institutions are ever sent to prison for their crime! Yet the statistics show that those very same people who are released come back again and again to the bar of justice, after committing more crimes, thus repeating the endless cycle. Forty-five percent are arrested again within eighteen months, which is three times higher than the general criminal population, and 60 percent of those are returned to mental institutions.

The situation is somewhat better in the states of Michigan and Indiana where courts are using the "insane but guilty" verdict. This means that persons claiming mental illness will be treated in confinement until able to stand trial for their original crime, with the treatment being considered part of their sentence. In other words, if Hinckley pleads guilty, he would be treated in a hospital until able to stand trial for his crime of attempting to assassinate President Reagan. Certainly this approach is far more enlightened than what is currently general practice.

The next section serves as a *summary* and *transition.* Jodie tells her audience that her original question has been answered: criminals do use the insanity plea to "beat their raps." She then restates the three points that she hopes have been established with her listeners.

The evidence my research turned up just amazed me, and I hope you are horrified along with me. This is what happens to the multitudes who commit a major crime and plead insanity that you read about in the papers. My original question of whether or not they beat their raps seems to be answered in the affirmative. Their hospital sentences are shorter, they're in better environments, and upon being released from treatment are free to attack some innocent victim again, perhaps you or me.

Jodie's speech follows a classical arrangement format. She begins with an attention-getting introduction, narrates the facts, forecasts her development, confirms her thesis with argument and evidence, refutes possible opposing arguments, and ends with a conclusion. Jodie's refutation is brief, but she apparently feels that certain issues have enough possible prominence that she must deal with them. She doesn't actually refute the first point of whether or not "beating the rap" saves taxpayers' dollars. She simply states that she would be willing to pay more. It would have been useful if she had sought to determine if imprisonment actually costs more than hospitalization. She handles the second point better. She supports her refutation with statistics showing that hospitalization does not diminish subsequent criminal careers more effectively than does imprisonment.

Although I find it hard to believe, arguments have been given in favor of this system of "beating the rap." One such argument is that fewer cases are heard in the courts, thus saving taxpayers' dollars. I, for one, am more than willing to pay more for my protection, as well as seeing to it that criminals are justly punished for the crimes they commit. A second argument is that hospitalization diminishes subsequent criminal careers by not allowing extensive contact with other criminals. There are several inherent problems in this theory, one being that the statistics show otherwise. As I've already said, of those released from mental hospitals, 45 percent commit another crime within eighteen months, which is three times greater than those released from prison. Secondly, if that is the reasoning we are to follow—namely, that criminals beget criminals, then wouldn't it be just as undesirable to put them with other truly mentally ill people? Following that theory, we would have more insane people on our hands! It seems the best solution would be to leave them in society where they might be positively influenced by the law abiding citizens!

The Conclusion

Jodie initiates her conclusion by referring back to Joseph Baldi as personification of the problem. Of course, mentioning someone by name makes the problem seem more real than a general reference to people who plead insanity. She then flatly states, "Something must be done." Lest some members of the audience feel that she is advocating a return to barbaric and unusually cruel treatment of criminals, Jodie makes it clear that she is not opposed to psychiatric treatment—she simply wants to change the system so as to protect the innocent. She tries to involve the listener directly in the problem and ends by repeating the title of her speech, "Insane or Guilty," which she suggests could perhaps be changed to read, "Insane *but* Guilty." This technique gives the speech a strong ending note.

Clearly people such as Joseph Baldi should be imprisoned for their horrendous crimes rather than be allowed to "beat the rap" by pleading insanity. Something must be done. I am not in favor of "putting away" criminals in primitive prisons without chance of rehabilitation. I am not opposed to psychiatric treatment. I simply want to protect the innocent.

I don't know the exact solution to the problem. I'll leave that up to people who are more knowledgeable and have more experience with these matters than I. But I do feel that nothing will be done about the problem unless citizens such as you and I show some concern for it. It is society's right to have a person who is charged with a crime to be detained until able to lead a nonviolent life, one that will bring no harm to people, such as you and me, who have done him no harm—except perhaps in the long run if we allow him back on the streets to repeat his cycle of crime. "Insane or guilty?" Perhaps it doesn't have to be one or the other. Perhaps it can be "insane *but* guilty."

Criteria for Your Problem Speech

1. Is the problem clearly identified?

2. Is the nature of the problem explored effectively?

3. Is the problem of sufficient scope and magnitude to warrant collective action?

4. Has the speaker related the problem to the specific audience?

5. Is the speaker's use of evidence convincing?

6. Are constraining forces dealt with adequately?

7. Is the speaker's call for action effective?

EXAMPLE OF A PROBLEM-SOLUTION SPEECH

We have chosen a speech entitled "A Bill of Rights for the Severely Communicatively Disabled" given by Professor Russell J. Love as an example of a problem-solution speech.[1] Professor Love teaches in the Division of Hearing and Speech Sciences at the Vanderbilt University School of Medicine. He delivered this address at a Speech, Hearing, and Deafness Awareness Dinner, May 14, 1981. The fact that Professor Love was handicapped at birth by cerebral palsy, a condition that drew him to the field of speech pathology, audiology, and deafness, makes this speech especially compelling. Professor Love certainly is addressing his audience as a competent and credible observer of speech and hearing problems; he is a professional expert in the field and he himself has experienced the handicap and its accompanying problems that his speech discusses. His personal authenticity would seem to be great.

The Introduction

Professor Love begins his speech with a direct statement of the topic; he gives the listener his thesis in the first sentence. The rest of the opening paragraph consists of a forecast of how he is going to develop his speech.

My talk tonight is concerned with the rights of the handicapped—
particularly those people with severe communication disabilities. I
will be presenting what I call a bill of rights for the severely
communicatively disabled. But before I present this bill of rights to
you, I want to talk briefly about the whole notion of civil rights and
entitlement to human privileges as they apply to the disabled. The
idea of civil rights and entitlement is relatively new in the field of the
handicapped. We are all familiar with the civil rights movement for
blacks of the 1960s and '70s, but I'm not sure we all understand the
consequences of a civil rights movement for the handicapped.

Does it bother you that the speaker begins his speech without a
full introduction? Since the speech was given at a Speech, Hearing, and
Deafness Awareness Dinner, in all probability, an interest-provoking
introduction was unnecessary; the audience was already vitally concerned with the subject. Professor Love doubtlessly was aware of this,
and hence Professor Love moved directly into a discussion of the subject.
But what if this same speech were to be given to an audience without *a
priori* concern for the subject, would an introduction then prove useful?
As a class exercise, you may want to imagine adapting this speech to a
disinterested audience and prepare what you consider to be an appropriate introduction that would arouse interest and generate concern for
the subject.

The second part of the introduction is a personal narrative in
which the speaker reveals his handicap to the audience. Love's professional credentials were given to the audience by the person who introduced him prior to the speech; all that remained was to tell the listeners
of the "personal" credentials which his personal experience provided.
The final sentence of the personal narrative provides a transition to the
central thesis of civil rights for the handicapped and the problem phase
of the speech.

To indicate the newness of these ideas, let me put them in a time
perspective for you. If you will allow me, I will use a personal
timetable to make more concrete how really new the ideas are.
    I was born fifty years ago and was handicapped at birth by
cerebral palsy. Approximately thirty years ago I became acquainted
with the field of speech pathology, audiology, and deafness when I
entered a university speech clinic to receive therapy for my own
speech disorder. I became interested in the field of communication
disorders and earned my first professional degree twenty-five years
ago. I worked in the field for twenty years without hearing one single
word about civil rights for the handicapped.

The Body of the Speech

Love begins the problem phase of his speech by telling his audience about the attitudes people generally hold toward a handicapped person: They view it as "a personal tragedy rather than a legal rights problem," and although they usually feel sympathy and compassion toward such a person, they view the individual as inferior. Love then *compares* the plight of the handicapped with that of a minority group based on race or ethnicity. He suggests that in like manner stereotypical thinking about the handicapped produces prejudice and discrimination. It is this analogy that allows the speaker to make the leap from a physical handicap to a civil rights issue. Not only does the comparison provide extra understanding of the problem but it also gives legitimacy to the speaker's position.

It was a mere five years ago that I became acquainted with the concept of mandated rights and privileges for the disabled.

How did this new and powerful concept arise in the field of rehabilitation and special education for the handicapped? I think it is fair to say that the overwhelming attitude that most people held toward a handicap was that it was a personal tragedy rather than a legal rights problem. The typical responses that most nondisabled people felt toward the disabled were feelings of sympathy and compassion because of this personal tragedy. But many people have had mixed feelings toward the person with a disability. Although most people express sympathy and compassion, the handicapping condition also marks a disabled person as inferior and deviant in the eyes of many people. For these people, and it is a sizable number of our population, the disabled are a minority group similar to any ethnic or racial minority. As such, the disabled person is often seen in terms of stereotypes and frequently becomes the object of discrimination and prejudice because of apparent deviancy and supposed inferiority resulting from their disability. Consciously or unconsciously, the majority of the population treats them as a neglected, forgotten, and shunned subgroup in our society. They become split off from the mainstream of American life because of a series of barriers that exclude them from enjoying the rights and privileges that the nondisabled persons in our nation take for granted. Thus disability is more than personal tragedy; it is a civil rights problem. A major barrier facing the disabled of all categories is that they lack easy and convenient access to public buildings and transportation.

In the next section of his speech Professor Love dissects the problems the handicapped person encounters. In the first place, deaf or severely hard-of-hearing people find it difficult to operate in our society because we tend to give them few helpful visual signal systems. Fire warnings, for example, are almost always based upon sound systems. The speaker illustrates in various ways the point he is trying to develop. These examples tend to be startling because people who have use of all their faculties don't tend to think of these problems.

If you are deaf or severely hard-of-hearing, you do not always have appropriate visual displays of information that are equivalent alternates to information transmitted via public address systems in large public buildings such as hospitals, schools, and airports. In other words, deaf and hard-of-hearing persons often miss a crucial page or message on the public address system. Rarely do the deaf and hard-of-hearing find visual signal systems in hotel or motel rooms to alert them to fire or other emergencies. Manual interpreters for the deaf are provided for only a handful of meetings and conferences in large public buildings. We are beginning to see teletypewriters for the deaf in some offices, stores, and public buildings but there are too few of them to really relieve the frustration of the deaf person who must communicate his needs over long distances quickly.

Furthermore, churches, courtrooms, small hotels, motels, and meeting rooms often do not provide adequate public address systems for the laryngectomee who cannot increase the volume of the voice to communicate before an audience or in a crowd. In fact people with communication disorders are almost a hidden subgroup in the larger neglected minority of disabled persons.

For instance, the person in a wheelchair or on crutches, or the blind individual with a white cane may have a more visible handicap than the person with a communication disorder, but he or she fares only slightly better. People in wheelchairs or those who have orthopedic problems like myself still are overwhelmed by stairs and high curbs. To be sure, there are now curbcuts, ramps, special parking places, and elevators designed for the disabled, but they are scattered willy-nilly over the landscape in such a random fashion that they are usually more of an irritation than an aid for the handicapped person who must transverse a busy city to complete everyday errands. The movement for accessible mass transportation for the disabled in this country has come to a screeching halt lately because of budget constraints on transportation funding. In brief, architectural and transportation barriers, despite the Architectural Barriers Act of 1968, are still with us and there is currently little relief in sight for the disabled in this area.

The second dimension of the problem that communicatively handicapped people face is the difficulty of obtaining an equal and appropriate higher education. Although this barrier has received considerable attention in the courts, rulings have generally been conservative and not in favor of the deaf or handicapped in general. The speaker cites no specific examples of court rulings. We think that one or two citations would strengthen this point.

In 1976 Public Law 94-142 was enacted. The fundamental thrust of this law required public schools to provide an adequate educational base for the handicapped. The law intends that handicapped children be kept in their own homes, communities, and neighborhood schools whenever possible, and that alternative education programs be available to meet each individual's needs. However, the speaker suggests, there is a "strong move afoot in Washington to cut funds to programs supported by this legislation," and such action would make "gains in the movement of civil rights for the handicapped . . . more illusionary than real." The speaker is trying to establish the point that legal support for the handicapped, whatever there may be, is eroding, and that this returns the handicapped to a relatively primitive environment.

The handicapped, particularly the communicatively disabled, also face the barrier of discrimination in obtaining an equal and appropriate higher education. Despite the Rehabilitation Act of 1973 which compels colleges and universities receiving federal funds to make their educational programs accessible to the handicapped, very slow progress has been made. This particular barrier has received considerable attention in the courts and several cases concern deaf plaintiffs. Cases that have reached the U.S. Supreme Court have dealt with issues of deaf persons asking for university support of manual interpreters in the classroom or the rights of admission to certain professional programs despite the problem of deafness. The issues involved are, of course, complex and I will not detail them here, but I think it is fair to say that so far the rulings have been conservative and have not been in favor of the deaf or handicapped in general.

The passage of Public Law 94-142 assuring not only education but appropriate education for all handicapped children was emancipating federal legislation because it struck a blow at the discrimination and oppression that handicapped children faced under certain local school systems. The PL 94-142 and the Rehabilitation Act of 1973 established a basis in federal statutes for a systematic civil rights approach to the development and funding of educational programs for the handicapped rather than the unsystematic earlier approach which relied on sympathetic and compassionate appeals to local school systems for appropriate special education programs. Now there is a strong move afoot in Washington to cut funds to programs supported by this legislation. If you take these proposed budget cuts seriously, you might well wonder whether the recent and dramatic gains in the movement of civil rights for the handicapped are more illusionary than real.

The speaker at this point has tried to generate concern for the handicapped in two ways: First, by pointing to the extreme difficulty the handicapped have in functioning in our society, and second, that much of society tends to discriminate against them by viewing them as inferior deviates. Both situations should be strong impelling forces.

Professor Love now wants to narrow his speech to the real essence of his topic: the communicatively impaired. He suggests that statements of rights have been developed by advocates of various handicapped groups, but that no speech, hearing, or deaf specialist has ever presented "a bill of rights for the severely communicatively impaired." This is what he plans to do in the remainder of his speech. The next paragraph thus is essentially a transition from the problem phase to the solution phase of the speech. Professor Love's solution will consist of a Bill of Rights for the communicatively impaired.

Up to this point, I have talked about the civil rights movement for the handicapped as it applies to all disabled persons. Now I want to talk specifically about the severely communicatively disabled and their special rights. Recently advocates of special handicapped groups have developed statements of rights that apply to these special groups. As yet no speech, hearing, or deaf specialist that I know of has presented a bill of rights for the severely communicatively impaired that summarizes the humanistic concerns we might have about them. Our bill of rights is aimed at the practices of the individuals who help the communicatively impaired. As this group begins to realize that their clients are entitled to certain rights and are sometimes denied them, they will begin to scrutinize their own professional behaviors in terms of a civil rights viewpoint. Although our list of rights may not be complete or exhaustive, it is offered in the spirit of awakening the conscience of the professionals and the public to the issues of rights and justice for the communicatively disabled. I do want to acknowledge the major contribution of Dr. Wanda Webb, a colleague of mine at Vanderbilt University, for the development of the following bill of rights.

Professor Love's Bill of Rights consists of ten points. He clearly states each point and then briefly explains it. As you read each statement, and its accompanying explanation, ask yourself the following three questions: (1) Does this aspect of the Bill of Rights help to meet the need outlined in the problem phase of the speech? In other words, assess if the impelling forces Professor Love identifies can be eliminated by the ten points of his solution. (2) Is it workable? Does the speaker do anything to make you believe that each point of his plan is workable? (3) Is it beneficial? Will each point of the plan significantly assist the communicatively handicapped in coping with their environment?

A Bill of Rights for the Severely Communicatively Disabled

1. *The right to a trial at treatment despite the severity of the communicative impairment.*

Very frequently communication specialists use diagnostic classifications such as extreme severity or irreversibility as indicators that therapeutic trials are unnecessary and useless. I would maintain that no individual possesses behavior that cannot be changed. It is important to seek out these modifiable behaviors and channel them toward some type of communicative system, simple and primitive though it may be. Often small changes in an individual's ability to communicate can significantly enhance adjustment to the world.

2. *The right to select a means of communication, vocal or nonvocal.*

Recently communication specialists have adopted the philosophy that communication is their goal, rather than the development of spoken language. This has resulted in the development of nonvocal communication devices such as conversation boards, electronic instrumentation, and secondary language systems, like sign language and Bliss symbols. Communication has been made possible for severely involved individuals where it was not possible in the past. The advent of new technology brings with it a need to consider the right of the individual in using technical advances. First, the disabled individual must be made aware of these devices so that he is not limited only to the option of spoken language for communication. Second, the disabled individual must be involved in the decision-making process and selection of the type of nonvocal communication system that must be mastered. We have observed that as communication specialists become familiar with these nonoral techniques, they often tend to make value judgments about them and are inclined to decide which nonvocal method is best for the client without extensive consultation of clients and their families. Caution must be taken to individualize these nonvocal techniques to meet the psychological and environmental needs of each client.

3. *The right to comprehensive evaluation by several professionals if necessary.*

Although it is common practice to employ team evaluations or require multidisciplinary evaluation for individuals with severe communication disorders, on occasion the complexities of diagnosis are missed and clients are led to believe that a single diagnostic approach has solved their problems and more comprehensive evaluation should not be sought. At times communication specialists fail to recognize the changing nature of the problems with which they are confronted and do not institute further referral for comprehensive evaluation when necessary. We would argue that the client should be entitled to the right of comprehensive evaluation at all times.

4. *The right to a quality and equal education even though the medium of aural and oral communication is impaired.*

The right to equal education is now, of course, insured by public law. However, we are still concerned about barriers of attitude in education. Many classroom teachers, we believe, feel that an extremely important part of education is instructional exchange through spoken language. The teacher who is not familiar with the child's hearing loss or expressive speech disorder is likely to slight this child, and not allow him to demonstrate this knowledge through nonconventional means. We must insure that the burden for providing a means of communication in the classroom is on the teacher, the communication specialist, and the school administration, *not* upon the disabled child.

5. *The right to financial assistance if necessary for support of speech, language, and hearing services.*

Although several agencies in our society support speech and hearing services for the communicatively disabled, there always remain needy individuals who do not meet the specific requirements of these agencies. It is becoming increasingly apparent that the cost of certain health care services cannot always be solely borne by the individual. The rights of the severely communicatively disabled to treatment must not be denied on budgetary grounds.

6. *The right to a manual interpreter when needed.*

Clearly there must be an acceleration in providing manual interpreter services for the deaf. These services currently are available in most large and moderately large urban communities, but they are not always available in smaller communities. We would encourage wider use of signing by interpreters and captioning on major television networks at prime viewing times. The limited examples of signing and captioning on television suggests that these would be acceptable and nonintrusive to the normal hearing viewer.

7. *The right to a second opinion about the nature of the communication problem.*

This right should be obvious, but several factors limit its full exercise. Although the number of professionals in the field of communication disorders is increasing, many clients are in situations where seeking a second opinion from another communication specialist is difficult. This may be due to a limited number of communication specialists in a given locale or to problems of transportation. Clients are often apprehensive and unsure about the need for seeking further opinions about the management of their communication problems. If a client is dissatisfied, he often seeks an opinion of a professional in a related discipline such as medicine or psychology rather than another communication specialist. A member of a related discipline may or may not be sufficiently knowledgeable about a given communication problem to give a judicial opinion. The right to a second opinion is as important in communication disorders as it is in medicine.

8. *The right to supportive therapy even though maximum progress has been made.*

Since communication is such a vital aspect of living, a significant communicative disorder or defect leaves the individual isolated and alienated. In some cases communication has been improved by therapy or education, but the communication attempts may remain ineffective or minimally effective. We believe that instead of dismissing such a client from therapy with the comment that there is poor prognosis for further recovery, the communication specialist must shoulder the burden of helping the client to accept his or her limitations and must also work with the family to structure the environment to enable as effective communication as possible.

Another aspect of this issue is the need for appropriate follow-up after maximum progress has been made. All clients do not maintain maximum levels of performance; regressions may occur after initial termination. We believe that part of supportive therapy involves periodic recall of clients with severe problems to determine if such regression has taken place.

9. *The right to gainful employment despite the communication disability.*

We fully realize that many occupations demand intelligible communication with others. Many employers, however, do not realize that the intelligibility of speech need not be perfect to be functional and meaningful. We urge reasonable accommodation for individuals who have communication disorders in which intelligibility is less than ideal. It may be the responsibility of the communication specialist to outline for the employer the limitations resulting from the communication disorder and the potentialities for successful communication within the work setting.

10. *The right to a normal life-style with counseling support as needed.*

We need not detail the effects on emotional health of a communication disorder in as complex and highly verbal a society as ours. Certainly the psychological effects often make it difficult for the severely communicatively disordered individual to maintain a normal life-style. The aphasic, the severely handicapped cerebral palsied, the mentally retarded, the deaf individual, as well as others, often find it difficult to achieve life-styles which provide them with the quality of life that members of our society have come to expect. Provision must be made for establishing long-term care for severely involved individuals. Involvement in long-term planning above and beyond the communication disorder is part of the responsibility of the communication specialist in order to insure an adequate quality of life-style for the client. Periodic professional counseling may be needed when the communicatively handicapped meet life crises. The communication specialist should be instrumental in guiding the individual to marital, family, vocational, psychological, or psychiatric counseling when needed.

The Conclusion

Having explained his Bill of Rights, Professor Love directly signals his audience that he is moving into his conclusion: "In conclusion, I hope I have sensitized you . . ." The conclusion has two themes: First, it makes a closing appeal in behalf of the handicapped, and second, it asks listeners to contact their senators and congressmen "to resist budget cuts in Public Law 94-142 and the Rehabilitation Act of 1973." Love ends his speech on an upbeat when he says: "We recently gained a vision of what the world might become for the disabled. Now that we have such a vision we must not allow it to be clouded by darkness." Good speakers strive to end their addresses on a strong and memorable ending note. We think that Professor Love does this quite effectively.

In conclusion, I hope I have sensitized you to some of the special rights of the communicatively impaired, but more important, I hope that I have alerted you to the need for a civil rights viewpoint in dealing with the problems of disabling conditions. I believe it important that we do not focus too narrowly on the issues of speech, hearing, and deafness but that we form coalitions with other handicapped groups to keep the rights movement alive. Many of us concerned about handicapped rights have felt that in the past five or so years we have made significant strides in creating a new beginning for the disabled. However, recent actions in Washington have convinced me that we still have a long, hard battle before us.

I believe that it is totally inexcusable and unacceptable to deny civil and legal rights to the handicapped on the grounds that the federal budget is currently too fat. In essence this is to say that a disabled person cannot be a first-class citizen in our country, with all the rights and privileges of a nondisabled person, because it is just too expensive to insure justice and equality under the law. I urge you to contact your senators and congressmen to resist budget cuts in Public Law 94-142 and the Rehabilitation Act of 1973. We cannot allow ourselves to assume the inferior and neglected minority status we are just beginning to shed. We recently gained a vision of what the world might become for the disabled. Now that we have such a vision we must not allow it to be clouded by darkness.

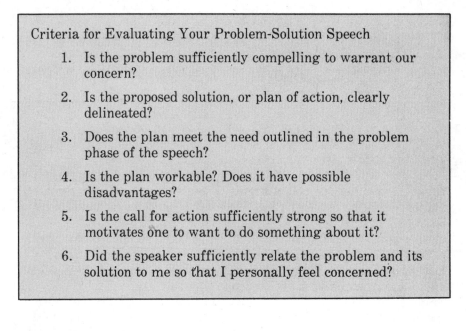

Criteria for Evaluating Your Problem-Solution Speech

1. Is the problem sufficiently compelling to warrant our concern?

2. Is the proposed solution, or plan of action, clearly delineated?

3. Does the plan meet the need outlined in the problem phase of the speech?

4. Is the plan workable? Does it have possible disadvantages?

5. Is the call for action sufficiently strong so that it motivates one to want to do something about it?

6. Did the speaker sufficiently relate the problem and its solution to me so that I personally feel concerned?

SUMMARY

In this chapter we have examined two examples of persuasive presentations: one involving awareness of and concern for a problem, and the second identifying a problem and presenting a workable solution. It is hoped that our critiques of these speeches will help you as you prepare your persuasive speeches. We think that the example speeches we have analyzed in this chapter should help clarify the concepts that we have presented in the previous chapter.

You are now ready to integrate the concepts emphasized through this book and to prepare to help an audience reach a decision concerning a common problem. One way to summarize the major thesis of this chapter, and of the entire book, is: "*You* are the message." In the speeches by Jodie Wallace and Professor Russell Love, the content and substance of the speeches came from their thinking and the feelings that they were willing to share. The content and delivery cannot be separated. Your concern for problems and willingness to offer solutions must come from your experiences, knowledge, reflection, and capacities to verbalize. Delivery is then the framing of your thinking into words.

LEARNING EXPERIENCES

Objectives

After studying this chapter, you should be able to *do* the following:

1. Critique the efforts of others as they present problem speeches.

2. Prepare and present a speech on a problem that greatly concerns you.
3. Analyze a speech that fits a problem-solution model.
4. Prepare and present a problem-solution speech based upon careful analysis and preparation.

Exercises

1. Present a five- to eight-minute speech alleging the existence of a problem.
2. Elicit and provide feedback on the speeches in your class.
3. Present a ten-minute problem-solution speech exemplifying the analysis presented in Chapter 12. This speech should be the culmination of your best efforts to help your classmates make a decision.
4. Evaluate your efforts based upon feedback given by your instructor and classmates. What changes or improvements would you make if you were to give the speech again?

NOTES

[1]"A Bill of Rights for the Severely Communicatively Disabled" by Russell J. Love. Given at a Speech, Hearing, and Deafness Awareness Dinner, May 14, 1981. Reprinted by permission of Russell J. Love.

Speeches for Study and Analysis

The acquisition of public speaking skills is best achieved through three complementary lines of study: *theory,* from which you gain a basic understanding of communication; *example,* through which you evaluate the theory in light of real and varied instances of public communication; and *practice,* in which you apply communication principles to the actual creation of speeches. In the previous sections of this textbook you learned the theory, analyzed the examples, and participated in the practice. These experiences will prepare you for the many varied opportunities you will have to speak in public.

Another important aspect of this course is the capacity to be an intelligent, responsible consumer of public speeches. You will listen to far more speeches than you will deliver, so learn to apply the principles and guidelines you have learned to the messages you will hear.

In many ways, the following three speeches exemplify responsible and effective public speaking. Study and evaluate them in terms of the knowledge of public speaking that you have gained. Think through the communicative choices made by these speakers. They will help you make your own.

CULTURE UNDER CANVAS

E. C. Buehler

This is a lecture given by Professor Emeritus Ezra Christian
Buehler on July 16, 1969, at South Dakota State University, Brookings,
South Dakota. The occasion is a program of cultural enrichment. On
May 13, 1982 Buehler celebrated his eighty-eighth birthday.

Thank you, Bob Oliver, for those kind, gracious remarks that you have made
about me. I feel honored indeed to be on the same program with Dr. Robert Oliver.
In a seminar at the University of Kansas in the fall semester, we took a private poll
as to who were the outstanding men in our profession, and Robert Oliver was in
the top ten. I am deeply pleased, of course, to be up here in South Dakota, this
land where your state is famous for its stone faces and for Crazy Horse and Sitting
Bull. You know that my adopted state and your state would be adjoining neighbors if it hadn't been for my native state, Nebraska, that got in between us. Well I
am happy to report that the sunflowers of Kansas are blowing kisses across the
badlands of Nebraska to you coyotes up here in South Dakota. Yes, I know, I too
have wondered at times what good can come from Kansas, for isn't that the state
where they have more political crackpots and more grasshoppers and jack-
rabbits than any state in the union? Well, it isn't all bad down there in this land of
the Wizard of Oz, the land of cyclones and dust storms. For out of all this muck and
turmoil come beautiful women, for Kansas leads the nation in producing winners
in the Miss America contest. I thought I'd better mention this so you wouldn't get
the impression that we are all wind down there. Of course I feel all set to be called
off the bench. I am, I suppose, an experienced benchwarmer, and I feel proud to
get out here and feel the plains. /1

      I feel lucky that I was assigned to speak on a position where I feel at
home, the chautauqua, for the chautauqua really means a lot to me. The
chautauqua played a unique role in my life and has left a marked impression upon
me. This is where I acquired a nickname, "Bill," and of course this name really
became my real name among colleagues and friends. My wife always calls me Bill
except once in a while when there's some crisis or some difficulty, when she will
say, "Now listen, Ezra Christian . . ." But it was the chautauqua that really
influenced me to move toward college and get a college education, and later it
was a major influence that led me finally into the field of teaching speech. It was
my good fortune in my youth to hear many famous men from the public platform. I
became an ardent fan of public speakers of both lyceum and chautauqua. I think I
was a very serious-minded lad, and somehow or another I preferred oratory to
some of the famous bands and symphony orchestras. I remember walking out on
John Philip Sousa, so I would have enough energy and strength to listen to a
lecture later on in the program. /2

      Let's examine the anatomy of the chautauqua. Let's take a look at this
American phenomenon on the last frontier. Let's ask some questions. First, what
is this thing called chautauqua? Originally the name was spelled with a capital
letter, referring to a lake 30 miles long and five to eight miles wide in New York
about 75 miles south of Niagara Falls. But spelled with a small letter, it has four
parts to its meaning: an idea, an institution, a movement, a system. It was born

with the idea of a Methodist minister who thought it would be a good thing to have a summer camp meeting of two weeks for Sunday School workers. Now this is not to be confused with an evangelistic crusade. The idea was very successful and was very popular; 25 states and seven foreign countries responded. And in a short time it grew to be a program that included many other courses and covered eight weeks. In a sense it became a kind of liberal arts college in the summer and followed through with courses of study during the winter. Thomas Edison and Albert Hubbard were among those who got diplomas, and over 8,000 people received these certificates and diplomas of recognition. It was so well-established that the New York legislature gave it the dignity of an institution, and it recognized by legislative act that it should be governed by a board of trustees of twenty-four members who served without pay.   /3

Now the movement part of the definition covers a half century: 1874 to 1924. It includes both the stationary or independent chautauqua, which was usually around a lake, a grove of trees, or a stream, and this eventually spread to 500 towns and communities all the way from New York to Oregon. And it also includes the traveling chautauqua, which ultimately reached 12,000 communities, serving perhaps 35 million people—two-fifths of the adult population of the United States.   /4

The system refers to the tent chautauqua or the circuit chautauqua, which was the traveling chautauqua. The chautauqua was as American as baseball and apple pie and flourished primarily among the rural areas of the Midwest and the western states.   /5

Second, let's ask how come the chautauqua came into being. Well, there was hunger and starvation across the land. Oh, not the kind the newspapers and politicians holler about today, but people were looking for something to feed their minds and their souls. They yearned for something outside of themselves, something to latch onto to improve their lot in life. They felt they were missing something. They felt a bit gypped or underprivileged in matters of education, social belonging and gracious living. In my farm community of 44 families, I could point to only one person who had more than an eighth-grade education, and he was the preacher. The Bible and the Sears Roebuck catalog were the chief books in the home library, and of course you know the Sears Roebuck catalog served many purposes. A train ride was a rare experience and parlor entertainment consisted largely of a family album, familiar views, and victrola records. Telephones were still a novelty; inside plumbing was a rare luxury even in town. No wonder the crowds gathered at the railroad station when the trains came in. No wonder the girls, in the words of Carl Sandburg "leaned their heads against the bars and wondered where the trains ran to." Because there might be a place where there is romance and real dreams that never go smash. As Victor Hugo once wrote, "Greater than an army is an idea whose time has come." The time was ripe for the coming of the chautauqua.   /6

Then let us ask a third question: What did the chautauqua have to offer? Well, here are some of its claims. It claimed that it would build a cooperating community spirit and remove some of the barriers of politics and church denominationalism. It claimed to bring entertainment of a better sort—better than that offered by the carnival and the circus. It claimed its major function was educational, to spread information, to challenge thought, and to inspire better living. And it claimed to give children guidance and experience in playground recreation and creative expression. Now it fulfilled most of these claims by offering a balanced program of music, theatre, and lectures. The backbone of the chautauqua was the lecture, and there were three kinds: the lecture to challenge thought, the lecture to inform, and the lecture to inspire. And, yes, the lecture to inspire was dominant—it was the most sure-fire. These programs were interspersed with music, plays, chalk-talks, magic, etcetera. /7

But to get the sweep and the feel of the chautauqua one must look at the vacant lot on the edge of town where the tall weeds are—this spot of wilderness. It has just been mowed the day before and cleared of all the boxes and debris. And then on that next morning when the stores begin to open you could hear the voices saying, "Here comes the chautauqua!" The big gray wagon loaded with balls of canvas, stakes, ropes, and tools rolled up the street and out on the chautauqua grounds, and materials are scattered in measured spots forming a big oval where the tent will stand. Crew-boys, the platform superintendent, local helpers came to hoist the center poles like masts on a ship. Guy ropes, pulleys, anchor stakes make up the skeleton rigging. Now all hands turn to unfolding the large balls of canvas and laying them out to match so that they can be laced, hooked, and snapped together into one huge piece that will cover 2,000 people. And now with the blocks and tackle and a special team of strong men, the great tent is raised at the center poles to form the kind of A-shaped roof, and the few anchor ropes and the eave poles are adjusted. In a matter of a few minutes we can say, "Ah, there she stands—the majestic temple of joy and learning!" And now all is ready for the seats, and this takes many more hours. The platform, the piano, and the wiring—this is all a good day's work with no time out for lunch. /8

In the next five or six days trains will be bringing in talent, and these talented people have an aura of glamor. They're always fine looking, well-dressed, and well-mannered people. There will be the musicians, the actors, the Alpine Yodelers, the jubilee singers, the cartoonists, the magicians, and the platform orators. And, yes, there may be some very prominent people: Mme. Schumann-Heinck, William Jennings Bryan, William Howard Taft, Joe Cannon, Catherine Ridgeway, who was a very famous reader. All this gives promise to bring cheer to many a nook and corner of farm homes and stores around Main Street. The image of the chautauqua was good. The image was a success. Even the struggling carnivals latched onto this image by calling their own show the Chautauqua Carnival. At a town in Texas sponsoring a poultry show they were a little skeptical about its success, so they advertised, "Come to the poultry chautauqua." /9

Now the fourth question: How did it work and what made it go? For me, this is still a source of mystery and wonderment. To me it still stands as a miracle. The chautauqua business called for men and women of vision, of faith, of courage, of initiative, of endless patience, and a lot of hard labor and great endurance. It certainly was no place for the lazy, and no place for the weak or faint-hearted. And at the top of the structure was the owner. He was the chief executive who furnished the money; he risked his fortune; he hired the talent; he arranged and set up the program and ran the home office. There were only a dozen to 20 of these in the entire nation. The owner hired and trained the circuit manager, who was his key man, and this man was in charge of operations of a territory that usually covered 75 to 100 towns. The Redpath Horner chautauquas had three of these managers. The circuit managers hired the traveling superintendent, the crew, and the advance men, and the key man in this line-up was the superintendent or the local platform manager. He had to be a tough top sergeant, a diplomat, a salesman; he had to be a public relations expert and general trouble-shooter. His big job was, of course, to get the iron-clad contract for next year, and he was hired and fired largely on that basis. He was expected to get ninety percent of the towns he served to renew the contract for next year. He also introduced the talent, arranged their travel schedule, and their hotel accommodations. The crew was made up of some husky, athletic college boys, not the Phi Beta Kappas. And then there was the junior supervisor called the "chautauqua girl," who was usually 30 or 40 years old. The crew had charge of ticket-selling, lighting the tents, seating, and all the equipment usually valued at about $20,000. Now the advance men were the loners. They came into the town two weeks before the chautauqua opened and shored up the publicity and the season ticket sale. Such is a brief sketch of the capital, the executive officers, the organizational structure, and the promotional and chore people. /10

Now, what were some of the trials and tribulations of the crew and talent? We must remember that there was an unwritten law that everybody lived by. This law read: "The show must go on. This is show business." The talent faced a new town every day and the crew a new town every week. And don't forget that these were the "good ole days." There was no air conditioning. The big tent in the afternoons got awfully hot, and so did the hotels and the restaurants. A hotel toilet and bath was a rare luxury, and the train accommodations along the prairie towns were awful. Four or five hours of sleep in a bed was a blessed experience, and the biggest headache of all, of course, was transportation. And next to transportation were the rain storms and the wind storms that threatened to blow the tent into shreds. And of course the mosquitoes and the flies were everywhere, and stomach upsets were very common. But the show must go on! Well, there was a daring experience of a superintendent that I knew—this was in Mexico. He couldn't get the local agent to flag the 2:00 a.m. mail train to make the only possible connection for the evening's talent people to get to the next place in western Oklahoma. So he tried the Mission Impossible. He bought a big flashlight, got the talent people down around the railroad station with all the baggage, and in more or less the manner of a train robbery he flagged the train. And this he did six nights in a row. /11

And there was William Jennings Bryan who had to go by auto over dirt roads for 80 miles when the floods washed out the tracks of the train that he was to ride. Arrangements had been made for driving two cars, one as a spare, to complete the mission of the railroad. William Jennings Bryan, being such a leading figure, sparked the idea of making this a party which created a caravan of five automobiles. Away they went on the great tour of 80 miles. But every car either broke down or got stuck in the mud except one, and Bryan had to be shifted from car to car, to the one that was still left. They finally made it, but it was 10:30 p.m. instead of 8:00! But there was the audience, cheering on his arrival. And on another occasion Bryan was on a train headed for Sioux Falls, 103 miles away. Thirty miles out the car on his own train ran off the track, and Bryan sent a telegram asking for a fast automobile to pick him up. But the car got stuck on the wagon roads, and they finally got a farmer out of bed to pull them out. Later the car got lost on the road and lost some more time, but they finally got to their destination—12:10 midnight! And the audience was still there and shouting. Bryan closed that speech at 2:08 a.m. /12

And there's the case of the Sunflower Girls from the state of Kansas. The trio gave a show one evening in Texas. This was in the month of May. They had to drive a Ford 150 miles to Amarillo to catch a train at 3:00 in the morning. They were warned the driver often fell asleep, but these girls made up their minds they would keep him awake with entertainment and questions and prod him along. Nobody was worried that he'd run off the road or hit another car or an abutment of a culvert. They were worried he might hit a cow, for three-fourths of the journey was over the open prairie.   /13

Now next to the transportation was the headache of winds and storms. One girl violinist was in three tent blow-downs in one season. She didn't worry about life and limb; she worried about her precious violin. And she always managed to duck under the grand piano. But there were other casualties from exhaustion. These were more numerous than the casualties from storms. Talent could not stand the pace and heat. Joe Cannon, Speaker of the House, collapsed while speaking in Winfield, Kansas, on July 16, 1910. Colonel Cooper, a veteran of the platform, died from exhaustion while lecturing in Bloomington, Illinois, and several other deaths were caused by sheer drain of physical strength. Lecturing on the chautauqua platform was indeed an occupational hazard.   /14

Now, question six: What brought on the rapid decline of the chautauqua? What made it fall apart like the one-horse shay? The rapid decline of the chautauqua was due to many things that seemed to converge almost at the same time. First, there were better roads, and concurrently, that meant more automobiles and better automobiles. Concurrently, the movies were coming along with their spectacular pictures—"Ben Hur," "The Birth of a Nation." And then there was the rapid growth of the civic clubs. The community itself had the thing that discouraged the chautauquas, because of the growth of the Rotary Club, the Kiwanis Club, and the Lions Club. These clubs pulled in a lot of talent from outside and therefore the community didn't need the programs that they used to have. And then came, of course, the radio with its Amos 'n Andy and the silly little shows in the afternoon. But the clincher that ruined the chautauqua movement was the 10 percent amusement tax. This hurt. Local people felt that the chautauqua was educational; that's what they were told. It was not for amusement. And therefore the local supporters soured on the chautauqua managers and blamed them rather than the government for letting this happen.   /15

The final question: What were the markings upon our culture? What were the fruits of this heritage of the last frontier? Well, first, it was a force in awakening a desire for better education. It was a catalyst for the introduction and expansion of correspondence courses, of study courses by mail, and of the university extension programs. The University of Chicago almost lifted bodily the correspondence courses of study that were set up in Chautauqua, New York, and the University of Chicago has long been the center of correspondence study courses. And for one whole decade at the university where I taught in Lawrence, Kansas, there were more students enrolled in correspondence study than there were in the regular university.   /16

Second, it was a significant pioneer force for the development of recreational services for the youth. It pointed the way for the supervised playgrounds and for recreational centers, and it was a great boost to the Boy Scout movement and Campfire Girls activities. And this, I think, is of some interest to theatre people—the chautauqua took the sin out of the theatre. The theatre in those days was really an object of suspect. The theatre was looked upon as the invention of the devil with its painted women who showed their ankles and occasionally their knees, and the men actors were kind of strange. People would say, what a shame that these able-bodied men aren't working in field and factory. But the plays like "Turn to the Right," "The Shepherd of the Hills," and "A Man from Home" had strong moral overtones. And the Benn Greek Players and the Caldron Players who played Shakespeare did much to bring Shakespeare to the hinterland. The chautauqua was a spawning ground for meaningful self-expression by means of the spoken word. The chautauqua provided a favorable climate for the rise and development of skills that apply to public address, rhetoric, and theatre arts. It offered root concepts for the germination and growth of those disciplines which found their way into the college classrooms. Theatre, oral interpretation, and rhetoric, with all their ramifications, found that the chautauqua not only helped to open the door to bring speech as an academic discipline to the colleges, it helped to keep it there. And I suspect that for a quarter of a century, from 1930 to 1955, more than half of the source materials for M.A. and Ph.D. theses were devoted to men and women who won distinction on the lyceum and chautauqua platform.   /17

Finally, the chautauqua and lyceum did much to pave the way for the liberal and progressive legislative reforms. Here many concepts were germinated and cultivated for the rise of the social conscience that became manifest in the twentieth century—women's suffrage, income tax, anti-trust laws, child labor laws, and other laws for labor welfare, Philippine independence, control of public utilities and railroads. The chautauqua always had an open season for anyone who wanted to take pot shots at Wall Street. And the chautauqua did much to cut down the power of Wall Street and give the common man a better chance. And although science and machines have altered the rise of the last frontier in the context of material things, it was the last frontier that left us the heritage of social and human values preserved by many laws which enrich our culture in this day of jet sets, protest marches, and moon rockets.   /18

THE SPEAKER AND THE GHOST
The Speaker Is the Speech

Carolyn Lomax-Cooke,
Communications Specialist, Cities Service Company

Delivered to the Tulsa Chapter of the International Association of
Business Communicators, Tulsa, Oklahoma, October 20, 1981

First of all, I must confess that I'd like to ask all of the speechwriters in the audience to get up and leave. The number one rule of speechmaking is this: Never speak to your professional peers. It scares you to death! That's why economists are in such demand as speakers. No one understands economics, so economists feel very comfortable talking to everyone. They even feel comfortable talking to each other because they all disagree. /1

Actually, we are all speechmakers—and we all practice our speeches in our imaginations before we actually deliver them to our husbands, wives, and children. My mother was the first speechmaker that I really noticed. Did you ever notice how mothers deliver speeches to their children? I think that they all secretly long for a podium. My mother's first speech was the one about my face. (Mothers have a way of getting personal in their speeches right away.) She would say, "Look at that expression on your face. Do you want your face to freeze into that expression? Go look in the mirror—you're about to step on your lip." Then came the speech about how faces are a reflection of the person's spirit. I'm sure your mothers had speeches, too. And those speeches were delivered with such frequency and conviction that you remember them.   /2

But how many other speeches do you remember? How many other speeches would you actually consider "good"? Tonight I want to talk candidly about what makes a good speech, a good speaker, and a good speechwriter. Please notice that I am emphasizing "good" in each instance. We have all heard unimpressive speeches. But what we want to look at tonight is that special quality that makes a speech memorable.   /3

My message is very simple—for the good speech, the good speaker, and the good speechwriter all center around one understanding of the speech occasion. And that understanding is this: the speaker IS the speech. The man IS the message. The woman IS her words. If the speaker and the speechwriter understand this fundamental of a good speech, all will go well. If the partners fail at this point, so will the speech.   /4

But what do I mean—the speaker IS the speech? I mean that the listener cannot separate the content of the message from the character of the speaker. During a speech, the message itself and the vehicle through which it is delivered (the speaker) are so integrated that when the audience evaluates one, it automatically evaluates the other. The speaker and the speech are one and the same. /5

Communications professors get fancy about theory at this point. They say that speeches appeal on three levels. One level is source credibility, called

"The Speaker and the Ghost" by Carolyn Lomax-Cooke from *Vital Speeches of the Day* (Vol. XLVIII, No. 4, December 1, 1981). Reprinted by permission of *Vital Speeches of the Day*.

"ethos." Another is the emotional appeal of the speech, called "pathos." Third is the so-called "logos" level, which relates to the rational, factual appeal of the speech. But when you subtract the Greek from this theory, you will find that professors are saying some very simple things about the human nature involved in listening to a speech. The listener asks three questions as he listens to a speechmaker. He asks: "Is this speaker reliable? Do I like him? Can I trust his facts?" And whether the speaker likes it or not, these questions will be answered through his own personality and character as he delivers the speech—not through statistics, charts, or intricate explanations of technical data. /6

Since the audience responds to personality and character, the good speaker will take care that the speech truly reveals his character. Personality, life, conviction, excitement, or despair—these must shine through the speech as a reflection of the speaker. The audience recognizes such honesty and always responds to personal stories, anecdotes about the speaker's family, or a reference to a book that the speaker has read. Because let's face it, the audience came to hear the speaker—not to watch a human body mouth the words of a written treatise. /7

When Hannah introduced me, she said that I have written more than 40 speeches during the past three years. What she didn't tell you is that many of those speeches are unimpressive, simply because they fail at this point of integrating the speech and the speaker. /8

And I can tell you right now that if you are interested in being a speechwriter, you will face this same difficulty. Many corporate speechmakers simply do not want to reveal any hints about themselves as people. They want to strike all references to their outside activities, to their opinions, to their personal experiences. They honestly believe that the audiences want facts—not warm human beings. Also, these guys are just plain modest. They don't want to draw any attention to themselves. And, like all other speakers, they are nervous. I read in the *Wall Street Journal* that Maurice Granville, former chairman of Texaco, complained to his wife about his nervousness when speaking. Her advice for him was wonderful. She said: Look out there and just imagine all those people in their underwear, and that will make you feel better about it. Granville reports he tried it and it worked. But mostly executives just want to deliver the facts and get off the stage. /9

What is the result of these corporate speeches? When the speaker is *not* the speech—when the content of the speech does *not* reflect the character of the speaker—the audience responds with the same emptiness which the speaker delivered. Mistrust and lack of persuasion result. /10

Just look at oil industry speaking activities. The American Petroleum Institute has calculated that during 1980 more than 4,000 oil industry speakers addressed more than 18,500 different audiences. If those audiences held an average of 50 people, then oil industry spokesmen talked to almost 1 million people in 1980 alone! And oil industry people have had active speaking programs for years. /11

Yet what are the results of this activity? Studies show that almost 80 percent of the general American public still believe that oil industry profits are out of line. Only 13 percent of the public is "very confident" of the industry. And half of the public still thinks the oil industry should be broken up into separate producing, transportation, refining, and retail companies. /12

Somewhere along the line, oil industry speakers have failed to impress their audiences with their thinking—and I am willing to bet that they have failed because they did not recognize the one fundamental which I have stressed: that, the man IS his message, and that his personality must shine through the content of his speech in order for him to be believable.   /13

Conversely, every truly impressive speech that you can remember is memorable because of the melding of speech content with the speaker's character and life experiences.   /14

For instance, no one but Aleksandr Solzhenitsyn could have delivered his stirring Harvard commencement address in 1978. No one but this great Russian author—rejected by officials of his nation, imprisoned for his writing and finally exiled from his country—could speak so convincingly about the important things in life such as honor, courage, strength, and conviction about eternal things. Who but Solzhenitsyn could say this to Harvard graduates, "I could not recommend your society as an ideal for the transformation of ours. Through deep suffering, people in our country have now achieved a spiritual development of such intensity that the Western system in its present state of spiritual exhaustion does not look attractive." Only he could say this—out of his own experience.   /15

And who but Barbara Jordan could have delivered her powerful keynote address at the 1976 Democratic Convention? This black Congresswoman, with her forceful voice, said: "A lot of years have passed since 1832 (when the first Democratic Convention met to nominate a Presidential candidate), and during that time it would have been most unusual for any national political party to ask that a Barbara Jordan deliver a keynote address . . . but tonight here I am, and I feel that notwithstanding the past that my presence here is one additional bit of evidence that the American Dream need not forever be deferred." From that point on, the audience was hers. She was the speech and the message was hers alone. No one else could have delivered it.   /16

. . . You can see through these examples that when the speech is good, it is because the speaker is the speech, the woman is her words. But if the speech must reveal the speaker in a personal way in order to be effective—what is the role of the speechwriter?   /17

I said earlier that the speaker and the speechwriter are partners. They are, but the ghost writer is the silent partner. A behind-the-scenes person. In fact, almost an invisible person.   /18

The speechwriter is a server—one who serves the speaker in a variety of ways. Foremost, the speechwriter must keep in mind the fundamental which I have harped on for the past ten minutes—that the speech and the speaker are one. The ghost writer must reach into the man or woman to find the message. The ghost writer must make the message come alive through anecdotes, testimonies, humor from the speaker's point of view. The executive will likely resist efforts to personalize his or her comments. Your job as a speechwriter is to encourage him and persuade him that the audience asked to hear his ideas—not yours.   /19

Then—and only then—should the writer focus on the practical aspects of speechwriting. The speechwriter's first service is to do extensive research. You must become an expert in the speaker's fields of interest. It is your job to keep up with daily developments in those areas. This involves a lot of newspaper and journal reading.   /20

Secondly, the speechwriter serves by writing with the flair and polish that the corporate speaker generally lacks. You must learn to write for the ear, not the eye. You are not a novelist, not a journalist, not an editor of a company newspaper.

You are a speechwriter—and speeches require a different cadence, a different vigor than do editorials and news articles. You can learn this skill by reading other good speeches, by writing a lot of bad speeches and getting embarrassed when they fail, and by delivering speeches yourself to see what works.   /21

And now, I want to give you some tips about how to actually create the speech. Write this first tip indelibly upon your hearts and minds—no matter what your boss says, *call* the speaker before researching or writing one word of a speech. Even if you have to do it on the sly (and many of us have done it that way), call the speaker and ask him what he wants to say to this particular audience. Set up a meeting with him so that you can establish a rapport with him, and so that you can help him develop his ideas. I must warn you that he may not have any ideas. It happens—frequently.   /22

Then it is your job to do as much research as time allows. Check newspapers, books, polling services, professional organizations, interview experts in the field—any source which might have material that involves the subject of the speech. Read the material as time allows. Don't spend a lot of time taking notes, because when you actually write the speech your message must be painstakingly simple.

Next, write your outline. You should be able to summarize a good speech in one or two sentences. Then develop that main idea all you want. Use illustrations, quotes, facts to amplify the idea. But do not have five main points and ten subpoints which you want to make. Your audience will never remember past point number one. And your speaker will get lost in the intricacy of his message.   /23

This actually happened to a corporate executive recently. He was speaking to a large group—using a very impersonal, well-written speech with complicated information and lots of slides. When he was through, a woman stood up and asked him what his purpose was in talking to her group. He couldn't answer the question. He couldn't remember why he was there! He even tried to turn the question over to the moderator. He lost all credibility through that exchange.   /24

You've summarized your main points and outlined the speech. Now is the time to put ink on paper. To exercise the creative power of words. This is the time to use all the flair and skill you have as a writer. This is the time to use those personal tidbits you have collected which reveal the speaker. Don't let yourself lapse into that special lingo called "corporate English." We laugh at our office about the guys in the Company who write that they have "jumboized" their tankers. Others are in the process of "prioritizing inputs." I implore you to say what you mean in straightforward English. Audiences shouldn't be called upon to translate speeches as they listen to them.   /25

Many writers worry about length of the speech. Most speeches run about 20 minutes, but audiences have been mesmerized for more than an hour by speakers who really have a message for them—so worry about the message, not length when you are writing the speech.   /26

Finally, you must face the approval process. Here a new series of difficulties begin—internal politics. Send the speech to the speaker and your bosses AT THE SAME TIME. A good speech cannot survive a long approval line. All corrections (except for factual changes) should be made directly between yourself and the speaker. Otherwise, all liveliness and honesty will evaporate from your words.   /27

Does this process sound time-consuming? It is. A reporter once asked Truman Capote why he could not produce a book in two weeks, as another writer claimed he could. Capote retorted: "That's not writing, that's typing!" /28

Speechwriting takes time, too—it's not a matter of "just typing." The final product is the speechwriter's reward: A speech occasion where the speaker is the speech and the audience responds warmly to the life of the message. /29

Finally, a word of encouragement. If you do not think you can tolerate ghost writing speeches—become a mother or father instead. Then you can practice and deliver your own speeches to a captive audience! And if you are fortunate, you may even see some good results coming from your performances! /30

FIVE GREAT POWERS OF A FREE LIBERAL ARTS EDUCATION
The Backward Scenario

Richard M. Eastman,
Chairman of General Studies, North Central College, Naperville, Illinois

Delivered as the Commencement Address, North Central College, June 13, 1981

Many of you have read Kurt Vonnegut's novel *Slaughterhouse-Five* on the Second World War. At one point Billy Pilgrim, the central character, watches a movie about Americans bombing a German city. But Billy's sense of time is all mixed up, so that he sees the film backward. A German city is in flames; then the bombs rise upward back into the bombers as the flames shrink. Then the American planes, loaded with corpses and wounded men shot by antiaircraft fire, fly backward to land in Britain with all crews in good health. The bombs are sent back to America, where they are dismantled and their destructive ingredients are buried once again in the green earth. /1

The effect of seeing all this backward is to shock us with the stupidity of war's destruction, which could and ought to be reversed, to recover this whole and wonderful world. /2

Now instead of the common Commencement tactic of showing you the life about to unfold before you, I'm going to borrow from Vonnegut by constructing a backward scenario of your lives. You are now 70 years old. The year is 2031. I've chosen two of you to follow backward. To protect the innocent and the guilty, I'll call them Dick and Jane. They long ago graduated in 1981 as biology majors. (No praise or blame is intended for biology majors; I needed the kind of flexible example which biology can provide.) /3

To begin: 2031. Dick and Jane have retired about two years back. Dick is having a bad time of it. All of his working life was spent as a technical biological engineer. What can he do with that, now that he has received the Golden Handshake? He has finished his puttering agenda—rescreened the porch, painted the kitchen. He plays solitaire. He glues himself to the TV set. I'm sorry to report that he waits all day for the martinis he likes to have before dinner. Sometimes he doesn't wait. He reads the obituaries to see if he's still alive. Dick is now equivalent of the bombed German city in *Slaughterhouse-Five*. /4

Jane—this is better news—hasn't really retired. Since leaving her law firm, she has set up as legal consultant for older people who don't know what to do about their health problems. She has become friends with many of them. She reads a good many books. She would enjoy re-tasting old times with Dick, but hesitates, because Dick doesn't think old times were that interesting. /5

A point to be drawn here is that Jane's education, both at North Central and since, has opened up a complete life for her, not merely a job. Unlike Dick, she *has rich uses for leisure.* /6

"Five Great Powers of a Free Liberal Arts Education" by Richard M. Eastman from *Vital Speeches of the Day* (Vol. XLVIII, No. 1, October 15, 1981). Reprinted by permission of *Vital Speeches of the Day*.

Let's crank backward now to age 60, the year 2021. Jane has been using the "empty nest" years to study the lives of great lawyers—William Blackstone, Oliver Wendell Holmes, Clarence Darrow. She's curious about the history of law, how its concepts grew. This has led her into a couple of courses in Greek and Roman culture at the Continuing Education center of a nearby college (maybe this one). /7

Dick couldn't care less about the history of his field, biology. He knows about biology now—that is, the part he works with. That's what brings in the pay check. He does know last week's general history from the newspapers and TV. All these stories about street crime, drugs, teenage sex, business slumps, have made him pessimistic and paranoid. He keeps saying, "Ah, the young don't have values any more. The world's going to hell in a handbasket." (Jane isn't so sure about that. She remembers the international terrorism of her college years in the '70s, the Vietnam sadness, as well as the barbarities of the far past. She has also read of humanity's unquenchable aspiration to rebuild, to reform. The world for her offers some hope.) /8

A second point about liberal education can be drawn here: that an understanding of the past leads to the rediscovery of great insights and personalities. *To have a sense of one's past is to have a keener sense of one's future.* Otherwise, as George Santayana has warned, "Those who ignore the past are condemned to repeat it." /9

Our scenario rolls backward to the year 2011. Most of you are now 50. Dick's company, which manufactures agricultural nutrients, has been caught on a bad environmental pollution rap. Dick's own section was the source of the pollution. When Dick is called up before his superiors and the government inspectors, he disclaims any real blame. The company has always handled its wastes this way, he argues. Besides, sewage is a community problem; the company shouldn't be in the business of the welfare state. Dick keeps his job, thanks to his record of loyal service. But his remaining years will be clouded. /10

Jane's law work has meanwhile led her among slums, the hopelessly sick, the aged, the criminals. She sees how social problems do affect the clients she works with. This understanding leads to greater success in her cases. She acquires a small reputation in working for legal reform. /11

A third point shows up here: that *a liberal education should not only clarify the past but orient us in the big problems of right now—health service, environment, race, sexism, crime, the impact of technology, the economy.* Dominic Martia of Roosevelt University has put it this way: "With life becoming more complex and technical, the nation needs a citizenry better versed in key issues so that it collectively can exercise better informed public opinion on political, ethical, and social questions." (Cited in the *Chicago Tribune,* 7 Sep 77) /12

Backward again, now to age 40, the year 2001. We find Dick suffering his first major life disappointment. Though his work as biology technician has been thoroughly competent (he was well trained), he is passed over for promotion to high executive rank. His superiors have been watching him supportively and giving him chances to expand. But they conclude that Dick has little sense of the larger dimensions of the industry. He doesn't really think beyond his special skills. /13

You'll expect a contrast with Jane, but maybe not the one which takes place. She had started out as a high school science teacher, and is now offered a principalship. But she takes a major life risk. She leaves teaching. She has become increasingly excited about law and the problems it solves or doesn't solve. With the encouragement of a woman lawyer friend, she successfully applies for law school—a big jump but not an impossible one for a well-rounded science teacher. /14

A liberal education should produce career flexibility. This is the fourth point we can make. Few of us end up in the jobs for which we trained in college. *Liberal education provides a general background which makes reorientation easier.* By stressing the theory of a subject-matter, it avoids imprisonment in the narrow applications which may soon be obsolete. It makes leadership easier for those of us who need the wide perspective for leading. /15

Now back to 1991, ten years away. Jane takes her first major risk. She's a science teacher at a badly run school—bureaucratic, crowded; everything about it shows lack of respect for the conditions of learning. Jane knows what a good school should be, what a good principal should be. She remembers what George Bernard Shaw said about working in bad conditions—either change them or get out. She arranges, at some sacrifice, a transfer to a school she knows to be better. /16

Dick is struggling bravely in a high-paid but unpleasant position in industrial biology. The job does use his special skills. But his present supervisor is unimaginative and spiteful—a dark lens through which Dick must see his work. So he neither changes his bad conditions nor leaves them. He staunchly plods ahead, reserving his jobs for the week-ends. /17

Point 5 and last: *The ability to recognize excellence (or the lack of it) is a hallmark of the educated person.* The great psychologist William James tells us: "The purpose of a liberal education is to teach you to recognize a good person"— or, I might add, a good achievement. We should learn to recognize excellence in our own field; excellence in other fields (especially those in which we may play a part, such as government, education, religion); and finally excellence (or the lack of it) in ourselves. /18

Five great powers of a true liberal arts education: openness to a complete life (including its leisure); an understanding of the past which shapes us; a grasp of the current social issues we must help to solve; flexibility in life commitment; the ability to recognize excellence wherever we look or act. /19

Now we are back on this college campus, June 13, 1981. The backward scenario is over. I see Dick and Jane out there, in all their triumph and bloom on this Commencement Day—a bloom all the brighter because they have plans to marry. You're sitting near them, maybe closer than you realize. /20

As your own films now start forward, I hope you'll be able to follow the kind of scenario which we at North Central College have all wanted for you. We can't guarantee it, but we have offered some notes for the plot. So we wish you success in working it out, in finding a life story of personal fulfillment and of power to participate fully in a free society. /21

Lights! Camera! Roll 'em! /22

Index